Tourism: People, Places and Products

Tourism: People, Places and Products

edited by

Geoffrey Wall

Department of Geography Publication Series

Series Editor   Clare Mitchell
Series Manager   Kate Evans
Cover Design   Monica Lynch
Printing   M & T Insta-Print (K-W) Ltd.

ISBN 0-921083-66-1   ISSN 0843-7386

National Library of Canada Cataloguing in Publication Data

Tourism : people, places and products / edited by Geoffrey Wall.

(Department of Geography occasional paper ; #19)
Includes bibliographical references.
ISBN 0-921083-66-1

1. Tourism. I. Wall, Geoffrey II. University of Waterloo.
Dept. of Geography III. Series.

G155.A1T683 2003   338.4'791   C2003-902408-3

Preface

This book provides an overview of contemporary perspectives on tourism by recognized scholars. Each chapter was originally an invited lecture presented in a Geography/Recreation course held at the University of Waterloo in 2000 and organized and instructed by Professor Geoff Wall. The course approach came about because the Faculty of Environmental Studies wished to highlight the tourism teaching and research endeavours at the University of Waterloo. The course was a success and has been run in this format ever since. The book, *Tourism: People, Places and Products*, is the outcome of the second offering of this course and it is hoped that each time the course is offered there will be an edited compilation of the invited lectures. In fact the third volume is at the editing stage.

As interest in the field of tourism continues to grow, I am delighted that my colleague Geoff Wall had the vision for such a course and for its tangible outcome in book form. *Tourism: People, Places and Products* will, I am sure, further stimulate the development in tourism studies.

Geoff McBoyle
Dean, Faculty of Environmental Studies

Acknowledgements

This book would not have come into existence in the absence of the commitment and patience of a number of people.

First I wish to thank the speakers who gave freely of their time and knowledge to travel to Waterloo to make their presentations. Without exception, their stimulating presentations raised awareness of the complexity and variety of tourism issues.

Dr. Geoff McBoyle, Dean, Faculty of Environment Studies, has been and continues to be an enthusiastic supporter of tourism research and education. His support has been tangible, through provision of resources to support this initiative, and also personal, including regular attendance at the Lecture Series.

Dr. Clare Mitchell, a colleague in the Department of Geography, and editor of the Department of Geography Publication Series, read the entire manuscript. The work has been enhanced by her meticulous attention to detail.

Kate Evans skillfully turned a collection of manuscripts into a book and kept the faith when little progress was being made and when it probably appeared that the editor was not doing his job.

While the preparation of the manuscript has been laborious, participation in the Lecture Series was a delight. It is my hope that the students, colleagues and members of the public who attended the lectures will have been stimulated by their content and that this document will be a record of one of many such Lecture Series.

Geoffrey Wall

Table of Contents

Figures

Tables

Chapter 1

The Nature of Tourism

Geoffrey Wall
University of Waterloo

Tourism is a complex, open-ended, system. It is complex because it brings together many different people and places. It is open-ended because it is difficult to put clear boundaries around what is to be considered tourism and what is not. For example, both permanent residents and visitors may participate in the same events, such as festivals and concerts, and may use the same services, such as taxis and restaurants.

One simple but useful perspective on tourism is to view it as consisting of three main elements that are linked through the behaviours of tourists: origins, destinations and travel between the two (Cooper *et al.*, 1993) (Figure 1.1). Origins are the places from which tourists come. Given that most people now live in urban areas, it follows that most tourists emanate from urban areas. It is here that important decisions are made about whether or not to become tourists, where and when to go, who to go with, whether to travel independently or to join a package tour and so on. It is here, too, that businesses are found, such as travel agents, that can help in the making of such decisions.

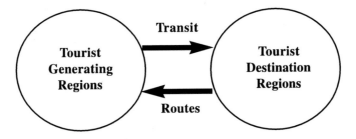

Figure 1.1: The Geographical Elements of Tourism.

Destinations are the places that tourists visit. They contain tourist attractions of various kinds and supporting infrastructure, and they may be other urban areas, specialized resorts, natural areas, or a host of other settings that tourists go to satisfy their needs and wants.

Origins and destinations are linked by transportation. In fact, travel is a prerequisite of tourism. While some speak of virtual tourism, and one may "tour" some destinations through video or websites, a real tourist must leave home to go to some other place. This requires the use of transportation systems: cars, planes, trains, boats etc.

Another way of viewing this triad of system components is demand (which emanates from origins), supply (which is concentrated in destinations), and the intervening distances that must be overcome by transportation.

Four observations are in order concerning this system:

- First, while it is perhaps natural to focus on destinations in the attempt to understand the behaviours of tourists and the implications for people, economy and environment in those places, to do so to the exclusion of other aspects of the system is to get an incomplete picture of tourism.

- Second, the system operates at a wide variety of scales. Thus both origins and destinations can be viewed as continents, countries, provinces, cities and towns, or even specific sites. Given the mix of scales and the movement of people, money, products and ideas that occur between origins and destinations, tourism is an example of globalization, exhibiting many forms of global-local interaction. However, the movements are not simply from origins to destinations for there is a reverse flow of advertising, ideas, impressions, postcards, photographs and other souvenirs, as well as of those returning home.

- Thirdly, both tourism marketing and planning involve the manipulation of supply and demand to bring them into equilibrium. These are difficult tasks for demand and some aspects of supply vary greatly through time: from day to night, from weekday to weekend, before, during and after public holidays, and seasonally, in somewhat predictable ways and, less predictably, in response to events such as economic crises, natural hazards and wars. Furthermore, this equilibrium should be maintained while the system grows for most destinations want more, rather than the same or fewer future tourists and investors in tourism. Under-supply leads to congestion and over-use of facilities whereas over-supply results in economic inefficiencies. However, the units of supply have tended to grow in size making a balance between supply and demand more difficult to achieve. For example, modern hotels and cruise ships have hundreds of rooms so that introduction of a new one may, in fact, constitute a massive increase in supply in one aspect of the system, with implications for others, such as transportation, labour, water demands and waste assimilation capacity.

- Fourth, the headings demand, supply and distance each refer to complex subsystems. For example, demand is influenced by socio-economic and psychological factors, supply is made up of a multitude of interlinked components that will be discussed below, and accessibility may be measured in distance, time, money or fatigue. Destinations may be competitive or complementary or both depending upon the market segment. Tourists may visit more than one destination on the same trip and the return journey may be by a different route or transportation mode from the outward one. Thus, the simple three-fold system needs to be embellished in many ways if it is to approximate reality.

THE TOURISM PRODUCT

There is debate whether or not tourism is an industry (Smith, 1988; 1994). Certainly, it does not produce a standardized product like many conventional industries. Sub-components of the tourism system may call themselves industries, such as the airline industry and the hotel industry, and there may be tangible products created, such as ski equipment or cooked food although, in themselves, these contribute to rather than encompass tourism. Other important players in tourism, such as the operators of museums, nature reserves and customs offices, may not see themselves as part of tourism at all! Nonetheless, it is still possible to talk about tourism products.

The products of tourism are experiences. When looked at from the perspectives of tourists, there are five phases to these experiences (Clawson and Knetsch, 1966).

1. Anticipation, which occurs primarily in the origin, as potential tourists make their decisions about their travel, make their bookings if these are required, and look forward to their trips.
2. Journey to the destination, which may be seen as an integral, positive, part of the experience as in sightseeing as part of a tour, or a necessary chore that must be endured to gain access to the delights of the destination area.
3. Experiences gained in the destination area as a result of visiting its attractions and drawing upon its infrastructure and supporting services.
4. The return journey, which is a different experience from the outward journey and not only because it involves travel in the opposite direction. It is travel undertaken with a different state of mind.

5. Recollection is the phase in which one re-lives the other
    experiences, often sharing them with others as one deliv-
    ers gifts and imposes one's photographs upon them.

While most research has been conducted on the destination
phase because of its obvious importance and the anticipation phase
because of its marketing implications, the total experience is made
up of all five phases and deficiencies in one may undermine what
otherwise might have been a more positive total experience. For
example, failure of one's baggage to arrive on time may lead to
additional expenses, wasted time and delayed arrival of recreational equipment. It may get the vacation off to a bad start from which
it may be difficult to recover, particularly if it is a short visit, or a
tour which makes it impossible for the bags to catch up with their
owners.

It is perhaps natural that much work has concentrated upon the
destination phase. Even here, the experience is complicated by the
fact that it is comprised from many different products and services:
attractions, accommodations, food and beverage, transportation,
utilities (water, sewage, electricity and communication systems),
guides and interpretation, to name some of the major ones. Whose
responsibility is it to ensure that the supply is sufficient in both
quantity and quality and who will ensure their coordination? What
are the consequences of deficiencies?

Switching the perspective from the demand to the supply side,
temporal change in tourism destinations has been a prominent
theme in tourism research, following the work of Butler (1980) and
there is an extensive literature that chronicles the evolution of
resorts, particularly coastal resorts (Agarwal, 1997; 2002).

At this point, it is worth making a distinction between a
tourism resource, a tourist attraction, and a tourism product. A
tourism resource can be natural or human-made attribute or a com-

bination of the two with the potential to contribute positively to tourists' experiences by satisfying their needs or wants. A tourist attraction refers to "all those elements of a 'non-home' place that draw discretionary travellers away from their homes" (Lew, 1987: 554). More specifically, according to MacCannell (1976: 109), tourist attractions consist of three components: tourists, a site to be viewed, and a marker or image that makes the site significant. Thus, a site-sacralization process is required to turn a resource into an attraction. However, a product is much more than an attraction: it is usually a combination of the varied offerings that together contribute to the tourists' experiences. It is made up of a collection of elements, both tangible and intangible, combined to form an ensemble that can be marketed and sold to tourists.

Of course, tourism does not end with such definitions; it has profound implications for both the tourists and the people and the communities that they visit, for the businesses that are set up to cater to their needs, and for the organizations, including governments at all levels, that attempt to encourage tourists to visit and to control tourists and tourism developers.

CONCLUSION

The purpose of this presentation has been to provide a context for the papers that follow. It has suggested that tourism is complex and that a broad perspective is required if one is to encompass its many attributes and manifestations. Tourism, by definition, involves travel to overcome the friction of distance between origin and destination areas. Thus, tourism is an inherently spatial concept with many overlapping scales. At the same time, whether one is focussing upon tourists or the places that they visit, a temporal dimension may be required and will certainly contribute to greater understanding of tourism phenomena.

In line with the the above plea for a broad perspective, the following definition of tourism is offered as a point of departure and context for the contributions that follow:

> Tourism is the temporary movement of people to destinations outside their normal places of work and residence, the activities undertaken during their stay in those destinations, and the facilities created to cater to their needs. The study of tourism is the study of people away from their usual habitat, of the establishments which respond to the requirements of travellers, and of the impacts that they have on the economic, physical and social well-being of their hosts. It involves the motivations and experiences of the tourists, the expectations of and adjustments made by residents of reception areas, and the roles played by the numerous agencies and institutions which intercede between them (Mathieson and Wall, 1982: 1).

REFERENCES

Agarwal, S. (1997) "The resort cycle and seaside tourism: an assessment of its application," *Tourism Management*, 18: 65-73.

Agarwal, S. (2002) "Restructuring seaside tourism; the resort life-cycle," *Annals of Tourism Research*, 29(1): 25-55.

Butler, R. (1980) "The concept of a tourist area cycle of evolution: implications for the management of resources," *Canadian Geographer*, 24(1): 5-12.

Clawson, M. and Knetsch, J.L. (1966) *Economics of Outdoor Recreation*, Baltimore: The Johns Hopkins Press.

Cooper, C., Fletcher, J., Gilbert, D. and Wanhill, S. (1993) *Tourism Principles and Practice*, London: Pitman.

Lew, A.A. (1987) "A framework of tourism attraction research," *Annals of Tourism Research*, 14(4): 553-575.

MacCannell, D. (1976) *The Tourist: A New Theory of the Leisure Class*, New York, NY: Schocken Books.

Mathieson, A. and Wall, G. (1982) *Tourism: Economic, Physical and Social Impacts*, Harlow, UK: Longman.

Smith, S.L.J. (1988) "Defining tourism: a supply side view," *Annals of Tourism Research*, 15(2): 179-190.

Smith, S.L.J. (1994) "The tourism product," *Annals of Tourism Research*, 21(3): 582-595.

Chapter 2

Tourism and the Canadian Economy: Trends, Cycles, and the Seasonal Variation in Tourism Demand

David Wilton
University of Waterloo

n June 1996, Statistics Canada and the Canadian Tourism Commission (CTC) began to publish National Tourism Indicators (NTIs), an important new database for Canadian tourism researchers. This chapter examines quarterly NTI data, both seasonally adjusted and not seasonally adjusted, for tourism demand in Canada, disaggregated into domestic tourism demand by Canadians and export tourism demand by foreign visitors. Tourism expenditures are further disaggregated into important tourism commodities, such as passenger air transport, vehicle rentals, hotels, food and beverage services, recreation and entertainment, and travel agency services. Trends, business cycles, and the seasonal variation in over 50 different tourism demand indicators are identified and discussed in this chapter.

The introductory part of the chapter provides background information on the NTIs and definitions of key tourism concepts. The next section presents a graphical overview of the trends and business cycles in tourism demand in Canada during the 1986-96 period (using seasonally adjusted data). The next two sections discuss trends and business cycles in tourism demand and provide answers to the following questions. What is the trend growth rate in tourism demand? Does the trend growth rate vary for different tourism commodities, such as passenger air transport, hotels, and travel agency services? Which sectors of the tourism industry have experienced the most rapid growth during the 1986-96 period? How does the trend in tourism export demand compare to the trend in tourism domestic demand? How much of the cyclical variation in tourism demand can be explained by the overall Canadian business cycle? Are the cyclical fluctuations in tourism demand relatively larger or smaller than the cyclical fluctuations in the overall Canadian economy? Which sectors of the tourism industry are most susceptible to the Canadian business cycle?

The last half of the chapter examines the seasonal variation in tourism demand, beginning with a graphical overview of the seasonal dimension in tourism demand. In the next section, regression analysis is used to estimate the magnitude of the seasonal component (seasonal factor) in tourism demand over the 1986 to 1997 period. This part of the chapter answers the following questions. Are the seasonal factors for each NTI significantly different for each quarter of the year? Is the seasonal factor for winter significantly lower than the seasonal factors for spring and summer? Is the seasonal pattern in one NTI (say tourism demand for hotels) different from the seasonal pattern in another NTI (say tourism demand for travel agency services)? Is the seasonal pattern for domestic tourism demand different from the seasonal pattern for export tourism demand? How much of the statistical variation in each NTI is explained by the seasonal component, by the trend component, and by the remaining business cycle and irregular components? Is the amplitude of the annual seasonal cycle in tourism larger than the amplitude of the business cycle? Are there any sectors of the tourism industry that are immune from seasonal fluctuations in demand?

The penultimate section of this chapter provides an exploratory examination of the effect of climate changes on the seasonal variation in tourism demand. Are the NTI seasonal factors immutable? Does a mild winter or a cool summer affect the magnitude of the seasonal factors in tourism demand? The final section summarizes the main conclusions of the chapter and considers what the NTIs tell us about Canadian tourism.

Background

Canada is the first country to develop and publish a Tourism Satellite Account (TSA) and National Tourism Indicators (NTIs). The Canadian TSA, developed by Statistics Canada and the Canadian Tourism Commission, provided a detailed picture of Canadian tourism in the year 1988. As discussed in Lise Beaulieu-Caron's article in Travel-log:

> A TSA is a structured information system that allows the statistics describing all the measurable aspects of tourism to be collected, classified and linked. The Tourism Satellite Account provides a measurement of the economic demand for, and production of, tourism commodities. For the first time, the information contained in this account makes it possible to evaluate the direct contribution of tourism expenses to Canada's Gross Domestic Product (GDP)... However, because of the complexity of the very detailed accounting framework required, the TSA cannot be updated more often than once every few years... To meet a requirement for more detailed and more recent data, the National Tourism Indicators were developed on the basis of the TSA.

The NTIs provide annual and quarterly data from 1986 for over 300 different Canadian tourism indicators. This gold mine of tourism data can be used to monitor the current state of tourism in Canada, to analyze the economic structure of tourism and its policy ramifications, and to study trends, business cycles and seasonal patterns in tourism (the objective of this chapter).

Defining and Measuring Tourism

Measuring tourism is a challenging task because tourism does not exist as a separate entity or as a distinct economic activity in the

System of National Accounts. The World Tourism Organization and the United Nations Statistical Commission define tourism as the activities of persons travelling to and staying in places outside their usual environment for not more than one consecutive year for leisure, business and other purposes.[1] In Canada this definition normally includes Canadians travelling in Canada 80 kilometres or more from their residence, Canadians travelling outside the country, and non-residents travelling in Canada.

To measure tourism demand, national income accountants focus on the activities of tourists (and same-day visitors) rather than on the intrinsic characteristics of the commodities purchased by tourists. For example, a restaurant meal can be consumed by both a tourist and someone who is not a tourist. The restaurant meal is the same irrespective of who consumes it, but is considered to be tourism only if it is consumed by a tourist (or same-day visitor). A further complication arises because tourists purchase some items that are not usually considered to be tourism commodities (such as groceries and clothing) from businesses (such as grocery and retail stores) that are not usually considered to be part of the tourism industry. Tourism demand cuts across a wide swath of industries (such as air transportation, accommodation, food and beverage services, recreation and entertainment) and can include some commodities (such as groceries and clothing) purchased from some industries (such as grocery and retail stores) that are not usually considered to be 'tourism.'

A good or service is classified as a tourism commodity if a significant part of its total demand comes from tourists and same-day visitors. Accommodation and restaurant meals are tourism commodities, but groceries and clothing bought in grocery and retail stores are not classified as tourism commodities (because purchases by tourists and same-day visitors represent a very small proportion of total grocery and clothing sales). Since tourism commodities, such as restaurant meals, also are purchased by people not classified as tourists and same-day visitors, the supply of tourism commodities exceeds tourism demand for tourism commodities.[2] Table 2.1 presents tourism shares (tourism demand as a percent of total supply) for eight major tourism commodities in 1998. Tourism shares for passenger air transport, hotels, motels, travel agency services and vehicle rentals range from 89 percent to 98 percent, while tourism shares for food and beverage services, recreation and entertainment, and vehicle fuel are between 23 percent and 25 percent.

Table 2.1: Tourism Demand and the Supply of Tourism Commodities
(Billions of dollars, 1998)

Tourism Commodity	Tourism Demand	Supply	Tourism Share
Passenger air transport	$10.581	$11.381	93%
Vehicle rentals	.959	1.081	89%
Vehicle fuel	3.533	14.855	24%
Hotel accommodation	4.997	5.322	94%
Motel accommodation	1.000	1.056	95%
Food and beverage services	7.716	32.868	23%
Recreation and entertainment	3.088	12.395	25%
Travel agency services	1.609	1.640	98%
All tourism commodities	$37.746	$95.470	40%

AN OVERVIEW OF TRENDS AND BUSINESS CYCLES IN TOURISM DEMAND[3]

This section of the chapter presents three figures that compare the trends and business cycles in tourism demand during the 1986 Q1 to 1996 Q4 period with the trends and cycles in the overall Canadian economy, as measured by Gross Domestic Product (GDP).

Tourism Demand in Canada

Figure 2.1 plots quarterly seasonally adjusted data for total tourism expenditures in Canada, tourism demand for total tourism commodities and GDP, each measured in constant prices. To facilitate graphical comparisons, GDP and tourism demand have been indexed to a value of 1.00 in the first quarter of 1986. Except for the 1991-93 recession period, the two index lines for tourism expenditures are higher than the index line for GDP. Actual tourism expenditures have risen at a slightly faster pace than GDP during the 1986-96 period.

The index lines in Figure 2.1 clearly show that the 'business cycle' is much more pronounced in the tourism sector than it is for the Canadian economy as a whole. Tourism expenditures and tourism demand for total tourism commodities declined by 9.0 percent and 10.6 percent respectively during the 1990-91 recession. Given that GDP fell by only 3.5 percent during this recession, the cyclical downswing in tourism demand is about three times larger than the cyclical downswing in the overall economy. The 1993-96 recovery also has been stronger for tourism demand than for the overall economy.

Domestic Tourism Demand

Aggregate data, such as total tourism expenditures plotted in Figure 2.1, can conceal more than they reveal. Domestic and export tourism expenditures exhibit very different trend, cyclical and seasonal patterns. There is a much more pronounced positive trend in tourism export data; as a proportion of total tourism expenditures, exports have increased from 23.8 percent of the total in 1986 Q1 to 30.1 percent in 1996 Q4. As we shall see, there is an obvious business cycle in domestic tourism expenditures but little evidence of a business cycle in export tourism expenditures. Furthermore, export tourism expenditures are subject to much more pronounced seasonal swings.

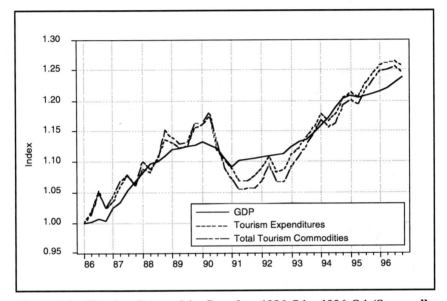

Figure 2.1: Tourism Demand in Canada - 1986 Q1 - 1996 Q4 (Seasonally Adjusted).

Figure 2.2 plots indexed domestic tourism expenditures data, along with indexed GDP data. Compared to cyclical movements in GDP, domestic tourism expenditures have a much more pronounced cycle during the recovery of the late 1980s and the 1990-91 recession (the 1990 Q1 peak to 1991 Q3 trough decline in domestic tourism expenditures is 8.6 percent, compared to a 3.5 percent peak to trough decline in GDP), but have grown more slowly during the 1993-96 recovery period.

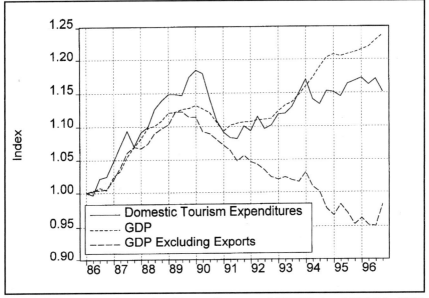

Figure 2.2: Domestic Tourism Expenditures and GDP Data - 1986 Q1 - 1996 Q4 (Seasonally Adjusted).

However, a comparison of domestic tourism expenditure growth with GDP growth is somewhat misleading. Exports have been excluded from tourism expenditures but are included in GDP. As shown in Figure 2.2, the index line for GDP excluding exports is very different from the index line for GDP during the 1990s. Without the tremendous surge in exports during the 1990s (because of a depreciating value of the Canadian dollar and the Canada-U.S. Free Trade Agreement), Canadian output would have declined. Removing exports from both tourism expenditures and GDP reveals that the 15 percent growth in domestic tourism expenditures during the 1986-1996 period substantially exceeded the growth in output for the domestic market.

Tourism Exports

Figure 2.3 for tourism export expenditures is very different from Figure 2.2 for tourism domestic expenditures. Tourism exports, which are purchases of Canadian commodities by foreign visitors, depend primarily on economic conditions in the foreign visitor's home country (not in Canada) and on the value of the foreign exchange rate.

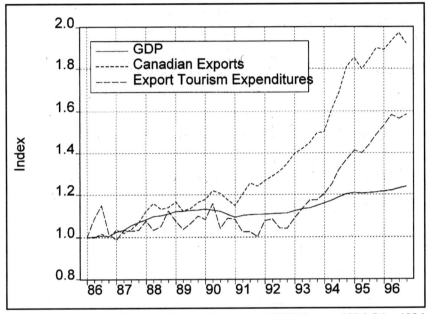

Figure 2.3: Export Tourism Expenditures and GDP Data - 1986 Q1 - 1996 Q4 (Seasonally Adjusted).

During the 1986-92 period there is no obvious trend or business cycle in tourism export expenditures, just a number of minor bumps. Two of the larger bumps are explained by special events in Canada. Expo86 resulted in a surge of tourism exports in the second and third quarters of 1986; third quarter tourism exports were 15 percent higher than in the first quarter. A smaller (4.2 percent) up-tick in tourism exports occurred during the Calgary Olympics, with passenger air transportation accounting for almost half of the 1988 Q1 increase in tourism export expenditures.

Tourism export expenditures end their bumpy trendless path in 1992 and begin to increase at a rapid rate. The strong positive trend in tourism export expenditures that began in 1992 is easily explained. The Canadian dollar depreciated from $0.89 U.S. in late 1991 to less than $0.71 in early 1995, reducing the foreign cost of a Canadian trip or holiday by about 20 percent for American visitors. There was an even greater depreciation in the value of the Canadian dollar when measured against the Japanese yen (47 percent), the German mark (31 percent), and the French franc (31 percent) during the 1991 to 1996 period. The positive effects from a depreciation in the external value of the Canadian dollar reinforced the positive income effects from the strong recovery taking place in the U.S. and world economies, resulting in a 58 percent increase in tourism export expenditures over the 1991 to 1996 period.

The growth in tourism export expenditures during the 1986-1996 period far exceeds the growth in GDP in Figure 2.3. However, the 58 percent increase in tourism export expenditures is less than the 92 percent increase in all Canadian exports. Three factors provided great stimulus to Canadian exports in the 1990s: a strong recovery in the U.S., the large depreciation in the external value of the Canadian dollar, and the signing of the Canada-U.S. Free Trade Agreement (FTA). Since most tourism expenditures are for services, which are not subject to tariffs, the FTA had a large positive effect on Canadian exports of goods but a minor effect on tourism expenditures. Thus, it is not surprising that the growth in tourism export expenditures during the 1990s is less than the growth in all exports. What is surprising is the magnitude of the increase in tourism export expenditures, particularly during the 1990s.

TREND ESTIMATES FOR TOURISM DEMAND
Many factors determine the magnitude of the trend increase in tourism demand over a particular period of time, factors such as the growth rate in the Canadian economy, a change in the value of the Canadian dollar, government deregulation (for example, an 'open skies' policy), and the introduction of casinos. Since these underly-

ing factors will change through time, estimates for the trend increase (decrease) in the NTIs are specific to a particular time period. The trend estimates[4] presented in Table 2.2 are for the 1986 - 1996 period and are not forecasts of future trends. In five cases the estimate for the trend is not significantly different from zero at the 5 percent error level (these five estimates are shown in bold type indicating that these trend increases/decreases are not significantly different from zero).

Table 2.2: Percentage Increase/Decrease in Trend Values (1986 Q1 - 1996 Q4)

	Tourism Demand in Canada	Tourism Domestic Demand	Tourism Exports
Transportation	8.21	**-0.17**	62.04
Passenger air transport	**3.61**	-6.83	55.85
Vehicle rental	20.05	-31.53	213.81
Vehicle repairs and parts	37.42	37.74	27.46
Vehicle fuel	13.90	13.13	21.75
Accommodation	39.10	30.23	56.40
Hotels	42.94	34.69	57.63
Motels	30.86	18.68	68.95
Food and beverage services	9.64	**-4.15**	42.18
From accommodation services	-14.60	-27.48	14.49
From food and beverage services	18.36	**4.09**	52.60
Other tourism commodities	41.70	40.69	44.81
Recreation and entertainment	**2.59**	-12.16	39.55
Travel agency services	224.60	222.68	
Total tourism commodities	16.93	7.13	53.03
Total other commodities	27.91	22.21	48.38
Tourism expenditures	19.18	10.21	52.06

Total Tourism Demand in Canada

Between 1986 and 1996 tourism expenditures (measured in constant prices) have an estimated trend increase of 19.18 percent. On average, tourism expenditures have trended upwards by almost 2 percent per year during this 11 year period.

The estimated trend increases (decreases) for the components of total tourism demand are reported in the first column of Table 2.2. The largest trend increase is for travel agency services, with an estimated trend increase of 224.60 percent. There are also large estimated trend increases in tourism demand for hotels (42.94 percent), motels (30.86 percent), vehicle repairs and parts (37.42 percent), vehicle rentals (20.05 percent) and food and beverage services from food and beverage establishments (18.36 percent). At the other end of the spectrum, there is an estimated 14.60 percent trend decrease in tourism demand for food and beverage services from accommodation establishments. Hotels and motels are increasingly in the room business, not the food and beverage business.

Domestic Tourism Expenditures

The estimated trend increase for domestic tourism expenditures is 10.21 percent, considerably less than the trend increase in total tourism expenditures. In the tourism domestic demand column in Table 2.2, travel agency services again has the largest estimated trend increase (222.68 percent). Large estimated trend increases are also found for tourism domestic demand for vehicle repairs and parts (37.74 percent), hotels (34.69 percent), motels (18.68 percent), and other commodities (22.21 percent). Four domestic demand components have negative trend increases: vehicle rentals (-31.53 percent), food and beverage services from accommodation establishments (-27.48 percent), recreation and entertainment (-12.16 percent) and passenger air transport (-6.83 percent).[5]

Tourism Export Demand

Tourism export demand is the driving force behind the upward trend in tourism expenditures in Canada. The estimated trend increase in tourism export expenditures over the 1986-96 period is 52.06 percent, compared to a much more modest estimated trend increase of 10.21 percent in domestic tourism expenditures. On average, tourism export expenditures have increased by almost 5 percent per year during the 1986-96 period.

The estimated trend increases for the components and sub-components of tourism export demand are, with one exception (vehicle repairs and parts), larger than the estimated trend increases for tourism domestic demand. The estimated trend increases for tourism export demand are largest for vehicle rentals (213.81 percent), accommodation (56.40 percent), passenger air transport (55.85 percent), and food and beverage services from food and beverage establishments (52.60 percent). The smallest estimated trend increases for tourism export demand are for food and beverage services from accommodation establishments (14.49 percent), vehicle fuel (21.75 percent) and vehicle repairs and parts (27.46 percent).

CYCLES IN TOURISM DEMAND

Most Canadian tourism demand indicators 'cycle' around a rising trend, with the cycles frequently swamping the trend. How much of the cyclical variation in tourism demand can be explained by the cyclical variation in the overall Canadian economy (*i.e.*, the Canadian business cycle)? Are the cyclical fluctuations in tourism demand relatively larger or smaller than the cyclical fluctuations in the overall Canadian economy? Table 2.3 summarizes the statistical answers to these 'cyclical' questions. The first three columns of numbers in Table 2.3 indicate the percent of the variation in the cyclical component[6] for a particular tourism indicator, which can be statistically explained by the cyclical variation in GDP. No entry is

Table 2.3: Cyclical Properties of Tourism - Demand and Supply Indicators

	Percent of Cyclical Variation Explained by GDP Cyclical Variation			Sensitivity Coefficients		
	Total Demand	Domestic Demand	Export Demand	Total Demand	Domestic Demand	Export Demand
Transportation	56	55	29	1.54	1.33	2.38
Passenger air transport	39	30	49	2.02	1.64	3.45
Vehicle rental	-	-	-	-	-	-
Vehicle repairs and parts	54	51	-	1.51	1.54	-
Vehicle fuel	-	-	-	-	-	-
Accommodation	33	21	-	0.88	1.58	-
Hotels	37	22	9	1.15	1.78	1.06
Motels	-	14	-	-	1.51	-
Food and beverage services	57	81	-	1.95	2.21	-
From accommodation services	27	50	39	1.72	1.94	1.91
From food and beverage services	67	78	-	2.04	2.34	-
Other tourism commodities	69	73	-	2.41	2.99	-
Recreation and entertainment	48	53	-	2.60	3.36	-
Travel agency services	57	58	-	2.96	3.09	-
Total tourism commodities	73	73	12	1.51	1.50	1.40
Total other commodities	18	10	-	0.40	0.36	-
Tourism expenditures	71	67	10	1.27	1.23	1.33

recorded in Table 2.3 if the statistical estimate is not significantly different from zero at the .05 level. The last three columns indicate the sensitivity of the tourism demand cycle to the GDP business cycle. A cyclical sensitivity coefficient greater than 1.00 indicates that the tourism demand cycle is relatively larger than the GDP business cycle. For example, a cyclical sensitivity coefficient of 1.5 indicates that the cyclical deviation in tourism demand is 1.5 times the size of the cyclical deviation in GDP.

The Total Picture

As illustrated in Figure 2.4, which plots the cyclical components of total tourism expenditures, total tourism commodities and GDP (all data are seasonally adjusted), tourism expenditures in Canada clearly cycle with the overall Canadian economy. Seventy-one percent of the cyclical variation in total tourism expenditures in Canada and 73 percent of the cyclical variation in the demand for

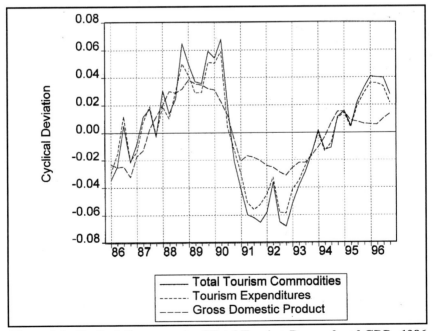

Figure 2.4: Cyclical Components of Total Tourism Demand and GDP - 1986 Q1 - 1996 Q4 (Seasonally Adjusted).

total tourism commodities can be explained by the cyclical variation in GDP (see Table 2.3).

The business cycle in tourism demand has greater amplitude than the business cycle in GDP. As shown in Figure 2.4, when the Canadian economy experienced a 3.5 percent GDP cyclical peak in 1989, the cyclical components of tourism demand peaked at 6 percent to 7 percent. The negative cyclical deviations in tourism demand in 1991-92 are also larger than the negative cyclical deviations in GDP in Figure 2.4. In Table 2.3 the cyclical sensitivity coefficients for tourism expenditures in Canada and tourism demand for total tourism commodities are 1.27 and 1.51 respectively.

Since domestic expenditures represent approximately three quarters of total tourism expenditures during the 1986-96 period, the cyclical story for domestic tourism demand is very similar to that found for total tourism demand in Canada. As shown in Table 2.3, 67 percent of the cyclical variation in domestic tourism expenditures and 73 percent of the cyclical variation in domestic demand for total tourism commodities can be explained by the cyclical variation in GDP. The cyclical sensitivity coefficients for domestic tourism expenditures and domestic demand for total tourism commodities are 1.23 and 1.50, again very similar to that found for total tourism demand.

A much different story emerges for tourism export demand. As discussed above, tourism exports depend primarily on economic conditions outside of Canada, on the value of the Canadian dollar, and on irregular events. Non-trend movements in tourism exports tend to be dominated by movements in the foreign exchange rate and special events such as Expos and Olympic Games. The cyclical variation in Canadian GDP explains only 10 percent of the variation in export tourism expenditures, and only 12 percent of the variation in export demand for total tourism commodities.

Cyclical Properties for Various Tourism Commodities

As shown in Table 2.3, there is considerable variation in the business cycle properties of different tourism commodities. We begin by reviewing the cyclical results for total tourism demand in Canada. Three tourism commodities have more than 50 percent of their cyclical variation in total tourism demand explained by the cyclical variation in GDP: food and beverage services from food and beverage establishments (67 percent), travel agency services (57 percent), and vehicle repairs and parts (54 percent). The cyclical sensitivity coefficients for these three tourism commodities are 2.04, 2.96, and 1.51 respectively. Two other tourism commodities have cyclical sensitivity coefficients for tourism demand in Canada above two, namely recreation and entertainment (2.60) and passenger air transport (2.02). Tourism demand in Canada for vehicle rentals, vehicle fuel, and motels is not significantly affected by cyclical swings in GDP.

The story is almost identical for tourism domestic demand. The tourism commodities that have more than 50 percent of their cyclical variation in domestic demand explained by the cyclical variation in GDP are food and beverage services from food and beverage establishments (78 percent), travel agency services (58 percent), recreation and entertainment (53 percent), and vehicle repairs and parts (51 percent). The cyclical sensitivity coefficients for these four tourism commodities are 2.34, 3.09, 3.36, and 1.54 respectively; in each case the cyclical sensitivity coefficient for domestic tourism demand is a little higher than the cyclical sensitivity coefficient for total tourism demand.

As discussed above, tourism export demand is dominated by irregular movements associated with changes in foreign exchange rates, foreign economic conditions, and special events. Only three tourism export commodities are significantly affected by cyclical movements in Canadian GDP and in each case the cyclical component of GDP explains a relatively small percentage of the cyclical variation in tourism export demand (9 percent for hotels, 39 percent for food and beverage services from accommodation establishments, and 49 percent for passenger air transport).

AN OVERVIEW OF THE SEASONAL VARIATION IN TOURISM DEMAND[7]

> Seasonality has long been recognized as one of the most distinctive features of tourism ... In spite of this concern over seasonality and its perceived generally negative effects upon tourism and destination areas, there has been relatively little research devoted to this topic which appears in the published literature. It is clear that, while there is often general agreement about the seasonality 'problem', comparatively little study has been made of its detailed nature.[8]

Over 20 years ago, BarOn[9] identified two basic causes of seasonality in tourism, 'natural' seasonality and 'institutionalized' seasonality. Natural seasonality is caused by seasonal variations in climate, such as temperature, hours of sunlight, and precipitation. High latitude countries, such as Canada, have very distinctive seasonal variations in climate, which affect many activities and industries. Recreational activities such as swimming and camping (and associated tourism expenditures) are obviously affected by seasonal climate changes. Institutionalized seasonality in tourism arises from statutory and school holidays. Many individuals choose to visit friends and relatives, or take brief vacations, on statutory holidays, such as Christmas/New Year, Easter, and Thanksgiving. The timing of statutory and school holidays has a major impact on the seasonal pattern of tourism expenditures.

Figures 2.5 through 2.9 provide graphs of key tourism demand indicators in Canada over the 1986 to 1997 period based on quarterly data that have not been seasonally adjusted. Three key statistical features are readily apparent in Figure 2.5, which presents

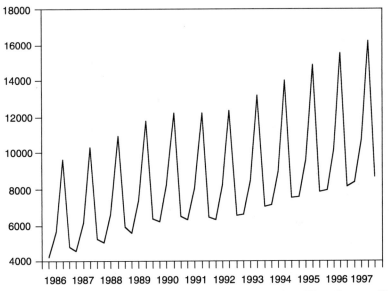

Figure 2.5: Total Tourism Expenditures in Canada (Not Seasonally Adjusted, Millions of Dollars).

'unadjusted' data for total tourism expenditures in Canada.

The Seasonal Component: The most obvious feature of Figure 2.5 is the seasonal 'saw-tooth' pattern. A third quarter (summer) peak is followed by a sharp decline in the fourth (autumn) and first (winter) quarters. For example, in 1997 first quarter tourism expenditures of $8,396 million are roughly one-half as large as third quarter tourism expenditures of $16,210 million. The 1997 seasonal peak to trough ratio is 1.93; total tourism expenditures are almost twice as large in the third quarter as in the first quarter.

The Trend Component: Given inflation and economic growth, there is an upward trend in total tourism expenditures. However, the increase in tourism expenditures from 12 years of economic growth and inflation is less than the annual summer to winter seasonal decline in tourism expenditures. The summer peak value in 1986 is considerably higher than the winter and autumn 'lows' in 1997.

<u>The Business Cycle Component</u>: Finally, there is a business cycle in tourism expenditures. One way to visualize the business cycle component is to join the summer peak points from 1986 to 1997 (to form an upper bound) and to join the winter trough points from 1986 to 1997 (to form a lower bound). The seasonal band for tourism expenditures has a small business cycle wave over the 1986 to 1997 period. However, compared to the sharp summer-winter seasonal decline each year, the cyclical decline from a business cycle peak in 1990 to a recession low in 1991-92 is barely discernible in Figure 2.5.[10] The 1990-91 cyclical decline in third quarter (summer) tourism expenditures is only $8 million, less than 0.1 percent of the $6,035 million seasonal decline in 1990.[11]

The seasonal 'saw-tooth' pattern in Figure 2.5 is by far the dominant statistical feature of total tourism expenditure data. Annual seasonal swings in tourism expenditures are much larger than business cycle fluctuations and the trend increase in tourism expenditures over the 12 year period from 1986 to 1997.

Figure 2.6 presents tourism expenditures for two key transportation tourism commodities, passenger air transport and vehicle rentals. While there is a seasonal saw-tooth pattern for tourism expenditures on passenger air transport, the seasonal fluctuations in Figure 2.6(A) are relatively small. The 1997 seasonal peak to trough ratio for tourism expenditures on passenger air transport is only 1.34 ($2,891 million divided by $2,165 million), much less than the 1.93 seasonal peak to trough ratio for total tourism expenditures. The trend increase in tourism expenditures on passenger air transport over the 12 years from 1986 to 1997 is larger than the annual seasonal fluctuation (the fall and winter trough observations in 1997 are considerably higher than the summer peak observations in the late 1980s). While the business cycle fluctuations are much more obvious in Figure 2.6(A) than in Figure 2.5, the annual seasonal decline in tourism expenditures on passenger air transport exceeds the cyclical decline during the 1991-92 recession (see

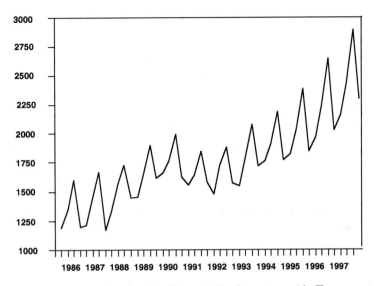

Figure 2.6A: Tourism Demand in Canada for Passenger Air Transport (Not Seasonally Adjusted, Millions of Dollars).

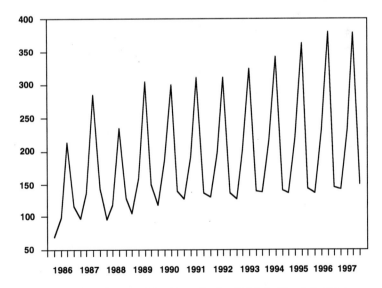

Figure 2.6B: Tourism Demand in Canada for Vehicle Rentals (Not Seasonally Adjusted, Millions of Dollars).

Table 2.5).

The seasonal 'saw-tooth' pattern is also the dominant feature
of tourism expenditures on vehicle rentals in Figure 2.6(B). The
huge annual seasonal decline from summer to autumn-winter
swamp any business cycle and long-run trends in tourism expenditures on vehicle rentals. The 1997 seasonal peak to trough ratio is
2.66 ($378 million divided by $142 million) for tourism expenditures on vehicle rentals.

Figure 2.7 presents the two key tourism commodities in the
accommodation category, hotels and motels. Again, there are very
large teeth in the 'saw-tooth' pattern for tourism expenditures on
hotels and motels. In both cases, the seasonal component swamps
the trend and business cycle components. Twelve years of inflation
and economic growth still leave the 1997 winter and autumn trough
observations considerably lower than the 1986 peak summer observation for tourism expenditures on hotels and motels. The seasonal
swing in tourism expenditures on hotels and motels is much larger
than the modest cyclical decline during the 1991-92 recession. In
relative terms, the annual seasonal decline in motel expenditures is
larger than the annual seasonal decline in hotel expenditures (the
1997 seasonal peak to trough ratio for motels is 3.22, compared to
1.98 for hotels).

Figure 2.8 presents tourism expenditures on (A) food and beverage services and (B) travel agency services. Again, the seasonal
'saw-tooth' pattern swamps business cycle and trend movements in
tourism expenditures on food and beverage services. The 1997 seasonal peak to trough ratio for tourism expenditures on food and
beverages is 2.19 ($2,714 million divided by $1,238 million).
Annual seasonal swings are much larger than the very slight business cycle fluctuation in tourism expenditures on food and beverage services. Twelve years of trend growth in tourism expenditures
on food and beverage services represent less than one-half of the

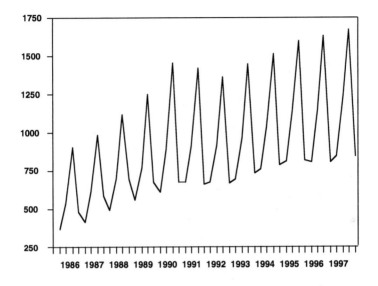

Figure 2.7A: Tourism Demand in Canada for Hotels (Not Seasonally Adjusted, Millions of Dollars).

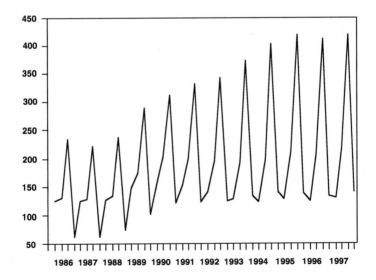

Figure 2.7B: Tourism Demand in Canada for Motels (Not Seasonally Adjusted, Millions of Dollars).

annual seasonal decline; the seasonal lows in 1997 are considerably lower than the seasonal peak in 1986.

The plot of tourism expenditures on travel agency services in Figure 2.8(B) reveals several interesting and important differences. First, there is a very strong positive trend in tourism expenditures on travel agency services; the seasonal low points in 1997 are considerably higher than the seasonal peaks during the late 1980s. Second, there is very little cyclical fluctuation in tourism expenditures on travel agency services; the 1991 Canadian recession is barely discernible in Figure 2.8(B). Third, unlike tourism expenditures on all other tourism commodities, which peak in the third quarter (summer) and bottom out in the fourth and first quarters of the year, tourism expenditures on travel agency services peak in the first quarter (winter) and bottom out in the third quarter (summer). The seasonal pattern for tourism expenditures on travel agency services is 'out of sync' with the seasonal pattern for all other tourism expenditures.

Tourism expenditures also can be disaggregated into domestic and export demand. Total tourism domestic expenditures and total tourism export expenditures are presented in Figure 2.9. Both exhibit a pronounced seasonal 'saw-tooth' pattern, peaking in the third quarter (summer) and bottoming out in the fourth and first quarters. In relative terms, seasonal swings in tourism export demand are twice as large as seasonal swings in tourism domestic demand. In 1997, the seasonal peak to trough ratio for total tourism export demand is 3.44 ($5,629 million divided by $1,635 million), compared to a seasonal peak to trough ratio for total tourism domestic demand of only 1.61 ($10,581 million divided by $6,585 million). Compared to tourism domestic demand, tourism export demand also has a much stronger upward trend (particularly in the 1990s) but no business cycle component.

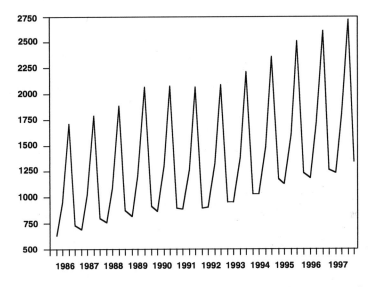

Figure 2.8A: Tourism Demand in Canada for Food & Beverage Services (Not Seasonally Adjusted, Millions of Dollars).

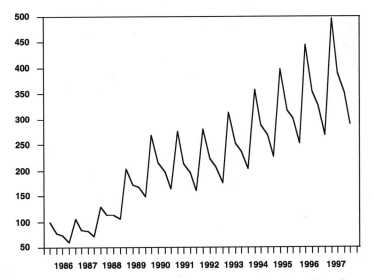

Figure 2.8B: Tourism Demand for Travel Agency Services (Not Seasonally Adjusted, Millions of Dollars).

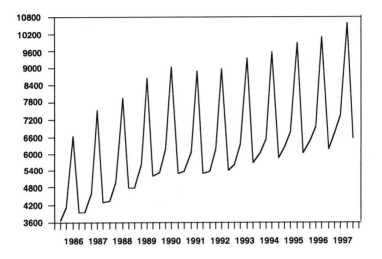

Figure 2.9A: Tourism Domestic Expenditures (Not Seasonally Adjusted, Millions of Dollars).

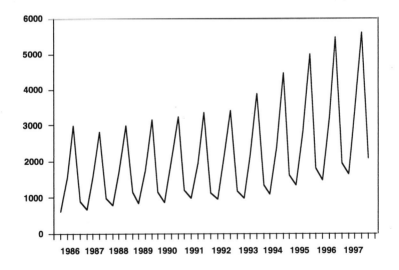

Figure 2.9B: Tourism Export Expenditures (Not Seasonally Adjusted, Millions of Dollars).

In summary, there is an obvious seasonal 'saw-tooth' pattern in Figures 2.5 to 2.9. Tourism is indeed very seasonal. However, the relative size and characteristics of the teeth in the 'saw-tooth' pattern vary from Figure to Figure. There are quite different seasonal patterns for different tourism commodities and for domestic versus export demand. Tourism expenditures on some tourism commodities (such as hotels, motels, and vehicle rentals) are much more 'seasonal' than tourism expenditures on other commodities (such as passenger air transport). And not all tourism expenditures peak in the summer; tourism expenditures on travel agency services peak in the winter season. The entire tourism sector does not swing together each year. Seasonality hits some parts of the tourism industry much harder than other parts.

MEASURING THE SEASONAL FACTORS IN TOURISM DEMAND DATA

Statistical regression analysis is used to estimate the magnitude of the seasonal factors (components) for tourism demand over the 1986 to 1997 period.[12] To facilitate comparisons between different NTIs, the estimated seasonal factors are constrained to sum to one. If there is no seasonality in the data, the estimates for the four seasonal factors would all be equal to .250, indicating that there is an equal amount of tourism expenditures in each quarter of the year. The magnitude of the seasonal variation in each tourism demand indicator is revealed by the deviation of the seasonal factor from .250, the 'no seasonality' benchmark case.

Tables 2.4, 2.6 and 2.7 present statistical estimates of the four seasonal factors for 75 tourism demand indicators.[13] The first column in each table records the average quarterly value for each tourism indicator. The last column in each table provides a summary measure of the degree of seasonality in each NTI. The four seasonal absolute deviations from .250 (the 'no seasonality' benchmark) are added together. For example, if the four estimated seasonal factors are .100, .250, .500, and .150, then the sum of the seasonal absolute deviations (SAD) is equal to .150 + .000 + .250 + .100 = .500. This SAD summary measure has a minimum value of .000 (no seasonality in the data) and a maximum value of 1.500 (all expenditures are in one quarter of the year). The higher the SAD number, the greater the degree of seasonality in the NTI. This SAD number is used to compare the magnitude of the seasonal variation in different tourism commodities.

Tourism Demand in Canada
Table 2.4 presents the seasonal factors and SAD number for the 25 NTIs for tourism demand. Starting with the bottom line, 42.6 percent of total tourism expenditures take place in the third quarter, compared to 16.5 percent in the first quarter, 17.1 percent in the fourth quarter, and 23.8 percent in the second quarter. The statistical estimates suggest that there are three different tourism seasons in Canada: a summer high, followed by a six months autumn-winter freeze and a spring thaw.

This pronounced seasonal pattern exists for nearly all tourism commodities. With one exception (travel agency services), tourism expenditures on each commodity peak in the third quarter and bottom out in the fourth and first quarters. In all cases the second quarter has the second highest seasonal factor, but the value of the second quarter seasonal is always closer to the 'low' seasonal factor rather than the 'peak' seasonal factor. All 75 seasonal factors for the first, third, and fourth quarters in Table 2.4 are significantly different[14] from .25, the 'no seasonality' benchmark case. For each tourism commodity, both the third quarter (summer) seasonal factor and the second quarter (spring) seasonal factor are significantly different from the first quarter (winter) seasonal factor.

While the individual tourism commodities presented in Table 2.4 all have a similar seasonal 'saw-tooth' pattern (see Figures 2.5, 2.6, 2.7 and 2.8), there are important differences. As noted above, tourism expenditures on travel agencies services peak in the first

Table 2.4 Seasonal Factors for Tourism Demand in Canada

	Mean Quarterly Value (Millions $)	Q1 Winter	Q2 Spring	Q3 Summer	Q4 Autumn	Sum of Seasonal Absolute Deviations
		Seasonal Factors				
Transportation	3439	.193	.241	.365	.201	.230
Passenger air transport	1779	.220	.256	.306	.219	.123
Passenger rail transport	46	.186	.238	.371	.205	.242
Interurban bus transport	120	.184	.255	.366	.195	.241
Vehicle rental	188	.130	.242	.473	.155	.446
Vehicle repairs and parts	418	.172	.215	.426	.187	.353
Vehicle fuel	761	.172	.221	.420	.187	.341
Other transportation	128	.157	.242	.431	.170	.361
Accommodation	1233	.136	.246	.481	.137	.463
Hotels	905	.150	.253	.437	.180	.381
Motels	191	.153	.237	.508	.102	.517
Other accommodation	136	.027	.214	.714	.046	.927
Food and beverage services	1363	.142	.247	.459	.152	.418
Meals, from accommodation	198	.124	.255	.494	.127	.499
Meals, from food/beverages	818	.146	.247	.451	.156	.401
Alcohol, from accommodation	117	.153	.247	.435	.165	.370
Alcohol, from food/beverages	186	.139	.244	.462	.155	.425
Meals and alcohol from other industries	44	.145	.221	.501	.133	.504
Other tourism commodities	751	.197	.225	.460	.118	.420
Recreation and entertainment	508	.138	.216	.513	.133	.526
Travel agency services	224	.550	.273	.177	.000	.645
Convention fees	20	.174	.257	.321	.248	.155
Total tourism commodities	6787	.173	.242	.413	.172	.325
Total other commodities	1730	.137	.225	.477	.161	.454
Tourism expenditures	8517	.165	.238	.426	.171	.352

quarter (55 percent of all expenditures), presumably reflecting the sale of air line ticket packages to Canadians flying south in search of warmer temperatures.

The degree of seasonality varies considerably for tourism expenditures on different commodities. Third quarter seasonal factors for tourism expenditures on tourism commodities other than travel agency services range from .306 to .714, and the SAD numbers range from .123 to .927. Tourism expenditures on other accommodation, such as tourist cabins, camping grounds, and trailer parks have the highest degree of seasonality, with the third quarter seasonal factor of .714 and a SAD number of .927. Other tourism expenditures with peak seasonal factors and SAD numbers larger than .500 are recreation and entertainment, motels, and travel agency services (the seasonal peak for travel agency services occurs in the first quarter, not the third quarter). Tourism expenditures on vehicle rentals, hotels, and food and beverage services have above average third quarter seasonal factors (in the .437 to .473 range) and above average SAD numbers (in the .381 to .446 range). At the other end of the spectrum, tourism expenditures on passenger air transport (the largest tourism expenditure component) have the lowest degree of seasonality, with a third quarter peak seasonal factor of .306 and a SAD number of only .123. Canadian air carriers have been able to smooth out seasonal demand patterns by offering off-season seat sales and by flying Canadians south in the winter season.

Any time-series, such as tourism expenditures on hotels, can be broken down into four statistical components: a seasonal component, a trend component, a business cycle component, and irregular or other movements in the data. The linear regression technique used to estimate the seasonal factors reported in Table 2.4 also can be used to determine how much of the statistical variation in each NTI is explained (1) by the seasonal component, (2) by the trend component, and (3) by the remaining business cycle and irregular components of the data.[15]

The first three columns in Table 2.5 present the percent of the statistical variation in the demand for each tourism commodity that is explained by the seasonal component, the trend component, and the business cycle and other components. The relative importance of the seasonal component can be determined by comparing these three numbers for each tourism commodity. The final two columns in Table 2.5 present the annual seasonal decline and the business cyclical decline in each NTI. The annual seasonal decline is measured by the percentage difference between the largest and smallest seasonal factor (as presented in Table 2.4). For most NTIs, the annual seasonal decline is the percentage decrease from the peak third quarter seasonal factor to the first quarter seasonal factor, the summer-winter effect. The cyclical decline for each NTI is measured by the percentage decrease from the 1989-90 business cycle peak to the bottom of the 1991-92 recession, using seasonally adjusted NTI data measured in constant prices.[16] By comparing the numbers in the final two columns of Table 2.5 we can determine whether the annual seasonal decline in tourism demand dominates the cyclical decline. Is the amplitude of the tourism seasonal cycle larger than the amplitude of the tourism business cycle?

The bottom line of Table 2.5 indicates that the seasonal component accounts for 75 percent of the statistical variation in total tourism expenditures. The 61.3 percent seasonal decline in tourism expenditures each year is almost seven times larger than the 9.0 percent cyclical decline during the 1991 recession. Seasonal swings in tourism demand account for most of the statistical variation in nearly all of the commodities listed in Table 2.5. With the exception of three tourism commodities (passenger air transport, travel agency services and convention fees), seasonal swings account for at least 66 percent of the statistical variation in tourism demand.

Table 2.5 Summary Statistics for Tourism Demand in Canada

	Percent of Variation Explained by				
	Seasonality	Trend	Cyclical/ Other	Seasonal Decline	Cyclical Decline
Transportation	64	33	3	47.1%	13.3%
Passenger air transport	24	66	10	28.4	23.0
Passenger rail transport	73	0	27	49.9	-
Interurban bus transport	73	17	10	49.7	29.1
Vehicle rental	83	11	6	72.5	9.1
Vehicle repairs and parts	78	18	4	59.6	12.7
Vehicle fuel	86	11	3	59.1	16.6
Other transportation	82	15	3	63.6	19.6
Accommodation	80	16	4	71.7	4.4
Hotels	70	25	5	65.7	7.1
Motels	81	10	9	79.9	7.0
Other accommodation	95	3	2	96.2	7.4
Food and beverage services	81	17	2	69.1	14.9
Meals, from accommodation	92	6	2	74.9	17.6
Meals, from food/beverages	77	22	1	67.6	14.8
Alcohol, from accommodation	96	2	2	64.8	21.6
Alcohol, from food/beverages	66	32	2	69.9	16.2
Meals and alcohol from other industries	76	19	5	73.5	19.4
Other tourism commodities	49	44	7	74.4	18.4
Recreation and entertainment	75	17	8	74.1	24.1
Travel agency services	13	82	5	100.0	7.0
Convention fees	29	63	8	17.1	11.8
Total tourism commodities	71	26	3	58.4	10.7
Total other commodities	85	14	1	71.3	7.8
Tourism expenditures	75	23	2	61.3	9.0

For every tourism commodity listed in Table 2.5, the annual seasonal decline is larger than the cyclical decline during the 1991 recession. For tourism expenditures on hotels, motels, other accommodation, travel agency services, and vehicle rentals, the annual seasonal decline is 8 to 14 times larger than the cyclical decline during the 1991 recession. Tourism expenditures on passenger air transport, the least seasonal of all tourism commodities, have an annual seasonal decline (28.4 percent) that is larger than the cyclical decline (23.0 percent) during the 1991 recession.

Tourism Domestic Demand in Canada

An interesting difference in seasonal patterns emerges when tourism expenditures are disaggregated into domestic versus export demand. Table 2.6 presents estimates for a comparable set of seasonal factors for tourism domestic demand, which represents about three-quarters of total tourism demand over the 1986 to 1997 period. Qualitatively, the seasonal pattern for tourism domestic demand is very similar to that found for total tourism demand.

With the exception of tourism domestic demand for travel agency services, tourism domestic demand for each commodity peaks in the third quarter and bottoms out in the fourth and first quarters. Sixty-nine of the 75 estimated seasonal factors for the first, third and fourth quarters in Table 2.6 are significantly different from .25, the 'no seasonality' benchmark. With the exception of tourism domestic demand for passenger air transport and convention fees, all of the third quarter (summer) seasonal factors are significantly different from the first quarter (winter) seasonal factors. And 21 of the 25 estimated second quarter (spring) seasonal factors are significantly different from the first quarter (winter) seasonal factor.

The relative ranking of SAD numbers for various tourism commodities in Table 2.6 is also very similar to the relative ranking in Table 2.4. In both tables the same five tourism commodities (other accommodation, travel agency services, recreation and entertainment, motels, and meals and alcohol from other industries) have the highest SAD numbers and the same two tourism commodities (passenger air transport and convention fees) have the lowest SAD numbers.

There is, however, an important quantitative difference between the seasonal factors in Table 2.4 and Table 2.6. The seasonal variation in tourism domestic demand is smaller than seasonal variation in total tourism demand. The third quarter peak sea-

Table 2.6 Seasonal Factors for Tourism Domestic Demand in Canada

		Seasonal Factors				
	Mean Quarterly Value (Millions $)	Q1 Winter	Q2 Spring	Q3 Summer	Q4 Autumn	Sum of Seasonal Absolute Deviations
Transportation	2884	.217	.235	.329	.218	.157
Passenger air transport	1457	.251	.249	.257	.243	.018
Passenger rail transport	34	.217	.243	.316	.224	.132
Interurban bus transport	96	.215	.244	.322	.219	.143
Vehicle rental	108	.193	.240	.357	.210	.214
Vehicle repairs and parts	405	.175	.214	.421	.190	.342
Vehicle fuel	688	.184	.218	.403	.195	.306
Other transportation	96	.188	.233	.378	.201	.255
Accommodation	774	.174	.231	.430	.165	.360
Hotels	551	.188	.243	.381	.188	.262
Motels	136	.200	.236	.436	.128	.373
Other accommodation	87	.045	.151	.723	.081	.946
Food and beverage services	882	.184	.237	.407	.172	.314
Meals, from accommodation	126	.181	.232	.412	.175	.323
Meals, from food/beverages	530	.182	.241	.405	.172	.309
Alcohol, from accommodation	74	.196	.234	.381	.189	.262
Alcohol, from food/beverages	123	.179	.238	.420	.163	.340
Meals and alcohol from other industries	29	.182	.241	.405	.138	.446
Other tourism commodities	561	.256	.205	.400	.139	.313
Recreation and entertainment	332	.184	.194	.462	.160	.424
Travel agency services	217	.578	.257	.144	.021	.670
Convention fees	12	.261	.195	.259	.285	.110
Total tourism commodities	5101	.206	.233	.364	.197	.228
Total other commodities	1302	.167	.218	.437	.178	.373
Tourism expenditures	6403	.199	.220	.379	.193	.258

sonal factor for tourism domestic expenditures is .379 (bottom line in Table 2.6) compared to .426 for total tourism expenditures (bottom line in Table 2.4). The SAD number for tourism domestic expenditures is only .258 compared to a SAD number of .352 for total tourism expenditures. With two exceptions, the SAD number for tourism domestic demand for each commodity in Table 2.6 is lower than the corresponding SAD number for total tourism demand in Table 2.4.[17]

Tourism Export Demand in Canada
Table 2.7 presents the estimated seasonal factors for tourism export demand. For every tourism commodity, tourism export demand peaks in the third quarter and bottoms out in the fourth and first quarters. For each tourism commodity, the first, third, and fourth seasonal factors are significantly different from .250. Both the peak third quarter (summer) seasonal factor and the second quarter (spring) seasonal factor are significantly different from the first quarter (winter) seasonal factor in every case.

The seasonal variation in tourism export demand is much larger than that found for tourism domestic demand. Comparing the bottom lines in Tables 2.4, 2.6, and 2.7, a SAD number of .788 for tourism export demand is two to three times larger than the SAD number for tourism domestic demand (.258) and total tourism demand (.352). The peak third quarter seasonal factor of .619 for tourism export demand is considerably larger than the peak third quarter seasonal factor for tourism domestic demand (.379) and total tourism demand (.426). For all tourism commodities, seasonal swings for tourism export demand are larger than that found for tourism domestic demand. All of the SAD numbers in Table 2.7 are larger than the corresponding SAD numbers in Tables 2.4 and 2.6. With one exception (other accommodation), the peak third quarter seasonal factor for tourism export demand is larger than the corresponding third quarter seasonal factor in Tables 2.4 and 2.6.

Table 2.7 Seasonal Factors for Tourism Exports - Canada

	Mean Quarterly Value (Millions $)	Seasonal Factors				Sum of Seasonal Absolute Deviations
		Q1 Winter	Q2 Spring	Q3 Summer	Q4 Autumn	
Transportation	555	.020	.282	.628	.070	.820
Passenger air transport	322	.050	.290	.564	.096	.709
Passenger rail transport	12	.017	.212	.668	.103	.835
Interurban bus transport	24	.000	.323	.677	.000	1.000
Vehicle rental	80	.000	.229	.771	.000	1.042
Vehicle repairs and parts	13	.042	.257	.608	.093	.729
Vehicle fuel	73	.041	.260	.604	.095	.728
Other transportation	32	.004	.287	.691	.018	.955
Accommodation	459	.049	.280	.598	.073	.756
Hotels	354	.069	.275	.556	.100	.662
Motels	55	.000	.241	.744	.014	.989
Other accommodation	50	.000	.333	.667	.000	1.000
Food and beverage services	482	.032	.275	.598	.095	.745
Meals, from accommodation	72	.000	.305	.677	.018	.964
Meals, from food/beverages	289	.045	.266	.576	.113	.684
Alcohol, from accommodation	43	.037	.284	.584	.095	.736
Alcohol, from food/beverages	63	.025	.264	.583	.128	.695
Meals and alcohol from other industries	16	.043	.259	.581	.117	.680
Other tourism commodities	191	.000	.291	.658	.050	.899
Recreation and entertainment	176	.008	.278	.657	.057	.869
Travel agency services	7	.000	.408	.591	.000	.999
Convention fees	8	.013	.372	.435	.180	.614
Total tourism commodities	1686	.030	.280	.614	.076	.789
Total other commodities	428	.017	.255	.637	.091	.783
Tourism expenditures	2114	.027	.275	.619	.079	.788

The bar charts in Figures 2.10 and 2.11 highlight the differences in the seasonal factors for tourism export demand and tourism domestic demand. In all cases, tourism export demand has a higher third quarter seasonal factor than tourism domestic demand. In all cases, tourism export demand has a lower seasonal factor in the first and fourth quarters than tourism domestic demand. The seasonal swings in tourism export demand are consistently much larger than the seasonal fluctuations in tourism domestic demand. Perhaps the two most interesting comparisons are for passenger air transport and travel agency services (in Figure 2.11). Compared to minimal seasonal variation in tourism domestic demand for passenger air transport, there is a very pronounced seasonal pattern in tourism export demand for passenger air transport (peaking at .564 in the third quarter). In the case of travel agency services, tourism export demand peaks at .592 in the third quarter while tourism domestic demand peaks at .578 in the first quarter. This is the only case where the seasonal patterns for domestic and export demand are not synchronized.

There are several interesting implications of the much more pronounced seasonal pattern in tourism export demand than in tourism domestic demand. First, given that tourism export demand has been increasing as a share of total tourism demand in Canada (rising from 22.8 percent in 1987 to 29.0 percent in 1997), seasonal fluctuations in tourism are likely greater in the 1990s than existed in the 1980s. The tourism industry is becoming more seasonal over time. Second, the export share of total tourism demand varies for different tourism commodities; for example, in 1997 export demand accounted for 60 percent of tourism expenditures on vehicle rentals, 48 percent of tourism expenditures on hotels, and 19 percent of tourism expenditures on passenger air transport. The export side of tourism demand is largely responsible for the seasonal pattern in total tourism expenditures on hotels, vehicle rentals, and passenger air transport.

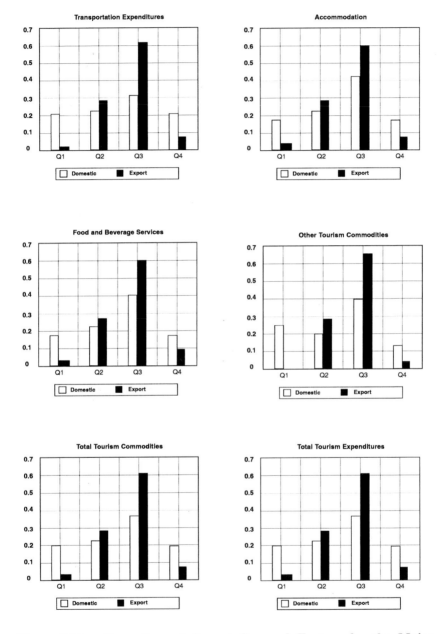

Figure 2.10: Domestic and Export Seasonal Factors for the Major Components of Tourism Expenditures.

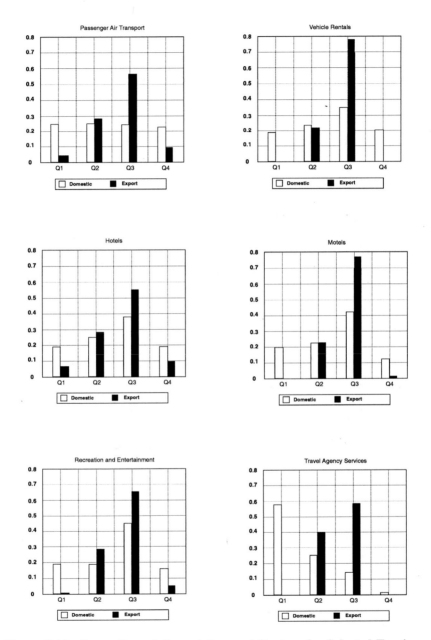

Figure 2.11: Domestic and Export Seasonal Factors for Selected Tourism Commodities.

ARE THE SEASONAL FACTORS IMMUTABLE?

Tables 2.4, 2.6 and 2.7 present estimates for the 'average' seasonal factors for 75 tourism demand indicators over the 1986 to 1997 period. Are these seasonal factors for tourism demand always the same each year? Could they change under a different set of circumstances? If so, what determines the magnitude of the seasonal factors for tourism demand each year? Do temperature deviations from seasonal norms cause the seasonal factors to deviate from their average values? Does a hot summer raise the peak summer tourism seasonal factor even higher? Does an unusually mild winter result in a lower (or higher) winter seasonal factor?

To answer these questions, additional explanatory variables are added to the statistical regression used to estimate the seasonal factors for tourism demand. For each season of the year, the *Climate Trends and Variations Bulletin for Canada* reports the deviation of the average Canadian temperature from the seasonal norm. This seasonal temperature deviation variable is used to test for an abnormal weather effect on the seasonal factors for each NTI.[18] A significant positive coefficient for a seasonal temperature deviation variable indicates that temperatures above the seasonal norm increase the seasonal factor. The size of the coefficient on the temperature deviation variable indicates the amount of additional tourism expenditures that is attributable to a temperature that is one degree above the seasonal norm. If the seasonal temperature variables have significant statistical effects, then the tourism seasonal factors will vary from year to year, depending on temperature deviations from seasonal norms.

The statistical evidence for the effects of seasonal temperature deviations on seasonal factors for the NTIs is mixed. For two seasons (spring and autumn), virtually all of the estimated coefficients for the temperature deviation variables are not significantly different from zero. For the first quarter of the year, temperature deviations from the seasonal norm have a statistically significant effect on the seasonal factor for only six of the 75 NTIs, and in each case the estimated coefficient is negative. For example, below normal winter temperatures appear to have a positive effect on domestic expenditures on travel agency services (more Canadians booking winter vacations in a warmer climate). However, the estimated coefficients for the winter temperature deviation variable are relatively small.

The strongest statistical results are for the third quarter of the year. Temperature deviations from the seasonal norm have a significant effect on the summer seasonal factors for 40 of the 75 NTIs (see Table 2.8). All of the estimated coefficients are positive; temperatures above the seasonal norm have a significant positive effect on the demand for many tourism commodities.

This positive summer temperature effect on tourism expenditures arises primarily on the domestic side of tourism demand. With one major exception, tourism export demand in the third quarter is not significantly affected by temperature deviations from the seasonal norm. However, the one exception is important. Tourism export demand for passenger air transport in the third quarter is significantly affected by temperature deviations in Canada. One degree Celsius above the summer seasonal norm results in an additional $71 million of export demand for Canadian passenger air transport ($71 million is over 8 percent of tourism export expenditures on passenger air transport in the third quarter of 1997).

Turning to domestic demand, almost all of the NTIs are significantly affected by summer temperature deviations from the seasonal norm. One degree Celsius above the summer seasonal norm results in an additional $405 million tourism domestic expenditures (which is 3.8 percent of tourism domestic expenditures in the third quarter of 1997), consisting of $110 million transportation expenditures, $115 million accommodation expenditures, $63 million food and beverage expenditures, $67 million other tourism commodities (mostly recreation and entertainment), and $51 million other commodities. Rather interestingly, the only important tourism commodity where domestic demand is not significantly affected by summer temperature deviations is passenger air transport. Above average summer temperatures result in Canadians making greater use of their cars for summer vacations, and not increasing their purchases of passenger air fares.

Table 2.8 The Effects of Temperature Deviations from the Seasonal Norm on the Third Quarter Seasonal Factor (Millions of Dollars)

	Total Tourism Demand	Tourism Domestic Demand	Tourism Export Demand
Transportation	215	110	105
Passenger air transport	-	-	71
Passenger rail transport	-	-	2
Interurban bus transport	-	-	-
Vehicle rental	21	-	-
Vehicle repairs and parts	57	56	-
Vehicle fuel	54	49	-
Other transportation	9	-	-
Accommodation	157	115	-
Hotels	105	72	-
Motels	27	22	-
Other accommodation	25	21	-
Food and beverage services	104	63	-
Meals, from accommodation	15	11	-
Meals, from food/beverages	63	36	-
Alcohol, from accommodation	-	-	-
Alcohol, from food/beverages	16	10	-
Meals and alcohol from other industries	6	4	-
Other tourism commodities	86	67	-
Recreation and entertainment	79	62	-
Travel agency services	-	-	-
Convention fees	2	-	-
Total tourism commodities	563	354	-
Total other commodities	94	51	-
Tourism expenditures	657	405	-

SUMMARY AND CONCLUSIONS

Tourism is a leading growth sector and job creator in the Canadian economy. Over the 1986 - 1996 period total tourism expenditures in Canada (measured in constant prices) increased by 26 percent. The high growth rate in tourism expenditures has been largely fuelled largely by a tremendous surge in tourism export demand, particularly since 1992. Tourism export expenditures increased by 58 percent from 1986 to 1996, more than double the increase in GDP. Turning to specific tourism commodities, during the 1986-96 period the estimated trend increases for the major components of tourism demand in Canada are 8.21 percent for transportation, 39.10 percent for accommodation, 9.64 percent for food and beverage services, and 41.70 percent for other tourism commodities. The variation in estimated trend increases is even larger when one compares various tourism commodity sub-components. A huge 224.60 percent trend increase in tourism demand for travel agency services leads the pack, followed by a 42.94 percent trend increase in tourism demand for hotels. While there is a 39.10 percent trend increase in tourism demand for accommodation, tourism demand for food and beverage services from accommodation establishments has an estimated trend decrease of 14.60 percent. The estimated trend increases for tourism export demand are, with one exception (vehicle repairs and parts), larger than the estimated trend increases for tourism domestic demand.

There are very pronounced business cycles in tourism demand; 73 percent of the cyclical variation in tourism demand in Canada can be statistically explained by the cyclical variation in Canadian GDP. The cyclical variation in tourism demand in Canada is about 1.5 times the size of the cyclical variation in GDP. However, the cyclical variation in Canadian GDP explains only 12 percent of the variation in tourism export demand; tourism export demand depends primarily on economic conditions outside of Canada, the value of the Canadian dollar, and on irregular events. There is considerable variation in the cyclical properties of different tourism commodities. The Canadian business cycle hits passenger air transport, food and beverage services, recreation and entertainment, and travel agency services particularly hard; the cyclical variation in tourism demand for these tourism commodities is more than twice as large as the cyclical variation in GDP. On the other hand, tourism demand for vehicle rentals, vehicle fuel, and motel accommodation appear to be relatively immune from the vicissitudes of the Canadian business cycle. Very little of the cyclical variation in these three tourism commodities can be explained by the cyclical variation in GDP.

There is a very sharp and pronounced seasonal pattern in Canadian tourism expenditures. Over the 1986 to 1997 period, third quarter (summer) tourism expenditures account for 43 percent of annual tourism expenditures, compared to only 17 percent in the first and fourth quarters. If Benjamin Franklin were a Canadian he undoubtedly would have said "nothing can be said to be certain, except death, taxes, and winter." Unfortunately, the Canadian winter appears to last six months; the seasonal factor for the fourth quarter is not significantly different from the seasonal factor for the first quarter. Seasonality explains 75 percent of the statistical variation in tourism expenditures and the annual seasonal decline in tourism expenditures from summer to winter is almost three times larger than the cyclical decline in tourism expenditures during the 1991 recession.

While there is a very distinctive seasonal pattern in tourism demand data, the nature and degree of seasonality varies considerably for different tourism commodities. Tourism expenditures on accommodation have the most severe degree of seasonality; third quarter tourism expenditures account for 44 percent of annual hotel expenditures, 51 percent of annual motel expenditures, and 71 percent of other accommodation expenditures. Tourism expenditures on vehicle rentals and recreation and entertainment also have a high degree of seasonality, with the third quarter accounting for 47 percent and 51 percent respectively of annual tourism expenditures. While tourism expenditures on travel agency services have a peak seasonal factor of 55 percent, the seasonal peak is in the first quarter (the winter season). Tourism expenditures on passenger air transport have the least degree of seasonality; the peak third quarter accounts for 31 percent of passenger air transport demand, compared to 22 percent in both the first and fourth quarters.

There is also a much more pronounced seasonal pattern for tourism export demand than for tourism domestic demand. Sixty-two percent of annual tourism export expenditures occur in the third quarter, with only 3 percent and 8 percent of annual tourism export expenditures occurring in the first and fourth quarters, compared to 38 percent of annual tourism domestic expenditures in the third quarter, with 20 percent and 19 percent in the first and fourth quarters. For all tourism commodities except convention fees, the third quarter accounts for more than 55 percent of annual tourism export demand. Given the rising share of tourism export demand in total tourism demand during the 1990s, the degree of seasonality in tourism expenditures is likely greater in the 1990s than in the 1980s.

Finally, temperature deviations from the seasonal norm appear to have a positive effect on tourism expenditures in the third quarter of the year. This positive summer temperature effect occurs predominantly on the domestic side of tourism demand. One degree Celsius above the summer seasonal norm is estimated to increase tourism domestic expenditures by $405 million, a 4 percent increase. The only important tourism commodity where domestic demand in not significantly affected by summer temperature deviations is passenger air transport. On the export side of tourism demand, passenger air transport is the only major tourism commodity that is affected by Canadian temperature deviations from the summer norm. While there is a significant positive temperature effect on summer tourism demand for many tourism commodities, temperatures above the seasonal norm do not appear to affect tourism expenditures in the second and fourth quarters of the year, and perhaps have a small negative effect on tourism expenditures in the first quarter of the year.

One final caveat. While tourism is a leading growth sector in the Canadian economy, there is considerable variation in trend growth rates, cyclical fluctuations and seasonal swings within the tourism sector. The entire tourism sector does not grow, cycle, and swing together. One should be careful in deriving implications for tourism policy and development based on aggregate tourism data.

End Notes:
[1]Not all travel constitutes tourism. For example, commuting and travelling for the purpose of studying or moving to a new work location is not considered to be tourism.

[2]For additional information on tourism concepts and methodology, see the *Guide to the National Tourism Indicators, Sources and Methods*, Statistics Canada, Ottawa, 1996.

[3]The initial sections of this chapter are based on D.A. Wilton, *Recent Developments in Tourism as Revealed by the National Tourism Indicators*, Canadian Tourism Commission Research Report, Ottawa, 1998.

[4]Estimates for the trend in each tourism indicator are produced using the 'least squares' regression technique. This statistical technique determines the 'best' trend line that can be fitted through all observations; it is 'best' in the sense that it produces the least sum of squared residuals, the deviations between the actual observations and the trend line. The trend increase in each tourism indicator is calculated by dividing the last observation on the trend line by the first observation on the trend line.

[5]The rise and fall of the Canadian dollar during this period is one possible explanation for a negative trend in the demand for passenger air transport. During the early 1986-90 period the Canadian dollar appreciated by approximately 20 percent against the U.S. dollar, prompting many Canadians to purchase passenger air fares on Canadian airlines to visit U.S. and foreign destinations in order to take advantage of the increased purchasing power of the Canadian dollar outside Canada. The reverse happened in the 1990s as the value of the Canadian dollar fell sharply against the U.S. dollar, prompting many Canadians to forego the purchase of passenger air transportation to U.S. destinations.

[6]The cyclical component, defined as (actual-trend)/trend, measures the deviation of the actual quarterly observation (seasonally adjusted) from the trend line.

[7]The final sections of this chapter are based on D.A. Wilton and T. Wirjanto, *An Analysis of the Seasonal Variation in the National Tourism Indicators*, Canadian Tourism Commission Research Report, Ottawa, 1999.

[8]R.W. Butler, "Seasonality in tourism: issues and problems," in *Tourism: State of the Art*, edited by A.V. Seaton *et al.*, Chichester, Wiley, 1994: 332.

[9]R.R.V. BarOn, *Seasonality in Tourism*, Economist Intelligence Unit, London, 1975.

[10]The data in Figure 2.5 are measured in *current* dollars, which includes the effects of inflation. If tourism expenditures were plotted in constant dollars, the 1991-92 recession would be more noticeable. Statistics Canada does not publish NTI data in *constant* dollars which are *not seasonally adjusted*.

[11]Measured in *constant* dollars, there was a 9.0 percent peak-to-trough cyclical decline in tourism expenditures during the 1991-92 recession (see Table 2.5).

[12]Each NTI is 'regressed' on four seasonal dummy variables and a time trend; the estimates for the seasonal factors are based on 'detrended' NTI data.

[13]While each of the 300 estimated seasonal factors should lie in the [0,1] interval, the statistical estimate for 11 seasonal factors is a small negative number. Since these negative estimates are not significantly different from zero, these 11 anomalous negative seasonal factors are constrained to have a .000 value. Most of these .000 value seasonal factors are for tourism commodities with relatively small expenditure levels, such as tourism export expenditures on bus transportation, motels, other accommodation, and travel agency services (see Table 2.7).

[14]'Significantly different' is used in the statistical sense that there is a 95 percent probability that the estimate of the seasonal factor is different from 0.25.

[15]Two regressions are run for each NTI. First, each NTI is regressed on four seasonal dummy variables; the R^2 from this regression indicates the percent of the variation in the NTI explained by the seasonal component. Second, a time trend is added to the regression; the increase in the R^2 indicates the percent of the variation in the NTI explained by the trend. The percent of the variation in the NTI explained by the business cycle and other irregular components is determined residually (the three numbers add up to 100 percent).

[16]The NTIs plotted in Figures 2.5 through 2.8 expressed in *current* dollars, not *constant* dollars.

[17]The two exceptions are for relatively small expenditure items, other accommodation and travel agency services, and the difference between the SAD numbers is very small.

[18]The above/below average temperature variable is multiplied by each of the four seasonal dummy variables and these four seasonal temperature variables are included in the statistical regression used to estimate the seasonal factors for each of the 75 NTIs. Unlike first quarter NTI data which begin on January 1, winter seasonal weather data begin on December 21. Quarterly seasonal weather data lead quarterly NTI data by about one-third of a month. Since it takes time for people to adjust their tourism plans to an unexpected change in the weather, quarterly NTI data should be regressed on weather data that begin prior to the start of the NTI quarter.

REFERENCES

BarOn, R.R.V. (1975) *Seasonality in Tourism*, London: Economist Intelligence Unit.

Beaulieu-Caron, L. (1997) "National tourism indicators: a new tool for analyzing tourism in Canada," Travel-log, Ottawa, ON: Statistics Canada, Catalogue No. 87-003-XPB, 1-6.

Butler, R.W. (1994) "Seasonality in tourism: issues and problems," in Seaton, A.V. *et al.* (eds.), *Tourism: State of the Art*, Chichester: Wiley, 332-339.

Guide to the National Tourism Indicators (1996) *Sources and Methods, System of National Accounts*, Ottawa, ON: Statistics Canada, Catalogue No. 13-594-GPE.

National Tourism Indicators (1996) *Historical Estimates 1986 to 1995*, Ottawa, ON: System of National Accounts, Statistics Canada, Catalogue No. 13-220-XPB.

_____ (1997) *Historical Estimates 1987 to 1996*, Ottawa, ON: System of National Accounts, Statistics Canada, Catalogue No. 13-220-XPB.

Wilton, D.A. (1998) *Recent Developments in Tourism as Revealed by the National Tourism Indicators*, Ottawa, ON: Canadian Tourism Commission Research Report.

Wilton, D.A. and Wirjanto, T. (1999) *An Analysis of the Seasonal Variation in the National Tourism Indicators*, Ottawa, ON: Canadian Tourism Commission Research Report.

Chapter 3

A Broad Context Model of Destination Development Scenarios

David B. Weaver
George Mason University
formerly at
Griffith University Gold Coast Campus

N o one can deny the remarkable expansion that has occurred in the global tourism industry during the latter half of the 20th century (World Tourism Organization (WTO), 1998). Similarly, it is difficult to challenge the primacy of Butler's resort cycle (Butler, 1980) as the most cited and empirically investigated model for describing the growth of tourism within particular destinations. Without discussing this literature in detail (recent literature reviews and useful critiques already have been provided by di Benedetto and Bojanic, 1993; Agarwal, 1994; Oppermann, 1995; Baum, 1998; and Russell and Faulkner, 1998), suffice it to say that few if any investigations either categorically accept or reject Butler's model. After almost 20 years of exposure, there seems to be an emerging consensus that the 'Butler sequence' represents but one evolutionary scenario among a range of destination possibilities, and that the concept of carrying capacity, upon which much of the model is based, is far more malleable, subjective, and complex than the sequence implies. In addition, there is a growing recognition of the model's utility as an 'ideal type' against which real-life deviations can be measured and assessed (Harrison, 1995). The purpose of this chapter is to introduce a broad context model of destination development, within which various scenarios, including the classic Butler sequence itself, can be situated and assessed in terms of their prevalence and likelihood. The implications of the model for the management of tourism destinations are also considered, and a specific demonstration made with respect to the Gold Coast of Australia.

THE BROAD CONTEXT MODEL

The proposed model initially consists of four inclusive tourism ideal types, based on the relationship between the level of tourism intensity or scale, and the amount of regulation associated with the tourism sector (Figure 3.1). Although it is recognized that these two variables are continuous in reality, the uses of discrete categories is

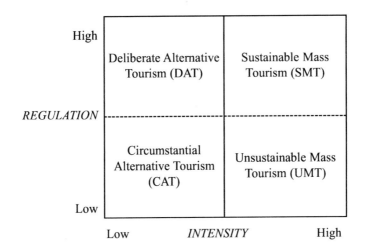

Figure 3.1: Destination Possibilities.

entirely appropriate for purposes of generalization and discussion. *Circumstantial Alternative Tourism* (CAT) destinations have a non-regulated, small-scale tourism sector that superficially resembles Alternative Tourism (Weaver, 1991). This latter concept, which has been much debated in the literature (Butler, 1989; Smith and Eadington, 1992; Romeril, 1994), can itself be presented as an ideal type contrasted with 'mass tourism' through a series of semantic differentials (Table 3.1). CAT destinations (as an ideal type) have the indicated Alternative Tourism characteristics for markets, accommodations, attractions and economic status, but lack the appropriate regulatory environment that ensures a higher probability of continued adherence to those traits. If conceived in terms of the Butler sequence, CAT destinations are simply locations situat-

Table 3.1 Ideal Types, Mass Tourism and Alternative Tourism

Characteristic	Mass Tourism	Alternative Tourism	Type of AT
Markets			
Segment	Psychocentric-midcentric	Allocentric-midcentric	CAT / DAT
Volume and Mode	High; package tours	Low; individual arrangements	
Seasonality	Distinct high and low seasons	No distinct seasonality	
Origins	A few dominant markets	No dominant markets	
Attractions			
Emphasis	Highly commercialized	Moderately commercialized	CAT / DAT
Character	Generic, 'contrived'	Area specific, 'authentic'	
Orientation	Tourists only or mainly	Tourists and locals	
Accommodation			
Size	Large-scale	Small-scale	CAT / DAT
Spatial pattern	Concentrated in 'tourist areas'	Dispersed throughout area	
Density	High density	Low density	
Architecture	'International' style; obtrusive, non-sympathetic	Vernacular style, unobtrusive, complementary	
Ownership	Non-local, large corporations	Local, small businesses	
Economic status			
Role of tourism	Dominates local economy	Complements existing activity	CAT / DAT
Linkages	Mainly external	Mainly internal	
Leakages	Extensive	Minimal	
Multiplier effect	Low	High	
Regulation			
Control	Non-local private sector	Local 'community'	DAT only
Amount	Minimal; to facilitate private sector	Extensive; to minimize local negative impacts	
Ideology	Free market forces	Public intervention	
Emphasis	Economic growth, profits; sector-specific	Community stability and well-being; integrated, holistic	
Timeframe	Short-term	Long-term	

Source: Adapted from Weaver (1993).

ed within the 'exploration' or 'involvement' stages, which are described as having similar characteristics (Butler, 1980). If however, those regulations are present, then a *Deliberate Alternative Tourism* (DAT) destination can be identified. Two 'mass tourism' possibilities are situated at the high intensity end of Figure 3.1. *Unsustainable Mass Tourism* (UMT), as predicted by Butler, is the logical outcome of continued tourism development that, in the absence of restrictive regulation, exceeds existing environmental and socio-cultural carrying capacities or limits of acceptable change. *Sustainable Mass Tourism* (SMT) destinations are those, in theory, where high intensity, large-scale tourism sectors are maintained within those carrying capacities or limits. This would entail some modification of mass tourism characteristics as iterated in Table 3.1, with a higher level of local control, retention of a mainly midcentric clientele, and encouragement of vernacular architecture all being examples of desirable outcomes indicative of sustainability. Intriguingly, the large corporations that dominate mass tourism destinations may actually be better positioned than their small-scale counterparts to facilitate sustainable practices, given internal economies of scale that allow for the allocation of resources toward audits and educational programs, and the generation of enough waste material to justify profitable and effective recycling practices (Clarke, 1997; Goodall, 1992).

In terms of their conception, these four possibilities can be linked to the sequential appearance of the tourism perspectives of 'platforms' proposed by Jafari (1989) (Table 3.2). Initially, the *advocacy* platform of the 1950s and 1960s implicitly supported mass tourism in assuming that destinations would attain far more benefits than costs from the development of the sector (thus, the more tourism the better). The *cautionary* platform of the 1970s emphasized the negative consequences of accelerated tourism development, and thus fostered the concept of UMT, though without explicitly employing the terminology of 'sustainability' as per the Brundtland Report (World Commission on Environment and

Table 3.2 Tourism Platforms and Associated Ideal Types

Platform	Ideal Types
Advocacy Cautionary Adaptancy Knowledge-based	Mass tourism UMT DAT SMT, CAT

Development, 1987). The DAT option (usually labelled simply as AT, with the deliberate regulatory aspect being implicit) emerged from the *adaptancy* platform of the early 1980s, which attempted to put forward new and sustainable tourism options in direct response to the criticisms of the cautionary perspective. Most recently, the *knowledge-based* platform has consciously utilized the rhetoric of sustainability to argue that mass tourism could potentially be a benign option for destinations if appropriate techniques of scientific management are applied (*e.g.*, Hawkes and Williams, 1993; Wight, 1994). Clarke (1997) emphasizes that the application of sustainability principles to the tourism equation has been a dynamic process initially involving a conception of mass tourism and alternative tourism as polar opposites, the former being perceived by the adaptancy platform as implicitly bad/unsustainable, and the latter as implicitly good/sustainable. The knowledge-based platform, in contrast, exemplifies Clarke's assertion of an emerging convergence between mass tourism and sustainability, wherein notions of 'good' and 'bad' are more ambiguous. (A similar subjectivity is apparent in the recognition of Limits of Acceptable Change (LAC) as a more appropriate indicator of impact than the notion of carrying capacity.) In this configuration, mass tourism can be conceived as a potentially desirable and sustainable option (*i.e.*, SMT), while, conversely, alternative tourism can be potentially unsustainable (*i.e.*, CAT). By accommodating sustainable and unsustainable options at both ends of the intensity spectrum, Figure 3.1 therefore demonstrates compatibility with both the knowledge-based platform and Clarke's notion of convergence.

BROAD CONTEXT SCENARIOS

The proposed model considers seven possible bilateral scenarios involving the transition of destinations from one Figure 3.1 situation to another (see Figure 3.2). Hypothetical options involving movement from high to low intensity configurations are excluded, as is the movement of a destination from DAT back to CAT, since such scenarios are unlikely to occur in reality. As a prelude to the presentation of these scenarios, comments need to be made regarding the status and occurrence of CAT destinations.

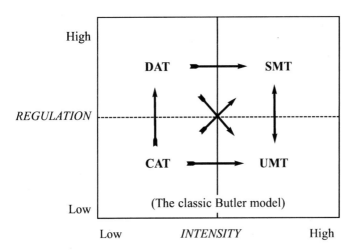

Figure 3.2: Destination Development Scenarios.

CAT Destinations

A major reason for considering an array of tourism development options is the expectation that destinations have the potential to move in a spontaneous or induced way beyond their status quo. While this is theoretically true, the issue of probability must be considered. Evolutionary tourism models, as with their equivalents in the development literature (*e.g.*, Rostow's modernization theory), seem to imply that all places are destined to progress conveyer-belt like through an entire evolutionary cycle. This determinism is often reflected in the tourism planning process, with managers in even the most unlikely would-be destinations sometimes behaving as if large-scale resort developments were imminent. While tourism has indeed experienced an impressive rate of growth since World War Two, its diffusion has been highly selective, and perhaps 95 percent of the world's surface is still occupied by CAT destinations. Furthermore, the vast majority of these destinations show no indication of progressing beyond that stage, due to a lack of tourism-related attributes and/or other impediments. Assuming that these low-potential destinations can be identified, this then raises the question as to whether any sort of tourism-related regulation is warranted under such circumstances, as discussed below.

CAT → UMT

The evolution from circumstantial alternative tourism to unsustainable mass tourism is the classic Butler S-shaped sequence, although similar progressions were earlier implicit in Christaller (1963), Miossec (1977) and Stansfield (1978). Destinations that have experienced this cycle, or an approximation thereof, include Atlantic City prior to its gaming-induced rejuvenation (Stansfield, 1978), parts of the French and Spanish Riviera (Pearce, 1995; Tyrakowski, 1986), the Caribbean Island of Antigua (Weaver, 1988) and portions of Australia's Gold Coast (Russell and Faulkner, 1998). The two main circumstances that favour this pattern of development include an absent or weak regulatory environment and proximity to actual or potential tourist attractions of sufficient magnitude to promote growth. While only a small portion of the world has followed or is likely to follow this trajectory, certain kinds of environment appear particularly susceptible. These include warmer coastal regions and islands, coastlines of densely populated developed countries, lakeshores and other land proximate to inland waters, urban hinterlands, and alpine valleys. At a global scale, the CAT-to-UMT scenario is perhaps best exemplified by the emergence and expansion of the 'pleasure periphery' region (Turner and Ash, 1975). Because it culminates in the environmental and socio-cultural deterioration, a declining tourism sector, and/or in the need to implement costly remedial measures (*i.e.*, retroactive or reactive management), the CAT-to-UMT sequence is never regarded as a desirable option for destinations.

CAT ⟶ DAT

The movement from circumstantial to deliberate alternative tourism essentially represents a truncation of the Butler sequence so as to avoid the 'development' and post-'development' stages in favour of a low level equilibrium at 'involvement'-type levels of intensity. Such an option may be appropriate for CAT destinations under the following circumstances, individually or in combination:

- location of destination in an environment (*e.g.*, coastal) susceptible to tourism intensification;
- location of destination within a low environmental and/or socio-cultural carrying capacity context, especially where these capacities are not amenable to upward adjustment;
- destination attributes are not considered attractive to the mass tourism market;
- evidence of Butler sequency-type progression beyond the involvement stage;
- community attitude that a low-to-intermediate level of tourism development (as opposed to high levels or none at all) is desirable in the medium term perspective; *i.e.*, limits of acceptable change are low from the local perspective; and
- desire for large-scale tourism, but recognition that DAT may be a desirable transitional stage to better ensure a sustainable mass tourism outcome.

Geographically, CAT-to-DAT scenarios are evident in rainforests or savannas adjacent to national parks, where local communities are mobilizing to accommodate the ecotourists who are attracted to those protected areas. This is especially apparent in lands occupied by indigenous people such as the Masai of Kenya (Sindiga, 1995), the Kuna Indians of Panama (Chapin, 1990), the Inuit of northern Canada (Hinch, 1995), and the Aboriginal people of Australia's Northern Territory (Altman and Finlayson, 1993), where increased tourism market demand intersects with the desire of indigenous people to capitalize on these opportunities without compromising the integrity of their culture or their control over the rate and method of development. The movement toward DAT on some small islands of the pleasure periphery is also interesting, given the prevalent regional trend toward 3S (sea, sand, sun) intensification. Usually, these strategies involve specific sub-regions such as peripheral islands, agricultural areas, remote coastlines, coral reefs, and mountainous interiors (Weaver, 1993; 1998). Less frequently, adoption is occurring at an all-encompassing national level. South Pacific examples of the latter include Samoa and Papua New Guinea (Weaver, 1998), while the Caribbean Island of Dominica is a classic case of an island that abandoned initial attempts toward large-scale 3S tourism in favour of a comprehensive nature and culture-based tourism product (Weaver, 1991). Prior to the destruction of its tourism industry by the eruption of a long-dormant volcano, Montserrat was also emerging as a DAT destination (Weaver, 1995).

CAT ⟶ SMT

Butler (1980) himself alluded to situations where the resort cycle could be accelerated or even circumvented altogether by the creation of 'instant' mega-resorts. If accompanied by a high level of regulation to ensure minimal environmental and social cost, this process may be described as a CAT-to-SMT scenario. These are relatively rare, though high profile examples initiated by either the public or private sector can be cited. Representative of the former possibility are the early development phases of Cancun and the other four coastal growth poles targeted by the Mexican government for 3S tourism purposes (Collins, 1979). Private sector examples arguably include South Africa's Sun City, and Florida's Disney

World. Implicit within this scenario is a deliberate and dramatic upward adjustment of carrying capacities so as to accommodate increased tourism intensity in a sustainable manner.

DAT ⟶ SMT

As suggested earlier, a destination may adopt DAT as a transitional stage toward sustainable mass tourism. In essence, this implies that the destination can gradually adapt to greater intensities of tourism activity on its own terms, and increase the limits of acceptable change, for example by gradually increasing its own environmental and socio-cultural carrying capacities (as for example through public and tourist education programs, infrastructure improvements, and local investment strategies to raise capital to expedite a high degree of local ownership over new product and accommodation development). Of course, this assumes the existence of a high market demand, which can derive from two circumstances. First, the destination may be situated in an area conducive to 3S or some other form of mass tourism, such as adjacent to a beach — the demand then is probably for a different kind of product than that currently offered by the destination. The second scenario is where the destination is perceived to be an exemplar of the DAT option, and therefore (and ironically), more and more visitors arrive to experience a product fundamentally based on small-scale dynamics. Both situations pose their own set of management challenges. In the former case, adjustments must be made in the available attractions, the type of clientele, etc. In the latter case, the challenge is to maintain the fundamental essence of the product, and to avoid an inadvertent transition to a different type of destination product, if that is considered undesirable.

As far as illustrations are concerned, the second option seems to describe Costa Rica's Monteverde Cloud Forest Reserve. Largely because of its reputation as an environmentally friendly destination, visitation to the Reserve increased from 300 in 1973 to 13,000 in 1987 and approximately 50,000 in 1993. While not entirely free from negative environmental or other impacts, the sustainability of the Monteverde product to date, as a result of effective management techniques, is widely conceded (Weaver, 1998). Recent increases in visitor numbers to Dominica may reflect a similar desire to accommodate a more intensive mode of tourism activity without sacrificing its ecotourism-based product.

DAT → UMT

DAT destinations may inadvertently evolve toward UMT if appropriate adjustments to local carrying capacities are not effected prior to visitation increases, or if the existing regulatory environment is relaxed or removed. The growth of visitor traffic in certain high profile protected areas such as Kenya's Amboseli National Park (Henry, 1980; Western, 1982), Costa Rica's Manuel Antonio National Park (Norris, 1994) and Canada's Banff National Park are suggestive of DAT-to-UMT dynamics, since the relevant protected areas were initially subject to a high degree of restriction on activities such as tourism.

SMT → UMT

The final two scenarios involve movement between the two high-intensity possibilities. As in the previous scenario, sustainable mass tourism can give way to unsustainable mass tourism if carrying capacity thresholds are not appropriately adjusted in response to intensification, or if regulations are relaxed. To some degree, this may be occurring inadvertently at Cancun as a result of deliberate government growth pole strategy. As with growth pole theory in general, government intervention is usually maintained until some critical threshold of population is attained that allows subsequent growth to be self-sustaining. This stage already has been achieved in Cancun, and government involvement is now increasingly giving way to *laissez faire* dynamics that are contributing to such problems as urban sprawl, overcrowding, increased crime and other problems associated with Butler's late development and consolidation state (Padgett, 1996). Another possibility is the contextual SMT-to-UMT transformation, which may occur when the broader external environment of a destination becomes over-developed (*i.e.*, possibly through a CAT-to-UMT progression), and therefore negatively affects an otherwise sustainable product. Such a scenario may be occurring at Florida's Disney World, due to the massive over-development of the surrounding landscape. One obvious implication is the need for planning and management to occur at a macro and inter-sectoral level rather than the micro and intro-sectoral scale, so that more of this external environment can be controlled.

UMT → SMT

In theory, the transition from unsustainable to sustainable mass tourism may be more difficult to effect than the reverse, because of the costs involved in rectifying damage already done (some of which may be irreversible). Important factors influencing the likelihood of this scenario, therefore, will include the extent of this damage, the amount of time and effort required to reverse the process, and the willingness of stakeholders to undertake the necessary changes. This, however, raises the more fundamental question as to what benchmark of sustainability is employed to judge whether this particular transition has actually been achieved. It could be argued that a mass tourism sector is sustainable as long as no further damage is incurred, even though the original environmental and cultural circumstances have been greatly altered (and thus, it is the revised circumstances, and their new carrying capacity thresholds, that are being sustained). Such basic issues (others would be the time period over which sustainability is measured, and the extent to which tourism can be directly or indirectly implicated in specific negative outcomes) probably can be resolved eventually; but even given the current 'state of the art' in sustainable tourism, few if any concrete examples of this transition, or attempts to implement such a transition, are evident in the tourism literature. One possibility is the British Channel Island dependency of Jersey, where mass tourism has long existed on the island in a manner inconsistent with limited local carrying capacities (Cooper, 1995). Jersey has been designated as the first 'Green Globe destination' by the Green Globe organization, which is an environmental management and awareness program established in 1994 by the World Travel and Tourism Council (WTTC) to facilitate the implementation of sustainable tourism principles. The Destination concept was introduced in 1997

> ... to recognize those tourist locations where there is a concerted effort by all those organizations involved in the local tourism industry to improve the quality of the environment. The Destination process provides a framework to guide tourist locations towards achieving sustainable development based on the principles of Agenda 21 (Green Globe, 1998).

Although based on the principles of voluntary adherence and free markets, a certification program with provision of independent verification is being developed, allowing for the expulsion of member destinations that no longer comply with designated standards (Green Globe, 1998). The Destination program, therefore, may facilitate a UMT-to-SMT transition in Jersey. The Mallorcan municipality of Calviá (which includes the well-known resort of Magaluf) also is attempting a similar transformation through its 21 Local Agenda initiative (Calviá, 1998).

IMPLICATIONS

The proposed model initially can be used to categorize the existing status of any particular destination. Where the latter involves a small-scale location (*e.g.*, a small island or town), a single category may be sufficient. Where the destination is larger and more complex (*e.g.*, a large country such as Spain or a region such as the Caribbean), a multi-category approach may be appropriate. The former status of the destination also should be identified to determine where some sort of transition already has occurred. Once this historical profile is compiled, the critical task for tourism managers is to assess all subsequent possibilities (including the status quo) in terms of their likelihood and desirability. On this basis, specific scenarios can be targeted, and management strategies designed accordingly.

Application to the Gold Coast of Australia

The Gold Coast is the major urban 3S resort of Australia, having hosted 2.7 million domestic and 979,000 inbound tourists in 1995 (Gold Coast Tourism Bureau, 1996). A very rapid average annual growth rate for all visitors of 28 percent was reported for the period from 1984 and 1993 (*vs.* 12 percent for Australia overall), indicating the presence of 'development'-stage dynamics as per the Butler sequence. However, growth has since slowed, suggesting the onset of 'consolidation' (Faulkner and Tideswell, 1996; 1997). Morphologically, the Gold Coast resembles other high-density urban resorts of the pleasure periphery, including Miami, Honolulu, Bali's Nusa Dua and parts of the Riviera. Concern has been expressed in recent years that levels of development and growth on the Gold Coast are not compatible with local carrying capacities. This is especially true with regard to the high intensity Surfers Paradise-to-Broadbeach strip, where levels of crime and congestion are on the increase along with irritation levels among local residents and negative perceptions of the Gold Coast among other Australians (Prideaux, 1996; Young, 1995). Furthermore, evidence of actual decline can be identified in the old resort node of Coolangatta, on the southern edge of the Gold Coast (Russell and Faulkner, 1998). These concerns have prompted major initiatives such as the Gold Coast Revisioning Project, a multi-dimensional research initiative introduced in 1998 under the rubric of the Co-operative Research Centre for Sustainable Tourism.

The model proposed in this paper could provide an overall framework for such initiatives by establishing the existing and desired tourism possibilities that pertain to the Gold Coast. As depicted in Figure 3.3, it is proposed that the Gold Coast is presently best described as a multi-category destination in which a coastal UMT sector gives way to CAT in the hinterland. Though the inclusion of the hinterland as a component of the Gold Coast product has long been recognized in promotional attempts such as the 'Green behind the Gold' slogan, the relationships between tourism on the coast and in the interior are at best informal and haphazard. It seems highly probable that the coast is moving toward environmental and social incompatibility, while the hinterland, because of its attractiveness and proximity to the urbanized coast, is one CAT destination that seems certain to experience further tourism-related development. Moreover, current trends and regulations point toward the likelihood of a Butler-type progression. Assuming that this status quo is undesirable for both the coast and the hinterland, a DAT-SMT spectrum is put forward as the most desirable policy and management outcome for the Gold Coast. In addition, the double-headed arrow signifies that a DAT hinterland and an SMT coast should be integrated into a single Gold Coast tourism system that capitalizes on the proximity of two distinct tourism products. The

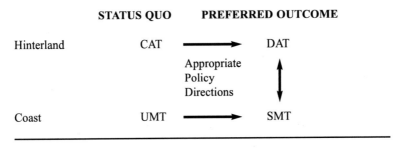

Figure 3.3: Application of the Broad Context Model to the Gold Coast of Australia.

kind of tangible interaction that could ensue from this partnership might include the restructuring of resort client itineraries to incorporate 'soft' ecotourism opportunities, and resort sponsorship of specific protected areas or other environmental attractions.

The broad context model, with its four tourism possibilities and eight evolutionary scenarios, and adherence to the knowledge-based platform and notions of mass tourism — sustainability convergence, is applicable to all destinations as a conceptual framework to facilitate the planning and management of the tourism sector. The much discussed Butler sequence is but one possible scenario within this model, which also recognizes that most CAT destinations are unlikely to evolve beyond their incipient status within the foreseeable future. The actual operationalization of the model will require extensive investigation into a number of relevant areas, but most importantly the establishment and measurement of criteria by which to gauge tourism intensity, regulation and sustainability (and, hence, allowing for the allocation of destinations to appropriate categories), and which in turn is linked to questions of carrying capacity, malleability and limits to acceptable change. Useful research initiatives also could be directed toward the means by which desirable scenarios can be realized, and to the probability that certain types of destination are likely to experience the various transitions.

ACKNOWLEDGEMENTS

Gratitude is expressed for funding from the Co-operative Research Centre in Sustainable Tourism (Griffith University Gold Coast Campus) to investigate the subject matter of this article. This chapter first appeared in *Tourism Management* and is published in this edition with the permission of the Editor of *Tourism Management*. The chapter was initially published as D. Weaver (2000) "A broad context model of destination development scenarios", *Tourism Management*, 21(3): 217-227.

REFERENCES

Agarwal, S. (1994) "The resort cycle revisited: implications for resorts", in C. Cooper and A. Lockwood (eds.), *Progress in Tourism, Recreation and Hospitality Management*, Volume 5, Chichester, UK: Wiley, 194-207.

Altman, J. and Finlayson, J. (1993) "Aborigines, tourism and sustainable development", *Journal of Tourism Studies*, 4(1): 38-50.

Baum, T. (1998) "Tourism marketing and the small island environment", in E. Laws, B. Faulkner and G. Moscardo (eds.), *Embracing and Managing Change in Tourism: International Case Studies*, London: Routledge, 116-137.

Butler, R.W. (1989) "Alternative tourism: pious hope or trojan horse?", *World Leisure and Recreation*, 31(4): 9-17.

_____ (1980) "The concept of a tourist area cycle of evolution: implications for management of resources", *Canadian Geographer*, 24(1): 4-12.

Calviá (1998) *Calviá 21 Locale Agenda*, (URL document) http://www.bitel.es/dir~calvia/kindice.htm (visited 22 December, 1998).

Chapin, M. (1990) "The silent jungle: ecotourism among the Kuna Indians of Panama", *Cultural Survival Quarterly*, 14(1): 42-45.

Christaller, W. (1963) "Some considerations of tourism location in Europe: the peripheral regions - under developed countries - recreation areas", *Regional Science Association Papers*, 12: 95-105.

Clarke, J. (1997) "A framework of approaches to sustainable tourism", *Journal of Sustainable Tourism*, 5(3): 224-233.

Collins, C. (1979) "Site and situation strategy in tourism planning: a Mexican case study", *Annals of Tourism Research*, 6(3): 351-366.

Cooper, C. (1995) "Strategic planning for sustainable tourism: the case of the offshore islands of the UK", *Journal of Sustainable Tourism*, 3(4): 191-209.

di Benedetto, C. and Bojanic, D. (1993) "Tourism area life cycle extensions", *Annals of Tourism Research*, 20(3): 557-570.

Faulkner, B. and Tideswell, C. (1997) "A framework for monitoring community impacts of tourism", *Journal of Sustainable Tourism*, 5(1): 3-28.

_____ (1996) "Gold Coast resident attitudes toward tourism: the influence of involvement in tourism, residential proximity and period of residency", in G. Prosser (ed.), *Proceedings from the Australian Tourism and Hospitality Research Conference*, Canberra: Bureau of Tourism Research, 19-35.

Gold Coast Tourism Bureau (1996) *Gold Coast Visitor Data - 1995*, Gold Coast: Gold Coast Tourism Bureau.

Goodall, B. (1992) "Environmental auditing for tourism", in C.P. Cooper and A. Lockwood (eds.), *Progress in Tourism, Recreation and Hospitality Management*, London: Belhaven Press, 60-74.

Green Globe (1998) *GREEN GLOBE Destinations*, (www document) ULR: http://www.wttc.org/WTTCGATE.NSF/06c49 762...ff648fc213c10025654f0050b9e4?OpenDocument (visited October 7).

Harrison, D. (1995) "Development of tourism in Swaziland", *Annals of Tourism Research*, 22(1): 135-156.

Hawkes, S. and Williams, P. (eds.) (1993) *The Greening of Tourism: From Principles to Practice*, Victoria, BC: Simon Fraser University.

Henry, W.R. (1980) "Patterns of tourist use in Kenya's Amboseli National Park: implications for planning and management", in D. Hawkins, E. Shafer and J. Rovelstad (eds.), *Tourism Marketing and Management Issues*, Washington, DC: George Washington University, 43-57.

Hinch, T. (1995) "Aboriginal people in the tourism economy of Canada's Northwest Territories", in C.M. Hall and M.E. Johnston (eds.), *Polar Tourism: Tourism in the Arctic and Antarctic Regions*, Chichester, UK: Wiley, 115-130.

Jafari, J. (1989) "An English language literature review", in J. Bystrzanowski (ed.), *Tourism as a Factor of Change: A Sociocultural Study*, Vienna: Centre for Research and Documentation in Social Sciences, 17-60.

Miossec, J. (1977) "Un modele de l'espace touristique", *L'espace Geographique*, 6(1): 41-48.

Norris, E. (1994) "Ecotourism in the national parks of Latin America", *National Parks*, 68(1/2): 33-37.

Oppermann, M. (1995) "Travel life cycles", *Annals of Tourism Research*, 22(3): 535-552.

Padgett, T. (1996) "The battle for the beach", *Newsweek*, 128(1): 58.

Pearce, D. (1995) *Tourism Today: A Geographical Analysis*, 2nd edition, Harlow, UK: Longman.

Prideaux, B. (1996) "The tourism crime cycle: a beach destination case study", in A. Pizam and Y. Mansfield (eds.), *Tourism, Crime and International Security Issues*, Chichester, UK: Wiley, 59-75.

Romeril, M. (1994) "Alternative tourism: the real tourism alternative?", in C. Cooper and A. Lockwood (eds.), *Progress in Tourism, Recreation and Hospitality Management*, Vol. 6, Chichester, UK: Wiley, 22-29.

Russell, R. and Faulkner, B. (1998) "Reliving the destination of life cycle in Coolangatta", in E. Laws, B. Faulkner and G. Moscardo (eds.), *Embracing and Managing Change in Tourism: International Case Studies*, London: Routledge, 95-115.

Sindiga, I. (1995) "Wildlife-based tourism in Kenya: land use conflicts and government compensation policies over protected areas", *Journal of Tourism Studies*, 6(2): 45-55.

Smith, V.L. and Eadington, W.R. (eds.) (1992) *Tourism Alternatives: Potentials and Problems in the Development of Tourism*, Philadelphia: University of Pennsylvania Press.

Stansfield, C. (1978) "Atlantic City and the resort cycle: background to the legalization of gambling", *Annals of Tourism Research*, 5(2): 238-251.

Turner, L. and Ash, J. (1975) *The Golden Hordes: International Tourism and the Pleasure Periphery*, London: Constable.

Tyrakowski, K. (1986) "The role of tourism in land utilization conflicts on the Spanish Mediterranean Coast", *GeoJournal*, 13(1): 19-26.

Weaver, D.B. (1998) *Ecotourism in the Less Developed World*, Wallingford, UK: CAB International.

_____ (1995) "Alternative tourism in Montserrat", *Tourism Management*, 16(8): 593-604.

_____ (1993) "Ecotourism in the small island Caribbean", *GeoJournal*, 31: 457-465.

_____ (1991) "Alternative to mass tourism in Dominica", *Annals of Tourism Research*, 18(3): 414-432.

_____ (1988) "The evolution of a 'plantation' tourism landscape on the Caribbean island of Antigua", *Tijdschrift voor Economische en Sociale Geografie*, 79(5): 319-331.

Western, D. (1982) "Amboseli National Park: enlisting landowners to conserve migratory wildlife", *Ambio*, 11(5): 302-308.

Wight, P. (1994) "The greening of the hospitality industry: economic and environmental good sense", in A.V. Seaton, C.L. Venkins, R.C. Wood, P.U. Dieke, M.M. Bennett, L.R. Maclellan and R. Smith (eds.), *Tourism: The State of the Art*, Chichester, UK: Wiley, 665-674.

World Commission on Environment and Development (1987) *Our Common Future*, Oxford: Oxford University Press.

WTO (1998) *Yearbook of Tourism Statistics*, (50th edition) Volume 1, Madrid: World Tourism Organization.

Young, M. (1995) "Evaluative constructs of domestic tourist places", *Australian Geographical Studies*, 33(2): 272-286.

Chapter 4

Border Regions as Tourist Destinations

Dallen J. Timothy
Arizona State University

By definition, a tourist is someone who crosses a political boundary — either international or subnational as they leave their home environment. Many travelers are bothered by the 'hassle' of crossing international frontiers, and the type and level of borders heavily influence the nature and extent of tourism that can develop in their vicinity. Furthermore, boundaries have long been a curiosity for travelers who seek to experience something out of the ordinary. It would appear then that political boundaries have significant impacts on tourism and that the relationships between them are manifold and complex. Nonetheless, the subject of borders and tourism has been traditionally ignored by both border and tourism scholars, with only a few notable exceptions (*e.g.*, Gruber *et al.*, 1979). In recent years, however, more researchers have begun to realize the vast and heretofore unexplored potential of this subject as an area of scholarly inquiry (*e.g.*, Arreola and Curtis, 1993; Timothy, 1995a; Paasi, 1996; Leimgruber, 1998; Paasi and Raivo, 1998; Arreola and Madsen, 1999).

One emerging theme in all this is borders and borderlands as tourist destinations. The purpose of this chapter is to discuss the notion of borderlands as tourist destinations, and to consider the range of features and activities that attract tourists to them. Many of the ideas presented here are taken from the author's previous work (Timothy, 1995a; 1995b; in press) and reflect an ongoing research interest in the relationships between political boundaries and tourism.

BORDERLANDS AS TOURIST DESTINATIONS

Tourism is a significant industry in many border regions, and some of the world's most popular attractions are located adjacent to, or directly on political boundaries (*e.g.*, Niagara Falls). According to Butler (1996), borderlands and their frequently associated remoteness appeal to tourists because they provide some of the most pristine natural landscapes in the world and incite a mythical frontier image in the human psyche. Christaller (1963) recognized this early on within the broader context of peripheral regions generally when he stated that "tourism is drawn to the periphery of settlement districts as it searches for a position on the highest mountain, in the most lonely woods, along the remotest beaches" (1963: 95).

Borderland tourism can be viewed from at least two spatial perspectives: tourism that focuses on the borderline itself and tourism that owes its existence to a border location but which does not focus directly on the border (Timothy, in press). The existence of political boundaries in a region creates unique political, economic and social conditions. In many instances these lead to the development of unique forms of tourism, particularly when an activity is permitted on one side of a border but not on the other, where laws pertaining to age limits vary from place to place, and when taxes and prices differ between sides. Activities of this type include gambling, prostitution, 'alcohol tourism', shopping, enclaves, and international parks. The following sections examine these types of borderlands tourism.

Borderlines

For some people, political boundaries invoke a unique type of fascination. Some tourist attractions have even been developed simply because they are a border, such as the Four Corners Monument in the United States, where Colorado, Utah, Arizona and New Mexico meet. The Navajo Nation has capitalized on this notion by charging an entry fee into the monument and establishing souvenir stands and food vendors. Dozens of other examples exist where frontier markers have become significant objects of tourist attention, such as the border gate between Macau and China, an interesting monument at the point where Finland, Norway and Sweden meet, and the Peace Arch, which straddles the border between the United States and Canada in Washington and British Columbia (Timothy, in press).

Even frontiers between rancorous neighbors can function as tourist attractions. While the demilitarized zone between North and South Korea is still a point of contention, it has become a significant destination. Each week, floods of South Koreans and foreigners arrive in Panmunjom, the village divided by the line where the treaty of armistice was signed (Pollack, 1996). Similarly, even amid a heated border dispute between Egypt and Israel in the 1980s over a small strip of beachfront property (Taba), the border and its related problems were an attraction. According to one resort manager in the disputed territory, the fact that guests could see four countries from their balconies was one of the primary allures of staying there. Also, in his own words, tourists were drawn towards Taba in part "because we are an international problem. How many people get to stay at an international problem?" (quoted in Drysdale, 1991: 205).

Several relict boundaries, or former boundaries that no longer function in their original political capacity but are still visible in the cultural landscape (Hartshorne, 1936), also have become significant attractions. Probably the most well-known example of this is the Great Wall of China, which was built as a fortification between China and Mongolia between 246 and 209 BC. The wall is one of China's most important tourist attractions, and few visitors to Beijing leave the area without having spent a day there (Toops, 1992). Hadrian's Wall is another example of an ancient relict boundary that has become a major tourist attraction. The wall, which is considered to be the finest vestige of Roman rule in Britain, was designated a UNESCO World Heritage Site in 1987, and a great deal of work has recently been done to map, delimit, manage and conserve the site (English Heritage, 1996; Turley, 1998).

A more recent example is the Berlin Wall. Soon after its demise in 1989, the wall became the focus of strenuous preservation efforts. While its downfall was a welcome event on both sides of the border, preservation enthusiasts immediately recognized the need to save the structure in some form for heritage purposes — to tell the story of the rise and fall of the Eastern regime. Today, Checkpoint Charlie, probably the best-known artifact of the Cold War, is now highlighted in a museum of the same name, which also contains other period artifacts such as parts of the wall itself (Borneman, 1998). Although the former east-west divide is rapidly disappearing from Berlin's urban landscape, the old border is so important in economic terms that the city "helps make ends meet by luring tourists who want to catch a glimpse of the cold war and whose first wish is to see where the wall used to be. So, to satisfy them, the city has devised a new east-west border — a red stripe painted through Berlin's heart along the route of the demolished wall" (Economist, 1997: 56).

Crossing borders may be the primary motivation for some people to travel. Frontier formalities and differences in landscape, language, and political systems add character to a trip. In the words of one traveler, "I love border crossings. They somehow make me feel as though I'm in a black-and-white movie with subtitles" (Harris, 1997: 12). Another commentator reminisces as follows:

> Borders have fascinated me since childhood. As a kid, I used to imagine border landscapes: dark rivers, watchtowers, and unknown lands lying beyond them...Over the years, as I started travelling, borders have been somewhat demystified, but now again, approaching the Finnish-Russian boundary, I was feel-

ing that boyish excitement, an anticipation of mystery (Medvedev, 1999: 43).

For some people straddling a border with one leg in two countries can be a memorable experience, and a person driving from coast to coast in North America would most likely observe travelers pulling aside to photograph themselves standing next to welcome signs at state or provincial lines as a way of documenting their trip (Timothy, 1998). At Four Corners visitors can simultaneously straddle the territory of four states — the only place in North America where this can be accomplished. Ryden (1993: 1) argues that this desire is based on the notion that straddling a border provides an experience of being in more than one place at once, something not physically possible in any other context.

This fascination with borders, according to Butler (1996), is likely grounded in the fact that boundaries are not part of most people's daily action space. It is this contrast from the ordinary that makes borders intriguing. In Ryden's (1993: 1) words:

> In a subtle and totally subjective way, each side of the border feels different; in the space of a few feet we pass from one geographical entity to another which looks exactly the same but is unique, has a different name, is in many ways a completely separate world from the one we just left...This sense of passing from one world to another, of encompassing within a few steps two realms of experience, enchants and fascinates.

Prostitution

Prostitution commonly develops alongside tourism, and borderlands are especially prone to its spontaneous growth. Timothy (in press) suggests that two conditions are the primary cause of this phenomenon. First, while many border areas are becoming heavily industrialized, as in the case of the US-Mexico and Eastern

European frontiers, borders generally remain unable to provide enough employment for the masses of people who migrate to them from the national interior. This drives many people into menial service occupations, including prostitution. Second, boundaries are prime locations for prostitution since visitors from neighboring regions do not have to go far into foreign territory to find their 'dens of iniquity'. This is particularly noticeable when large urban centers lie adjacent to, or within a reasonable driving distance of, the nearest border crossing.

The sex trade along the US-Mexico border fits this description. There, Mexican frontier communities became "convenient yet foreign playgrounds, tantalizingly near but beyond the prevailing morality and rule of law north of the border" (Curtis and Arreola, 1991: 340), where Americans could "provide relief to their sexual needs" (Fernandez, 1977: 127). This was especially so during the early and mid-1900s when dozens of US military installations were established near the border. However, by the 1970s, prostitution had become so extensive, even beyond the serviceman's fetish, that sex tourist guides were published for the general population. One publication boasts that:

> The one entrance and exit is carefully supervised by Nuevo Loredo's finest. Girls come from all over Mexico to work in the four or five nicest places. This is the best on the border...Most unique and pleasing structurally, both in building and clientele, is the Tamyko, a huge Japanese pagoda with outside patio and fishponds spanned by arched bridges, surrounded on two levels by bedrooms. The girls are almost all between 14 and 18 years old (West, 1973: 73).

In recent years, however, many people who previously worked as prostitutes have found more productive employment in the *maquiladora* industry. Additionally, according to Curtis and

Arreola (1991: 343), the growth of nude bars, increased sexual permissiveness, and the increased availability of pornography on the US side, as well as the increasing global fear of AIDS, have decreased the role of sex in the tourism product of Mexican border communities. Yet, prostitution still has its clientele of Americans who are attracted by lower prices and the 'exotic' setting (Bowman, 1994).

Similar conditions have developed in other parts of the world, as certain border regions have become notorious for attracting sex tourists from abroad. Lesotho and Swaziland are goods examples of this, as were the independent homelands, Bophuthatswana, Venda, Ciskei, and Transkei prior to their reintegration into South Africa in 1994.

Gambling

Like prostitution, gambling commonly develops — intentionally and spontaneously — at border crossings when one polity allows it but its neighbour does not. So specific are the border dimensions in gaming that casino parking lots are often bisected by political lines and front doors in some cases lie within a metre or two of the border (Timothy, in press). In the United States, this is common along Nevada's borders and in similar situations throughout the country (Jackson and Hudman, 1987; Sommers and Lounsbury, 1991). Bowman (1994: 52) observed, "the Nevada borderlands have, like a magnet, drawn new casinos to lure in gamblers as soon as they cross the state line".

On an international level, the same holds true. Monaco is an excellent example of this in Europe. Likewise, in the Middle East, the casino in Taba, Egypt, is thriving primarily on Israeli patronage (over 90 percent) (Felsenstein and Freeman, 1998). And, in North America, casinos recently have been built just inside Canada at important gateway cities like Niagara Falls and Windsor to attract Americans across the line (Smith and Hinch, 1996). These

Canadian efforts have been so successful in bringing Americans across, that US border cities, where gaming has heretofore been outlawed, have responded by gaining legislative approval and opening up competing facilities on their side of the border (Eadington, 1996).

'Alcohol Tourism'

In the presence of an international boundary, people will drink. Consumers by the thousands cross borders to purchase liquor for use at home or to spend time drinking in bars and taverns abroad. Cheaper alcoholic beverages, lower liquor taxes, longer opening hours, and lower drinking ages, if they exist at all, are the primary motivations for this type of behaviour (Timothy, in press).

Matley (1977: 25) termed this 'alcohol tourism' and argued that it is of dubious value, because it attracts the worst type of tourist and results in drunkenness, public disorder, violence, and vandalism. This behaviour is of particular concern when underage youth are involved. Bowman (1994) describes how American teenagers, some as young as 14, cross into Mexico on a regular basis to drink. Until recently, radio stations in Tucson, Arizona, advertised for Mexican bars that targeted Arizona teens. However, owing to public outrage, the city's stations no longer run advertisements for these types of establishments. Nonetheless, this situation is circumvented by bars paying students to distribute pamphlets at school (Bowman, 1994: 62).

Shopping

While cross-border shopping is common in all parts of the world, most academic attention has focused on its development in North America and Europe (e.g., Leimgruber, 1988; Weigand, 1990; Timothy and Butler, 1995; Di Matteo and Di Matteo, 1996; Patrick and Renforth, 1996; Asgary et al., 1997; Minghi, 1999; Timothy, 1999b).

Cross-border shopping occurs when economic and social conditions are right. Several causes for this activity have been identified by researchers: favorable exchange rates between currencies, higher taxes in the home region, more efficient distribution channels in adjacent nations, a wider variety of goods in the neighbouring area, and more flexible shopping hours across the border (Timothy, in press). In addition, that shopping can be as much a pleasurable activity as an economic one, adds an additional motivation for people to shop abroad (Timothy and Butler, 1995).

Cross-border shopping has long been a significant part of international tourism in North America. Canadian consumerism traditionally has been a significant economic boost for US border communities. However, in 1987, numbers and frequency of Canadian shopping trips began to soar, owing largely to the depreciation of the Canadian dollar (Di Matteo and Di Matteo, 1996). That year almost 31 million Canadian shopping trips to the United States were made, but the number nearly doubled in 1991 to 59 million. This phenomenon was blamed for thousands of lost jobs in Canada and billions of lost dollars in profits and tax revenues (Kemp, 1992). At the same time, though, the American frontier communities were thriving.

This trend was short lived, however, because in 1992 numbers began to fall, and by 1997 only 35 million Canadian shopping trips were taken. Today, the advantage has changed directions. Americans now flock north to Canadian border towns in record numbers to shop, dine out, watch a movie, and buy real estate (Bondi, 1998). American jobs are now being lost, and Canadian towns are booming. The present retail climate in US border towns is dismal. Dozens of shopping centres that were built during the zenith of Canadian shopping are now empty and falling into disrepair. Public officials and business owners are scrambling to find creative ways to bring Canadian business back.

Similar situations have existed for a long time at the US-Mexico border, as well as in other parts of the world. Exchange rate appears to be the most influential factor in this phenomenon, and even the slightest shift in conversion rates tends to have notable effects on the flow of shopping tourists (Asgary *et al.*, 1997; Di Matteo, 1999; Timothy, 1999b).

International Parks

While national parks have existed since the 1800s, the concept of international parks began in the early twentieth century with the passing of legislation in Czechoslovakia and Poland to establish binational parks between the two nations. Similar actions were taken in North America in 1932 when Waterton-Glacier International Peace Park was created on the Canada-United States border. The primary purpose of these entities was to conserve the natural ecosystems that lie astride international boundaries, although the promotion of peace was an additional concern in the North American context (Timothy, 1999a). Since that time, dozens of international parks have been established in various locations throughout the world, and many more are being considered (Thorsell and Harrison, 1990; Denisiuk *et al.*, 1997). International parks in this context are generally comprised of one or more pro-tected areas that lie adjacent to national frontiers or overlap them.

In many parts of the world, these cross-border parks are a sig-nificant component of the regional tourism product. For example, Waterton-Glacier International Peace Park is one of the most important tourist destinations, in visitor numbers and size, in the American and Canadian West. Niagara Falls, Victoria Falls, and Masaai Mara-Serengeti are just a few additional examples with global appeal that attract millions of visitors each year.

Despite their purpose to conserve the environment and pro-mote cooperation between neighbours, owing to their location astride international divides, these parks face a variety of management problems that few national parks rarely encounter (Blake, 1993; Timothy, 2000b). These include the following:

- cultural and political differences on opposite sides of the border often create communications' barriers and incompatible administrative practices;

- the cross-border parties involved are rarely willing to compromise in areas of collaboration because it might mean giving up some degree of sovereignty, or absolute territorial control;

- border fortifications and methods of demarcation, such as walls, fences and landmines, disrupt the holistic functioning of ecosystems and scar the natural landscape;

- differing levels of development between neighbouring states often result in varying environmental standards from side to side; and,

- the peripheral location of most borderlands commonly translates into political and socio-cultural marginality, and frontier areas are often excluded from economic development programs.

Despite these management constraints, numbers of international parks are continuing to grow, particularly as the traditional barrier roles of borders are giving way to higher levels of cooperation and integration (Minghi, 1991).

Enclaves/Exclaves
Exclaves, or enclaves, are small parts of one country surrounded completely by a neighbouring country. Pene-exclaves are similar in that they can only be accessed by wheeled traffic and only by passing through a neighbouring state. From the view of the country to

which the outlier belongs it is an exclave, but from the perspective
of the country where it is located, it is an enclave. Hundreds of
these unique communities exist in Europe, North America and
Asia.

Several international exclaves in Western Europe and North
America have a unique status as tourist destinations. In fact, the
economic base of some enclaves is comprised almost entirely of
tourism (*e.g.*, Northwest Angle, Llivia and Campione) (Catudal,
1979; Timothy, 1996). The primary attraction common to all
enclaves and pene-enclaves is their unusual political status.
However, each has its own additional appeal. For example,
Campione, Italy (located in Switzerland) is well-known for its
Casino Municipale. Llivia, Spain (located in France) is a base for
skiing enthusiasts in the Pyrenees, and it becomes a festival centre
each Spring. Point Roberts, Washington (USA-accessible by
wheeled traffic only through Canada), is popular among Canadians
for shopping, outdoor recreation and summer homes, while the
Northwest Angle, Minnesota (USA-also accessible only by
wheeled traffic through Canada), is home to over a dozen hunting
and fishing lodges that offer year-round outdoor activities
(Timothy, 1996).

While tourism is an important activity, like international parks,
these unique destinations face several factors that make the industry difficult to develop (Timothy, 1996). These include:

- small size leaves little room for spatial development;

- the enclaves are at the mercy of the host state for services
  and imports; and,

- most enclaves are physically isolated.

Miscellaneous Activities

Other types of attractions/destinations also exist in frontier regions whose appeal is not necessarily linked directly to their borderland locations. For example, several reputable beaches are intersected by international boundaries such as the eastern end of the Gulf of Aqaba, where attractive beaches are divided between Jordan, Israel and Egypt. Additionally, historic sites exist in several border areas like the case of Preah Vihear, an awe-inspiring ruin that lies only metres inside Cambodia near the Thailand border. Finally, owing to their often peripheral and frontier conditions, borderlands are ideal locations for the development of nature-based tourism. The rain forests adjacent to the Democratic Republic of Congo-Uganda and Costa Rica-Panama borders, for example, are recognized globally as some of the best ecotour regions in the world (Timothy, in press).

CONCLUSION

While political boundaries traditionally have acted as barriers to human interaction, they are in many cases becoming lines of cooperation and integration. As nations mend hostile relations that have plagued them for years, as in the case of Israel and Jordan, their borders will become less of a barrier and more of a facilitator of cross-frontier partnership, particularly in areas of tourism and natural resources. These changes will increase access among potential tourists to adjacent destinations across 'the line' and will thereby encourage the growth of tourist activities such as shopping, gambling, and in some cases, prostitution and drinking.

Clearly, activities and attractions like these that require people to cross borders will benefit from these developments. However, some hostile and less-crossable borders also function as primary attractions. The DMZ between North and South Korea and the former Berlin Wall are just two examples. These borderlines, which are/were arduous to cross, are/were popular attractions for southern and western tourists respectively. Part of the intrigue no doubt resulted from the tourists' inability to cross. So, it may be that improved relations and how they affect the border landscape may decrease the attractiveness of some borders for tourists.

This chapter, although cursory and descriptive in nature, has attempted to highlight some of the areas of research that might be pursued by border and tourism scholars. There is a dearth of knowledge about the relationships between borders and tourism, and research along these lines would make a valuable contribution to the literature in geopolitics, tourism and economic development. Given the examples and information presented here, it appears that as long as boundaries separate places in political, socio-cultural and economic terms, and as long as accessibility is assured, borderlands will continue to be a unique venue for tourist activities.

ACKNOWLEDGEMENTS
While some changes have been made to this paper, the majority of it has appeared in Timothy (2000a). Permission by the International Boundaries Research Unit at Durham University to reproduce the article is gratefully acknowledged.

REFERENCES
Arreola, D.D. and Curtis, J.R. (1993) *The Mexican Border Cities: Landscape Anatomy and Place Personality*, Tucson: University of Arizona Press.

Arreola, D.D. and Madsen, K. (1999) "Variability of tourist attractiveness along an international boundary, Sonora, Mexico border towns," *Visions in Leisure and Business*, 17(4): 19-31.

Asgary, N., de Los Santos, G., Vincent, V. and Davila, V. (1997) "The determinant of expenditures by Mexican visitors to the border cities of Texas," *Tourism Economics*, 3(4): 319-328.

Blake, G.H. (1993) "Transfrontier collaboration: a worldwide survey," in A.H. Westing (ed.), *Transfrontier Reserves for Peace and Nature: A Contribution to Human Security*, Nairobi: UNE, 35-48.

Bondi, N. (1998) "Bargain hunters hit Canada: loonie's record fall an economic windfall for American shopping across the border," *Detroit News*, 30 January.

Borneman, J. (1998) "Grenzregime (border regime): the Wall and its aftermath," in T.M. Wilson and H. Donnan (eds.), *Border Identities: National and State at International Frontiers*, Cambridge: Cambridge University Press, 162-190.

Bowman, K.S. (1994) "The border as locator and innovator of vice," *Journal of Borderlands Studies*, 9(1): 51-67.

Butler, R.W. (1996) "The development of tourism in frontier regions: issues and approaches," in Y. Gradus and H. Lithwick (eds.), *Frontiers in Regional Development*, Lanham, MD: Rowman & Littlefield, 213-229.

Catudal, H. (1979) *The Exclave Problem of Western Europe*, Tuscaloosa: University of Alabama Press.

Christaller, W. (1963) "Some considerations of tourism in Europe: the peripheral regions-underdeveloped countries-recreation areas," *Papers of the Regional Science Association*, 12: 95-105.

Curtis, J.R. and Arreola, D.D. (1991) "Zonas de tolerancia on the northern Mexican border," *Geographical Review*, 81(3): 333-346.

Denisiuk, Z., Stoyko, S. and Terray, J. (1997) "Experience in cross-border cooperation for national parks and protected areas in Central Europe," in J.G. Nelson and R. Serafin (eds.), *National Parks and Protected Areas: Keystones to Conservation and Sustainable Development*, Berlin: Springer, 145-150.

Di Matteo, L. (1999) "Cross-border trips by Canadians and Americans and the differential impact of the border," *Visions in Leisure and Business*, 17(4): 72-92.

Di Matteo, L. and Di Matteo, R. (1996) "An analysis of Canadian cross-border travel," *Annals of Tourism Research*, 23(1): 103-122.

Drysdale, A. (1991) "The Gulf of Aqaba coastline: an evolving border landscape," in D. Rumley and J.V. Minghi (eds.), *The Geography of Border Landscapes*, London: Routledge, 203-216.

Eadington, W.R. (1996) "The legalization of casinos: policy objectives, regulatory alternatives, and cost/benefit considerations," *Journal of Travel Research*, 34(3): 3-8.

Economist (1997) "Berliners see red," *The Economist*, 8 March: 56.

English Heritage (1996) *Hadrian's Wall World Heritage Site Management Plan*, London: English Heritage.

Felsenstein, D. and Freeman, D. (1998) "Simulating the impacts of gambling in a tourist location: some evidence from Israel," *Journal of Travel Research*, 37(2): 145-155.

Fernandez, R.A. (1977) *The United States-Mexico Border: A Politico-Economic Profile*, Notre Dame: University of Notre Dame Press.

Gruber, G., Lamping, H., Lutz, W., Matznetter, J. and Vorlaufer, K. (eds.) (1979) *Tourism and Borders: Proceedings of the Meeting of the IGU Working Group - Geography of Tourism and Recreation*, Frankfurt: Institut für Wirtschafts-und Sozialgeographie der Johann Wolfgang Goethe Universität.

Harris, M. (1997) "Spirited, independent Slovenia," *New York Times*, 11 May: 12.

Hartshorne, R. (1936) "Suggestions on the terminology of political boundaries," *Annals of the Association of American Geographers*, 26: 56-57.

Jackson, R.H. and Hudman, L.E. (1987) "Border towns, gambling and the Mormon culture region," *Journal of Cultural Geography*, 8(1): 35-48.

Kemp, K. (1992) "Cross-border shopping: trends and measurement issues," *Canadian Economic Observer*, 5: 1-13.

Leimgruber, W. (1988) "Border trade: the boundary as an incentive and an obstacle to shopping trips," *Nordia*, 22(1): 53-60.

_____ (1998) "Defying political boundaries: transborder tourism in a regional context," *Visions in Leisure and Business*, 17(3): 8-29.

Matley, I.M. (1977) "Physical and cultural factors influencing the location of tourism," in E.M. Kelly (ed.), *Domestic and International Tourism*, Wellesley, MA: The Institute of Certified Travel Agents, 16-25.

Medvedev, S. (1999) "Across the line: borders in post-Westphalian landscapes," in H. Eskelinen, I. Liikanen and J. Oksa (eds.), *Curtains of Iron and Gold: Reconstructing Borders and Scales of Interaction*, Aldershot: Ashgate, 43-56.

Minghi, J.V. (1991) "From conflict to harmony in border land-scapes," in D. Rumley and J.V. Minghi (eds.), *The Geography of Border Landscapes*, London: Routledge, 15-30.

_____ (1999) "Borderland 'day tourists' from the East: Trieste's transitory shopping fair," *Visions in Leisure and Business*, 17(4): 32-49.

Paasi, A. (1996) *Territories, Boundaries and Consciousness: The Changing Geographies of the Finnish-Russian Border*, Chichester: Wiley.

Paasi, A. and Raivo, P.J. (1998) "Boundaries as barriers and pro-moters: constructing the tourist landscapes of Finnish Karelia," *Visions in Leisure and Business*, 17(3): 30-45.

Patrick, J.M. and Renforth, W. (1996) "The effects of the peso devaluation on cross-border retailing," *Journal of Borderlands Studies*, 11(1): 25-41.

Pollack, A. (1996) "At the DMZ, another invasion: tourists," *New York Times*, 10 April: A10.

Ryden, K.C. (1993) *Mapping the Invisible Landscape: Folklore, Writing, and the Sense of Place*, Iowa City: University of Iowa Press.

Smith, G.J. and Hinch, T.D. (1996) "Canadian casinos as tourist attractions: chasing the pot of gold," *Journal of Travel Research*, 22(3): 37-39.

Sommers, L.M. and Lounsbury, J.F. (1991) "Border boom towns of Nevada," *Focus*, 41(4): 12-18.

Thorsell, J. and Harrison, J. (1990) "Parks that promote peace: a global inventory of transfrontier nature reserves," in J. Thorsell (ed.), *Parks on the Borderline: Experience in Transfrontier Conservation*, Gland: IUCN, 3-21.

Timothy, D.J. (1995a) "International boundaries: new frontiers for tourism research," *Progress in Tourism and Hospitality Research*, 1(2): 141-152.

_____ (1995b) "Political boundaries and tourism: borders as tourist attractions," *Tourism Management*, 16(7): 525-532.

_____ (1996) "Small and isolated: the politics of tourism in international exclaves," *Acta Turistica*, 8(2): 99-115.

_____ (1998) "Collecting places: geodetic lines in tourist space," *Journal of Travel and Tourism Marketing*, 7(4): 123-129.

_____ (1999a) "Cross-border partnership in tourism resource management: international parks along the US-Canada border," *Journal of Sustainable Tourism*, 7(3/4): 182-205.

_____ (1999b) "Cross-border shopping: tourism in the Canada-United States borderlands," *Visions in Leisure and Business*, 17(4): 4-18.

_____ (2000a) "Borderlands: an unlikely tourist destination?" *Boundary and Security Bulletin*, 8(1): 57-65.

_____ (2000b) "Tourism and international parks," in R.W. Butler and S.W. Boyd (eds.), *Tourism and National Parks: Issues and Implications*, Chichester: John Wiley and Sons, 263-282.

_____ (in press) "Tourism in the borderlands: economic development and cross-frontier cooperation," in S. Krakover and Y.

Gradus (eds.), *Tourism in Frontier Regions*, Baltimore, MD: Lexington Books.

_____ (in press) *Tourism and Political Boundaries*, London: Routledge.

Timothy, D.J. and Butler, R.W. (1995) "Cross-border shopping: a North American perspective," *Annals of Tourism Research*, 22(1): 16-34.

Toops, S.W. (1992) "Tourism in China and the impact of June 4, 1989," *Focus*, 42(1): 3-7.

Turley, S. (1998) "Hadrian's Wall (UK): managing the visitor experience at the Roman frontier," in M. Shackley (ed.), *Visitor Management: Case Studies from World Heritage Sites*, Oxford: Butterworth Heinemann, 100-120.

Weigand, K. (1990) "Drei Jahrzehtne Einkaufstourismus über die deutsch-dänische Grenze," *Geographische Rundschau*, 42(5): 286-290.

West, R. (1973) "Border towns: what to do and where to do it," *Texas Monthly*, 1: 62-73.

Chapter 5

Tourism and Agriculture and Strategic Alliances

David J. Telfer
Brock University

The development and management of strategic alliances have become increasingly important in the highly competitive tourism industry (Crotts *et al.*, 2000). From high profile global airline alliances to local tourism partnerships, strategic alliances between large and small companies have become widely recognized as an important strategy for accelerating growth, innovation (Botkin and Mathews, 1992) and the development of backward and forward economic linkages. Two sectors, which are increasingly recognizing the importance of collaboration, are tourism and agriculture. With the agricultural sector not only providing input into the tourism industry as well as providing rural attractions and landscapes, there is significant potential for collaboration between the two sectors.

The purpose of this paper is to investigate the importance of strategic alliances and, in part, the response of agricultural-related entrepreneurs to the development of tourism. The chapter begins by examining the relationship between tourism and food and the importance of strategic alliances. Examples will then be drawn from three countries. On the island of Lombok in Indonesia, local suppliers have responded to demands from large-scale hotels for local food supplies. A village to the north of Yogyakarta on Java has developed an agritourism site with tourists visiting a salak (small apple like fruit) plantation. In the Sierra Del Rosario Biosphere Reserve in Cuba, there are strong links between tourism and community development in the state-run ecotourism venture of Las Terrazas. Abandoned coffee plantations serve as part of the tourist attraction in the Biosphere Reserve. In Canada, "Tastes of

Niagara", is an evolving strategic alliance (Vision Niagara, 1996) among the regions' food producers, processors, distributors, hotels, wineries, restaurants and chefs. Similar to the initiatives in Indonesia, the objective of the alliance is to promote the use of local food products in the tourism industry. Finally, the Niagara Wine Route, comprising 50 wineries that have joined forces to promote wine tourism, further illustrates the importance of partnering to promote a regional product. The chapter will conclude by noting common issues facing strategic alliances and the importance of linking tourism and agriculture for local development.

FOOD AND TOURISM
The relationship between tourism and agriculture is complex (Telfer and Wall, 1996) with the agricultural sector providing input and attractions for the tourism industry. In terms of input, Belisle (1983) suggests that food represents approximately one-third of tourist expenditures and the degree to which the tourist industry relies on imported food can have a significant affect on the social and economic impacts of tourism. Studies warn of the leakages that can occur when the tourist industry relies on imported foods (Belisle, 1983; Wilkinson, 1987; Taylor *et al.*, 1991). The reasons for using imported agricultural products have been generalized as ones of availability, price, consistency and the quality of local products (Bowen *et al.*, 1991). The barriers to increasing local food production for input into the tourist industry include economic, technological, behavioural, physical and marketing obstacles (Belisle, 1983).

Figure 5.1 summarizes the relationship between tourism and agriculture as one that ranges from conflict to symbiosis. In conflict, both sectors compete for land, labour, water and access to fishing grounds. However if there is a more symbiotic relationship, then the local agricultural sector can act as input and an attraction. If strategic alliances develop, the benefits of the tourism industry will extend throughout the local agricultural economy. Telfer and

Wall (1996) have suggested that the degree to which local agriculturally-related firms have the ability to trade with the tourism industry is related to the scale of enterprises, the interrelationships between entrepreneurs with differing access to resources, and the sizes of enterprises and their associated linkages. As indicated in the following section, strategic alliances have become a viable option for agriculturally related firms to develop links to tourism. Examples later in the chapter highlight this growing trend.

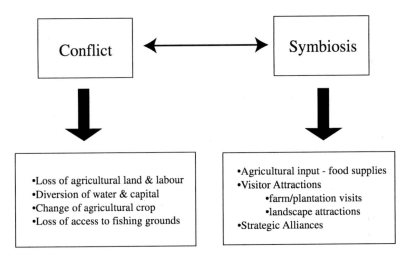

Figure 5.1: Relationship Between Tourism and Agriculture.

STRATEGIC ALLIANCES AND TOURISM

Magun (1996) argues that in the current competitive business environment, firms have three main alternate growth strategies including internal expansion and business start-up, acquisitions and mergers, and strategic alliances. Of the three options, strategic alliances have become increasingly prominent. Gulati (1998: 293) defines strategic alliances as "voluntary arrangements between firms involving exchange, sharing, or co-development of products, technologies, or services. They can occur as a result of a wide range of motives and goals and can take a variety of forms, and can occur across vertical and horizontal boundaries." Strategic alliances have started to receive increased attention in tourism research. The first issue of the journal *International Journal of Hospitality & Tourism Administration* was dedicated to the issue of global alliances. Within the context of strategic alliances the editors (Crotts *et al.*, 2000) highlight the following key factors in models of relationship building: reputation, performance capabilities, goal compatibility, trust, strategic advantage, amount of adaptations/non-retrievable investments, communication, cooperation and social bonding.

Steps have been taken to increase linkages in tourism between sectors such as the airline industry and between hotels, attractions and agriculture (see Crotts *et al.*, 2000). In the wine tourism industry, Hall *et al.* (2000) indicate that the relationship between wine and tourism is extremely significant at the regional level. Regionality provides for product branding, place promotion and economic development. The paper now turns to investigate examples from Indonesia, Cuba and Canada where strategic alliances have developed between agriculture and tourism.

EXAMPLES FROM INDONESIA
Lombok
Located between Bali and Sumbawa in the Province of West Nusa Tenggara (NTB), the island of Lombok has a population of 2.4 million people on a land area of 4,738 km^2 (Sofreavia, 1993). Corner (1989: 178) identified the provinces of East and West Nusa Tenggara as two of the poorest and least developed provinces of Indonesia primarily due to the lack of natural resources, poor soils, arid conditions and lack of suitable water storage for irrigation. Despite the difficult conditions, the economy of Lombok is primarily agriculturally-based. Tourism in Lombok is relatively recent and focused mainly on beach tourism. Senggigi Beach, located along the northwest coast of the island is the most developed tourist resort and home to the 156 room, four star Sheraton Senggigi Beach Resort. The hotel has four restaurants, 24-hour room service

and special theme buffets.

Whenever possible, the Sheraton has attempted to develop strategic alliances to purchase food locally avoiding the high costs of imports (Telfer and Wall, 1996). For example, the Sheraton relies heavily on two local fruit and vegetable suppliers who make daily deliveries to the Resort. They purchase supplies from one of the main local markets (Sweta or Ampenan) or directly from producers. Deliveries are made by public bemo (small public bus) or by a hired driver with a small truck. The Sheraton also buys fresh produce from a third company employing 10 people who work together providing fruit, vegetables and herbs to tourism establishments in Lombok. Six of the 10 people farm the land in nearby Narmada while the other four make deliveries to hotels and visit local markets to make purchases. Further generating links to the supplier network, this company has made agreements with other area farmers to grow crops specifically to be sold to hotels. In addition, rice and chicken are purchased locally by the Sheraton from small suppliers.

The Sheraton has established two unique strategic alliances with producers. Recognizing that the island of Lombok is surrounded with excellent fishing grounds, the Sheraton wanted to provide their guests with fresh local seafood. To ensure safe transport of the seafood to the hotel, a local fisherman was hired and provided with three coolers to supply all of the seafood to the Sheraton. He travels Lombok to the various fish markets and purchases fresh seafood for the hotel. The key to the project is insuring that there is a steady supply of fresh seafood. To ensure this, the Sheraton places small orders on a frequent basis. This strategic alliance has had significant impacts on both the Sheraton and the fisherman. The Sheraton has a reliable source of fresh seafood at an excellent price and by placing small orders on a frequent basis, high quality can be maintained. The fisherman has changed his employment from fisherman to fish supplier. His status has grown in the industry and his income has risen allowing him to purchase additional vehicles (Telfer and Wall, 1996).

The second unique strategic alliance was with a local farmer. The Executive Chef supplied the farmer with seeds from different countries for herbs and vegetables currently being imported. The farmer would grow the various crops exclusively for the hotel and, when ready, the Executive Chef would develop the menu around the available crops. Unfortunately this program is no longer running. When the author visited the two fields used in the project, one was already in the process of being converted back to rice and the second field was on the last harvest from the seeds provided. The farming project failed for several reasons. A cumulative effect seemed responsible for the ending of the project. The Executive Chef who initiated the project left to work at another Sheraton in Thailand. The project itself required constant supervision and a large commitment from the Resort whose primary business is running a hotel. The hotel occupancy rates fluctuated seasonally and the hotel would not always need the quantity of the product that the farmer had grown. The failure of this alliance illustrates the difficulties in maintaining strategic alliances between large multinational tourism companies and small local suppliers (Telfer and Wall, 1996). The chapter now turns to investigate the use of agriculture as a tourist attraction in a village on the island of Java.

Yogyakarta
The second Indonesian example of strategic alliances links local villagers and government in the development of a plantation as a tourist attraction. Located 20 kilometres to the north of the city of Yogyakarta, the village of Bangunkerto is situated in the highly productive agricultural lands of central Java. Altering their production to the more profitable salak crop, the villagers have established a plantation centre for tourists. The purpose of the project is not only to expose tourists to the natural environment but also to stimulate awareness and demand for the product thereby increasing local income and promoting community development (Telfer,

2000a).

The project began in 1980 with community farmers switching to salak fruit from traditional crops such as rambutan, mangoes, coconuts and bananas. Local residents developed the initial idea of establishing an agritourism venture and in 1984, the Provincial Agricultural Department assisted by giving the villagers 4,000 salak plants. A proposal was put forward to the local district government and in 1990 the agritourism site was selected in the village of Bangunkerto. Construction started on the 27 hectare site in 1992 and the local residents have made all of the agritourism facilities including a small guide centre, a small store, a dance platform and a fishing pond with a viewing platform. Visitors can take a guided tour or self-guided walk along the hand-made path through the plantation. Another example of cooperation is the use of student guides from the 12 surrounding villages at the site. Villagers also were observed working together laying stones for road foundations gathered from the site of a nearby recent volcanic eruption so that tourists could get through on mini-buses. Future construction projects include a home stay (small accommodation unit) and a swimming pool. Across the road, locals have responded to the new opportunities and have set up a small market to sell salak to the tourists (Telfer, 2000a).

The agritourism site is included on day trips combined with stops at nearby temples and money raised from entrance fees is used for staff salaries, new buildings and to help pay for the harvest of the salak from the tourist plantation. All aspects of the attraction are controlled at the local level thereby strengthening local identity and preserving cultural heritage as traditional dances are performed on site. While the project has not created a lot of income for the community directly from tourism, they are hoping to expand the facilities and markets. The alliances between the surrounding villages and the government have helped to develop and promote this agritourism initiative (Telfer, 2000a). The following example from

Cuba similarly builds on the agricultural base of the area as an attraction.

EXAMPLE FROM CUBA
Sierra Del Rosario Biosphere Reserve
Sierra Del Rosario, located in the northeast part of the province of Pinar del Rio, Cuba, was identified as a biosphere reserve by UNESCO in 1986. Within the biosphere, the community of Las Terrazas, with over 900 residents, and a growing tourist resort co-exist on the premise of sustainable tourism development. Advertised as an ecotourism destination, the area has strong links to the agricultural heritage of the past. The community of Las Terrazas was founded in 1971 in part, for the reforestation and the protection and enhancement of natural and cultural resources. Residents who were scattered across the region were encouraged to move into the state-built community and work as forestry officials, guides, teachers, merchants, gardeners, hotel employees, musicians and painters. One of the key factors in gathering the scattered population was to provide better community services such as schools, stores and medical care. Specialized courses have been developed on tourism and language for those who work in the tourism industry. The community itself has become an attraction as visitors are encouraged to walk through the community and crafts produced in the village are sold to tourists (Telfer, 2001a).

At the centre of the tourist complex is the Hotel Moka, a four star resort with 26 rooms and one suite built in 1991. Sympathetic architecture was used in the construction as trees rise from below the lobby emerging through the roof of the complex. In addition to the hotel, there are 54 camping bungalows at the foot of El Taburete hill. In some areas of the tourist complex, solar power is being utilized. The entire tourism complex receives approximately 7,000 visitors a year.

Along with the nature walks through the biosphere, there is a strong connection to the area's agricultural past. The Cañada del Infierno Trail, for example, links up with the ancient ruins of a coffee plantation. A French immigrant in the first half of the 19th century founded the Buena Vista Coffee Plantation, built at 240 metres above sea level. The ruins of the manor house have been partially restored and the site includes a specialized restaurant offering views of the surrounding countryside. Mill and coffee drying areas also have been restored. Other agricultural tourist products include a ranch, which acts as a tourist information stop, and a small farm set within the ruins of the Union Coffee Plantation, offering typical Cuban cuisine for individuals or group tours.

A symbiotic relationship has been built between the tourism industry, the community, the environment, the research centre and the agricultural past within the biosphere reserve. All of the residents work and live within the Las Terrazas complex and have benefited though increased community services and employment. Portions of the money raised through tourism go to the community and to reforestation projects run through the Research Centre. Tourists visiting the biosphere reserve have the benefit of trained guides and are able to view the plantation buildings that are currently being restored (Telfer, 2001a). The final two examples from Canada similarly highlight the potential of using agriculture as an attraction in the tourism industry.

EXAMPLES FROM CANADA
Tastes of Niagara
While the image of this Region is focused on Niagara Falls, it is also uniquely bordered by two Great Lakes (Erie and Ontario), the Niagara River and the Niagara Escarpment. The microclimate that is created, moderates the winters and extends the growing season, allowing the Region to produce a wide range of fruits and vegetables (Shaw, 1994). The diversity of agricultural practices has led to

the development of agritourism in the form of farm and winery tours. One of the key strategic alliances between tourism and agriculture, which depends on these favourable conditions, is Tastes of Niagara, an evolving strategic alliance among the Region's food producers, processors, distributors, hotels, wineries, restaurants and chefs. The objective of the alliance is to promote the use of local products in the tourism industry (Telfer, 2000b). The movement is based on developing a Niagara-based regional cuisine using high quality local products. The program started in 1993 and was initially focused on connecting chefs in the region's more expensive restaurants with some of its more unique food products. A series of tours of farms and food processing plants were held to introduce chefs to local area products.

The official trademark depicts a sunrise over fields and vineyards and it identifies members who meet local quality and quantity requirements and are dedicated to publicizing and promoting the use of high quality Niagara food products. Members are committed to maintaining *a chain of excellence* from the field to the table, which includes the farmer, the processor, the distributor, the chef, the server and finally the consumer. The Alliance has developed a number of initiatives to strengthen the links between agriculture and tourism-related industries. The Agri-Hospitality Resource Guide for Niagara (1998) contains a listing of the region's food producers, processors, chefs and restaurants (see Table 5.1). The Guide has been useful to local chefs in identifying sources of high quality local products as information is provided on when specific crops are generally ready for harvest. Chefs can quickly identify sources of local supply, rather than importing products (Telfer, 2000b).

Table 5.1: Number of Organizations Involved in Tastes of Niagara

Fruit and Vegetable Growers and Processors	50
Meat and Poultry Producers	22
Fish Producers	4
Dairy Producers and Processors	5
Farm Markets	5
Distributors	3
Other Producers and Processors and Services	10
Wineries	21
Restaurants/Chefs, Caterers and Cooking Schools	<u>23</u>
Total	143

Source: Tastes of Niagara Agri-Hospitality Resource Guide, 1998, Telfer, 2000b.

One of the most important events for the Tastes of Niagara program is the Annual Showcase (Telfer, 2000b). At the 4th Annual Showcase, 22 restaurants and 20 wineries took part and over 800 attended. Chefs prepared sample dishes using products from the Niagara Region as producers are paired with chefs and wineries. The event has grown from 120 visitors at the first Showcase. The cost of the evening is $45 CDN and the organization has recently established a second annual showcase. A recent advertising initiative has been the development of a guide to local area fruit and vegetable stands available to tourists. Many of the Tastes of Niagara members also belong to Rural Routes, which is an organization of producers that opens its doors to farm visits on one weekend during the summer. Recent interviews with members of Tastes of Niagara showed positive opinions on the program and members want to see additional cooperative efforts evolve (Telfer, 2000b). One of the key strategic alliances within the Tastes of Niagara program is the Wine Route. The importance of the Wine Route and the partnerships they have formed are outlined in the last example of this chapter.

Niagara Wine Route

The wineries in the Niagara Region receive an estimated 300,000 visitors a year (Chidley, 1998) and future estimates indicate that 450,000 visitors may tour the wineries annually (Wine Council of Ontario (WCO), 1998). Connecting over 50 wineries in the Region, the Wine Route offers guided tours, tastings, restaurants, special events and shopping. The wineries collaborate on a number of initiatives including advertising and special events. The premier event in the summer is the 'Six Unforgettable Weeks of Summer' organized by the Wine Council of Ontario, which starts at the end of June (Telfer, 2001b). Table 5.2 highlights some of the dozens of weekend events held at Niagara wineries. Many of the activities illustrate the growing link between food and wine and some of the events involve Tastes of Niagara members. As the wine route has developed, efforts have been made to make Niagara a culinary destination linking wine and food. Strewn Winery hosts The Wine Country Cooking School that presents various half-day cooking demonstrations on Saturdays and Sundays using local Niagara ingredients and wines. They recently have opened a hands-on cooking school where visitors do the cooking. Other important wine tourism events include the annual Niagara Grape and Wine Festival, which attracts over half a million visitors each year.

Some wineries have developed strategic alliances with tour operators to bring bus groups to their wineries. Wine Country Tours, for example, offers customized tours for groups and companies to wineries (Lawrason and Wilson, 1998) and Inniskillin Winery has strong links to the Japan Travel Bureau to bring Japanese tourists to their winery (Hashimoto and Telfer, 1999).

Table 5.2: Selected Wine Tourism Related Events - Six Unforgettable Weeks of Summer '99

Complimentary Tasting	Artist in the Vineyard
Hot Air Balloon Ride over the Vineyard	Wine and Jazz Night
Vineyard Barbeque	Backyard and Helicopter Vineyard Tour
Chef Series - Wine and Food Pairings	Hiking through the Vineyard
Comedy Weekend	Horseback Riding in the Vineyard
How to Taste Wine Seminar	Shakespeare in the Vineyard
Caribbean Candlelight Evening	Cigars, Wine and Sunsets
Weekend of Gardening and Wine	Mediterranean Lunches
Stargazing	Mexican Fiesta
Wine Country Golf Package	Music Festival
Icewine Sampling	Fresh Local Fruit and Wine
Wine and International Cheese Night	Dining Amongst the Vines
Antique and Classic Car Show	

Source: Wine Council of Ontario (1999), Telfer, 2001b.

The wineries collaborate both formally and informally illustrating both vertical and horizontal linkages. In interviews with approximately half of the wineries, the importance of working together with other sectors of the tourism industry was highlighted strongly by all (Telfer, 2001b). Joint initiatives between the wineries relate to association memberships, advertising, festivals and operations. At a very formal level, all of the wineries belong to a series of associations. The rules and regulations of the Vintners Quality Alliance (V.Q.A.) has helped in the development of high quality wine as well as making the Wine Route a highly marketable and identifiable entity. All of the wineries belong to the Wine Council of Ontario, which has joint marketing initiatives, festivals and special events. The wineries in southern Ontario also have linked up with wineries in New York State to create the Northeast Wine Route (Telfer, 2000c).

Along the Wine Route, agriculture acts as input in the form of food and wine and as an attraction in the form of vineyards and winery buildings. Horizontal strategic alliances include joint marketing and special events between wineries while vertical strategic alliances are illustrated in links with tour operators and local hotels. The Wine Route has raised the profile of the Niagara Region and helped diversify the tourism product.

CONCLUSION

Through a variety of examples, this chapter has illustrated the importance of strategic alliances between tourism and agriculture in order to promote local development. The Sheraton on Lombok makes it a policy to utilize local food products whenever possible. Their reliance on a variety of suppliers, who in turn purchase products from local markets or suppliers, increases the backward economic linkages of the hotel to the local economy. Over time, new supplier networks have developed and additional people are now linked to the economic benefits of tourism. The hotel has made specific strategic alliances with both a farmer and a fisherman. It is important to identify the strengths and weaknesses of these two specific alliances. By creating these two projects, the hotel has developed a source of fresh, inexpensive, high quality products. For those involved, it has created a new source of income and has increased their status in the community. However, as illustrated by the collapse of the farming project, it can be difficult for a small operator to fully meet the demands of a large tourism corporation. The ending of the project has forced the farmer to return to traditional farming methods and has had a significant impact on his income.

In the case of the salak plantation where agriculture is a tourist attraction, the strategic alliances between the nearby villages and the government have helped develop the site. By working together, the community has switched to a crop, which generates higher income, and they are now beginning to receive the benefits of tourism. Similarly, the example of Cuba illustrates the value of using agricultural heritage as a tourist attraction. The restoration of the coffee plantation buildings and coffee drying areas has established agriculture as one of the main attractions next to the natural environment. There is a strong level of symbiosis between the community of 900, the environment, agriculture and tourism, further illustrating the benefits of collaborative efforts.

In Niagara, both Tastes of Niagara and the Niagara Wine Route clearly illustrate the importance of firms working together to build a tourism product. The Tastes of Niagara initiative links firms across the production system thereby extending the benefits across a range of industries. Marketing is now done at a Regional level as firms take advantage of the shared marketing strategies. Similarly, the wineries link for marketing purposes as wine tourism continues to increase. The wineries offer not only input for tourism in the form of wine but the landscaped vineyards add value to the tourism product.

Within all the examples outlined above a series of common issues can be identified, which are highlighted in Figure 5.2. With weak local alliances, there is a lack of communication, which can lead to a use of imports thereby redirecting the economic benefits to other countries or regions. Those entering strategic alliances need to select their partners carefully to ensure a sustainable, reliable partnership is maintained. As presented in Figure 5.2, strong local alliances can lead to strong networking and new supply systems as entrepreneurs respond to new demands. The use of local products can stimulate greater economic multipliers as a result of tourism leading to potentially higher levels of local development. These case studies illustrate the importance of increased communication between the tourism industry and those involved in local agriculture. The development of regional branding can help establish a product and promote a region. The challenges within strategic alliances are to establish lasting linkages where small and large organizations can work together. The greater number of those involved in the alliance generates a greater degree of benefits.

Firms along with governments should take steps to help establish local supplier networks through tourism in order to promote greater local economic development.

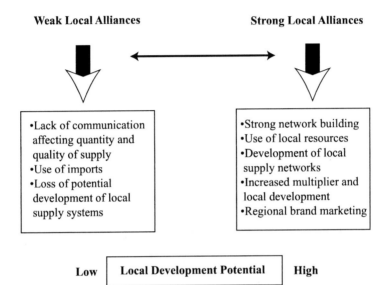

Figure 5.2: Importance of Strategic Alliances.

REFERENCES

Belisle, F.J. (1983) "Tourism and food production in the Caribbean," *Annals of Tourism Research*, 10(4): 497-513.

Botkin, J.W. and Mathews, J.B. (1992) *Winning Combinations: The Coming Wave of Entrepreneurial Partnerships Between Large and Small Companies*, Toronto: John Wiley & Sons.

Bowen, R., Cox, L. and Fox, M. (1991) "The interface between tourism and agriculture," *Journal of Tourism Studies*, 2 (2): 43-54.

Chidley, J. (1998) "Haute Canuck," *Maclean's*, 111(34): 36-40.

Corner, L. (1989) "East and West Nusa Tenggara: isolation and poverty," in H. Hill (ed.), *Unity and Diversity: Regional Economic Development In Indonesia Since 1970*, Singapore: Oxford University Press, 178-205.

Crotts, J.C., Buhalis, D. and March, R. (2000) "Introduction: global alliances in tourism and hospitality management," *International Journal of Hospitality & Tourism Management*, 1(1): 1-10.

Gulati, R. (1998) "Alliances and networks," *Strategic Management Journal*, 19: 293-317.

Hall, C.M., Johnson, G. and Mitchell, R. (2000) "Wine tourism and regional development," in C.M. Hall, L. Sharples, B. Cambourne and N. Macionis (eds.), *Wine Tourism Around the World: Development, Management and Markets*, Oxford: Butterworth Heinemann, 196-225.

Hashimoto, A. and Telfer, D.J. (1999) "Marketing icewine to Japanese tourists in Niagara: the case of Inniskillin Winery," *International Journal of Wine Marketing*, 11(2): 29-41.

Lawrason, D. and Wilson, K. (1998) "Canadian wine getaways," *Wine Access*, 8(4): 7-9.

Magun, S. (1996) *The Development of Strategic Alliances in Canadian Industries: A Micro Analysis*, Working Paper Number 13, Ottawa, ON: Industry Canada.

Shaw, T. B. (1994) "Climate of the Niagara Region," in H. Gayler, (ed.), Niagara's Changing Landscapes, Ottawa: Carleton University Press, 111-137.

Sofreavia in Association with PT. Asana Wirasta Setia and PT. Desigras (1993) *Feasibility Study For Airport Development In Lombok Master Plan Report Executive Summary*, February, Government of the Republic of Indonesia Ministry Of Communications Directorate General of Air Communications.

Tastes of Niagara Agri-Hospitality Resource Guide (1998) *Tastes of Niagara*, St. Catharines, ON: Vision Niagara Planning and Development Inc.

Taylor, B.E., Morison, J.B. and Fleming, E.M. (1991) "The economic impact of food import substitution in the Bahamas," *Social and Economic Studies*, 40(2): 45-62.

Telfer, D.J. (2001a) "Ecotourism and community development in a biosphere: Sierra Del Rosario, Cuba", *Annals of Tourism Research* (unpublished manuscript).

_____ (2001b) "Strategic alliances along the Niagara Wine Route", *Tourism Management*, 22(1): 21-30.

_____ (2000a) "Agritourism - a path to community development? The case of Bangunkerto, Indonesia," in G. Richards, and D. Hall (eds.), *Tourism and Sustainable Community Development*, London: Routledge, 242-257.

_____ (2000b) "Tastes of Niagara: building strategic alliances between tourism and agriculture," in J. Crotts, D. Buhalis and R. March (eds.), *Global Alliances in Tourism and Hospitality Management*, London: The Hawthorne Hospitality Press, 71-88.

_____ (2000c) "The northeast wine route: wine tourism in Ontario and Canada and New York State," in C.M. Hall, L. Sharples, B. Cambourne and N. Macionis (eds.), *Wine and Tourism*

Around the World, London: Butterworth Heinemann.

Telfer, D. J. and Wall, G. (1996) "Linkages between tourism and food production," *Annals of Tourism Research*, 23(3): 635-653.

Vision Niagara (1996) *Tastes of Niagara: A Quality Food Alliance Handbook*, St. Catharines, ON: Vision Niagara Planning and Development Inc.

Wilkinson, P.F. (1987) "Tourism in small island nations: a fragile dependence," *Leisure Studies*, 6(2): 128-146.

Wine Council of Ontario (1999) The Ontario Wine Industry: An Overview of Recent History, Wine Council of Ontario, [Brochure].

Chapter 6

Planning for Resource Protection and Tourism Management in Protected Areas: A Practical Perspective

Pamela Wight
Pam Wight & Associates

THE SUSTAINABLE DEVELOPMENT CONTEXT
Sustainable Tourism

Sustainable tourism needs to be viewed in the context of sustainable development. Sustainable development is not a fixed state; it is "a process of change in which the exploitation of resources, the direction of investments, the orientation of technological development, and institutional change are made consistent with future as well as present needs" (World Commission on Environment and Development, 1987: 9). Sustainable development is not a destination, rather, it is a journey. By now, the need to incorporate social, economic and environmental dimensions in sustainable tourism is relatively well known. However, sustainable development actually includes five interrelated components.

1. *Economic*: dealing with wealth creation and improved conditions of material life.
2. *Social*: measured as well-being in nutrition, health, education and housing.
3. *Political*: pointing to such values as human rights, political freedom, security, participation and some form of self-determination.
4. *Cultural*: in recognition of the fact that cultures confer identity and self-worth to people.
5. *Ecological*: recognizing the primacy of conserving the life-giving natural resources and processes on which all progress depends.

Developments have always tended to stress the first two conditions, particularly the economic. Environmental Assessment (EIA) has tended to stress the fifth. Protected areas (PAs) focus on environmental systems, but they cannot realistically exist in an operational vacuum; most environmental systems co-exist with economic development, and address the needs and aspirations of society in this mixed system, and cultural and political components may well shape social and economic conditions and values. This requires an integrative approach by all players. We need to consider *all* five of the dimensions discussed above to contribute most effectively to sustainable development and sustainable tourism.

Sustainable tourism is not equivalent to sustainable development. Tourism is only part of the whole idea of sustainable development (Wight, 1996). "Sustainable tourism" has become a form of shorthand for tourism that attempts to adhere to sustainable development principles.

Not all tourism has been, or is sustainable; nor has it always conformed to these principles. Sustainable tourism involves a challenge to develop quality tourism products without adversely affecting the natural and cultural environment that maintains and nurtures them, taking into account the political context of the community/society.

PLANNING FOR PROTECTED AREAS: INTEGRATING HUMAN USE AND PROTECTION

Canada's natural and wilderness areas feature an unequalled inventory of pristine environments, unique wildlife, spectacular scenery and distinct aboriginal cultures. Growing demand for these features make many of these areas tourism destinations in waiting. For such places, Hinch and Butler (1996:3) suggest that the "spread of tourism has been driven in part by a perpetual search for new destinations, and in part by an increasing interest in and marketing of things natural or unspoiled".

To understand all the dimensions of tourism in an area, planners and strategists must recognize that tourism is part of an interdependent system of causes and effects (McIntosh *et al.*, 1995). A truly sustainable tourism plan requires that all parties contribute toward achieving a shared set of outcomes; a vision that reflects their shared values.

Integrative Planning Approaches Required

More than 20 years ago, Mathieson and Wall (1982:182) pointed out the need "to integrate the analyses of social, economic and environmental effects of tourist development to derive an overall assessment of the desirability" of tourism development. Later Getz (1987) called for a "process, based on research and evaluation, which seeks to optimize the potential contribution of tourism to human welfare and environmental quality." Different tourism planning models have evolved (Table 6.1). With the exception of *Boosterism*, which is not a rational approach, each tradition represents responsible tourism planning from a single perspective. Taken alone, these perspectives cannot address the range of tourism impacts that an integrated approach requires.

Traditional tourism planning perspectives fail to address tourism impacts in all its dimensions. In general, these approaches seek to maximize or minimize tourism impacts from a single perspective, and tend to over-simplify. Wight (1998a) identified some of the attributes and constraints of various tourism planning tools, and the need for an integrated approach where the decision-making framework incorporates community values, appropriate scales, and broad-based public involvement in management and monitoring.

In Australia, an integrated approach called the Tourism Optimization Management Model (TOMM) was developed (Manidis Roberts, 1997). TOMM evolved from the Limits of Acceptable Change (LAC) model during tourism planning in South Australia, because LAC could not accommodate the perspective of those who sought an overall quality of life in the community.

Table 6.1 Traditions, Perspectives and Planning Issues for Tourism

Tradition	Perspective	Strategic Planning Issues and Questions
Boosterism	Tourism is good and should be developed.	How can more tourists be attracted? How can obstacles to growth be overcome?
Commercial	Tourism is a business that should provide a financial return to its investors.	How can profits and shareholder value be maximized?
Economic	Tourism creates employment and attracts foreign revenue.	How can tourism spur growth in the economy? How can employment and income be maximized?
Environmental	Tourism has an impact on resources, so should have an ecological basis. Tourism is a spatial phenomenon.	What is the physical carrying capacity of an area? How can travel patterns be manipulated to reduce environmental impacts? Should visitor use be concentrated or dispersed?
Community-based	Tourism is neither good nor bad. Its development should be guided by local wishes.	How can the community take control of tourism development? What are the impacts of tourism on the community?
Integrated	Tourism is part of a complete system that includes the environment, community, industry, economy, and the legislative environment. Its planning should be democratic and integrated with related planning processes. Its planning should help tourism to contribute to a community's well being.	How does the tourism system work in this area? What are the reasons for tourism in this area? How can the system be changed to optimize tourism's contribution, relative to shared goals?

McVetty, 1997, adapted from Getz, 1987.

The TOMM process involves developing a realistic set of tourism scenarios for a destination, including their benefits and disbenefits, and working with stakeholders to develop a set of outcomes for tourism and visitor use, together with realistic and measurable indicators. When implemented, these indicators are monitored, and may trigger a management response. TOMM, as a management tool, is consistent with the principles of integrated tourism planning, and addresses the broad set of tourism benefits and impacts based on community values, tourism assets and realistic market opportunities. It was designed to operate at a regional level, rather than a single site; serve a variety of stakeholders, rather than a single agency; and help foster a sustainable tourism industry, rather than focus on minimizing negative impacts.

Integrative Planning in Practice: Aulavik National Park

Aulavik National Park was established on Banks Island in 1992 (see Figure 6.1). The island's 140 residents are all clustered in Sachs Harbour, a Hamlet about 250 kilometres south of the park boundary (two hours by plane, and two or more days by land or water). The Inuvialuit were key players in the establishment of Aulavik National Park, and retain rights to traditional subsistence activities within park boundaries.

Figure 6.1: Aulavik National Park, Banks Island, Northwest Territories.

The park's establishment agreement directed that services and facilities would be developed in response to *market demand*. But Parks Canada recognized that not only does demand vary over time, it is also affected by the very establishment of a park. They also realized that demand would be further affected by the character of any facilities or services, and by marketing and packaging. To address this conundrum, Parks Canada commissioned a Visitor Market Analysis, using an integrated tourism planning approach, to help managers and stakeholders understand the influences and impacts of park-related tourism - in all its dimensions - and to develop a system to achieve those objectives (Pam Wight & Associates, 1998a). The approach included:

1. *A Situation Analysis.* This included:
- information review;
- community and stakeholder consultations;
- parks Canada staff interviews;
- commercial trends review (including a travel trade survey); and
- legislative and policy environment review.

By addressing the social, economic, environmental, cultural and political/legislative concerns, it ensured that all of the interrelated components of sustainable development were considered. The analysis found significant park-related tourism potential for the Aulavik and Banks Island area, but found the network of legislation, agreements and administrative bodies was, in some cases, creating barriers to the very outcomes that they were put in place to support.

2. *Developing A Shared Vision.* This vision represents a set of desired outcomes for tourism and visitor use, that are very similar for community residents, regional stakeholders and Parks Canada. Overall, the shared vision for tourism was summarized as a: "sustainable tourism indus-

try based on renewable resources and on cultural experiences, which is compatible with traditional values and activities, and where the community is enabled to participate optimally." (Pam Wight & Associates, 1998a)

3. *Alternative Visitor Use Scenarios.* These scenarios are based on the area's commercial realities and regulatory environment, and they were not based on growth, but on visitor type, and intended to optimize tourism outcomes. Outcomes investigated were:
    - no substantial change - no commercial operations in the park;
    - enabling outside companies to operate in the park; and
    - partnerships (between local and outside operators) to optimize tourism outcomes.

The TOMM process, as applied for Aulavik National Park, revealed that key stakeholders were unaware that their separate initiatives had produced minimal visitor use. Certainly, there had been few negative impacts, but there were even fewer benefits. These early stages of integrated planning helped Parks Canada and stakeholders to address this quandary, in ways that support the shared objectives of the park and its stakeholders. Integrated tourism planning has shown potential to bring Parks Canada and its local stakeholders together to manage their activities in ways that support a well-researched, realistic and shared set of desired outcomes.

Park managers then started planning the next phase in the TOMM/integrated planning process - developing an integrated suite of indicators for a monitoring and management programme to bring together the expertise of several disciplines. Without this integration into existing plans and policies, the efficacy of a single partner's efforts would be limited.

Integrative Planning in Practice: Gwaii Haanas

Gwaii Haanas National Park Reserve/Haida Heritage Site (Gwaii Haanas) is a rugged and remote wilderness area located on the Queen Charlotte Islands/Haida Gwaii (The Islands) of Northwest British Columbia.

Parks Canada and the Council of the Haida Nation cooperatively co-manage Gwaii Haanas. As with Aulavik, co-management adds complexity to the management of a protected area (PA). Previous tourism planning for Gwaii Haanas failed, because of community division, a strong resource extraction industry, low awareness of sustainable tourism and a feeling that the planning process was being driven by "off-Islanders."

More recently Parks Canada has been working with the tourism industry to refine tourism marketing for The Islands. In a search for alternatives to traditional tourism planning models, the integrated approach, TOMM in particular, was selected. Baseline research came from Parks Canada visitor surveys and focus groups, and was analyzed through market research and tourism opportunity analysis (Pam Wight & Associates, 1999). This baseline research forms the basis of the tourism planning process, and the results are used by Gwaii Haanas management and the local communities and tourism industry.

Research included:
- a review of attitudinal information (both of residents and visitors);
- a review of summer visitors to The Islands;
- a review of Vancouver and Calgary focus group results;
- research related to ecotourism, culture and aboriginal tourism markets;
- product evaluation; and
- issues evaluation.

The integrated planning approach helped to focus this complex research exercise, so information collection and presentation was designed to address many of the issues. The research examines Gwaii Haanas at a series of levels (the total Islands community, the regional and the global tourism industry). The Islands experience is also reviewed from the visitors' perspective. The report identifies for the Islands communities the shared values, shared concerns, opportunities and gaps in service, and current and potential visitor information.

The research shows that different groups of visitors have different benefits and costs. Thus, Park management developed plans to move into the next phases of their integrated planning process. For example, some plans target the high-yield, low-cost niches, while others reflect management's new view of sea kayaking as a market with potential and few costs.

One challenge for famous PAs is the impact of third-party media on tourism demand. The research found that the visitors' image of the destination was being shaped through a number of outside sources: the provincial tourism agency, travel media, news media and conservation groups. The focus has been on traditional icons, particularly the World Heritage Site SGaang Gwaii (which is an over-used image of mortuary poles along the beach). This can create visitor expectations of seeing totem poles everywhere. Current research is looking at this more closely, to help stakeholders to work more closely with the media and tourism industry partners to shift the focus away from the traditional icons. Within the context of this new thinking, the brand for The Islands and Gwaii Haanas should be considered. The images for travellers need not be grand or dominating (like the Eiffel Tower or the Pyramids); they may be windmills, rickshaws, palm trees or penguins (Figure 6.2).

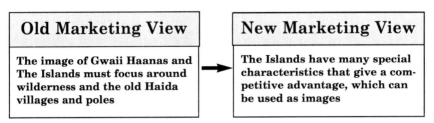

Figure 6.2: Shift in Views About Marketing Gwaii Haanas.

To address the stakeholders' range of perspectives, future research must synthesize the contributions of different disciplines into a cohesive decision-making framework. Local management feels that the integrated approach at an early stage helped them to better understand their visitors and the dynamic outcomes of their visits. It also might be useful for future research to consider an inverse approach - that of stakeholder articulation of *undesired* outcomes, which are to be avoided by the planning process.

TOOLS FOR MANAGING PARKS AND PROTECTED AREAS
Approaches to Protected Area Management
There are a number of management approaches to natural and protected areas, each of which could be used in isolation or in a complementary fashion. Approaches are shown in Figure 6.3:

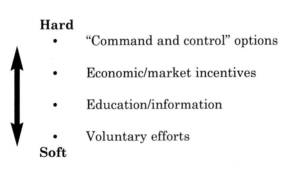

Figure 6.3: Management Approaches.

Management approaches range from "hard" to "soft". However, there has tended to be a high emphasis on the "command and control" approach in PAs.

Dealing with Problems in PAs

Some authors have recognized a number of environmental problems that are common in wilderness or natural areas and apply to tourism activities (Table 6.2).

Table 6.2 Problems Common in Wilderness/Natural Areas

Negative Impacts of Visitors on the Environment	
• Trail deterioration	• Habitat loss
• Campsite deterioration	• Noise & air pollution
• Litter	• Souvenir/firewood collection
• Crowding	• Aesthetic impacts
• Packstock impacts	• Over fishing, undersized fishing
• Human waste problems	• Impacts on vegetation
• Impacts on wildlife	• Damage to sand dunes/reefs
• User conflicts	• Soil compaction
• Water pollution	• Increased fire risk
• Overdevelopment	• Damage to archaeological sites

Source: Cole et al., 1987; McNeely and Thorsell, 1989; Buckley and Pannell, 1990; Dowling, 1993.

In the face of such actual or potential problems in protected areas, one of the commonest management responses is to put a limit on use. This often takes the form of limits to commercial or FIT (Free Independent Travel) activities through such means as limits on numbers of visitors (or facilities), group size limits, or use quotas. This is a relatively easy approach. However, it may well be inappropriate.

Taking a similar view, the literature has presented numerous calls for tourism carrying capacity to be determined, to appropriately plan, manage and control the direction and consequences of tourism and other activities (*e.g.*, McNeely and Thorsell, 1989; International Working Group on Indicators of Sustainable Tourism,

1993; Consulting and Audit Canada, 1995). Unfortunately, however, while the *concept* of carrying capacity is appealing, it has had limited success outside the field of wildlife management (where it was originally developed), and cannot deal with the complexity and diversity of issues associated with recreation and tourism (McCool, 1991; Bianchi, 1994; Wight, 1994, 1996, 1998a; Hall and McArthur, 1998). Some of the problems inherent in attempting to determine carrying capacity include:

*   *unrealistic expectations* (*e.g.*, that a technique can provide a magic number, limit or threshold);
*   *untenable assumptions* (*e.g.*, that there is a direct relationship between visitor use and impact; and that limiting use limits impact); and,
*   *imprecise and varying parameters* (*e.g.*, are we dealing with biophysical resources? the host community? visitors? what activities? how are they behaving?)

Although attractive in *conceptual* terms, in *practical* tourism terms carrying capacity is not an applicable concept. Research and programs are now focusing on managing the *resource*, the *visitors*, and the *impacts*, rather than carrying capacity.

With respect to the potential problems illustrated in Table 6.2, Cole *et al.* (1987) point out that there are a range of strategies which may be appropriate for managing these problems (Table 6.3).

Each management strategy has a number of tactics, of which only the first tactic of the first strategy is a form of carrying capacity. In fact, Cole *et al.* (1987) indicate that they have always found other *more effective* means to deal with problems, than applying carrying capacity (which is a strong "command and control" approach). As Table 6.3 suggests, there are many ways of managing for sustainability. Each of the tactics described relate to managing *resources*, *visitors*, or *impact* - or all three. This is essentially equivalent to managing the supply, the demand and the impact. These tactics were developed for terrestrial systems, but may be modified for management of marine protected areas. It should be noticed that a range of management approaches are incorporated in the "toolbag" of tactics, from hard to soft.

Table 6.3 Strategies and Tactics for Managing Wilderness, Natural and Protected Areas

Strategy	Management Tactics
1. Reduce Use of the Entire Wilderness/PA	1. Limit number of visitors in the entire wilderness/PA 2. Limit length of stay 3. Encourage use of other areas 4. Require certain skills and/or equipment 5. Charge a flat visitor fee 6. Make access more difficult in all wilderness
2. Reduce Use of Problem Areas	1. Inform about problem areas and alternative areas 2. Discourage or prohibit use of problem area 3. Limit number of visitors in problem areas 4. Encourage/require a stay limit in problem areas 5. Make access harder/easier to areas 6. Eliminate facilities/attractions in problem areas, improve facilities/attractions in alternative areas 7. Encourage off-trail travel 8. Establish different skill/equipment requirements 9. Charge differential visitor fees
3. Modify the Location of Use Within Problem Areas	1. Discourage/prohibit camping/stock use 2. Encourage/permit camping/stock in certain areas 3. Locate facilities on durable sites 4. Concentrate use through facility design or info 5. Discourage/prohibit off-trail travel 6. Segregate different types of visitors
4. Modify the Timing of Use	1. Encourage use outside of peak use periods 2. Discourage/ban use when impact potential high 3. Fees in periods of high use/high impact potential
5. Modify Type of Use and Visitor Behaviour	1. Discourage/ban damaging practices/equipment 2. Encourage/require behaviour, skills, equipment 3. Teach a wilderness ethic 4. Encourage/require a party size and/or stock limit 5. Discourage/prohibit stock 6. Discourage/prohibit pets 7. Discourage/prohibit overnight use
6. Modify Visitor Expectations	1. Inform visitors about appropriate wilderness/PA uses 2. Inform about potential conditions in wilderness/PA
7. Increase the Resistance of the Resource	1. Shield the site from impact 2. Strengthen the site
8. Maintain/Rehabilitate Resource	1. Remove problems 2. Maintain/rehabilitate impacted locations

Source: Cole et al., 1987.

Parks Canada's Management Challenges

Parks Canada has been increasingly mandated to focus on striking a more sustainable balance between the obligation to manage tourist destinations, and to provide visitors with meaningful experiences, and responsibilities to protect park ecosystems and the wildlife and natural processes dependent on them.

Criticism of Parks Canada usually goes hand in hand with the representation of the National Parks System as having the difficult task of meeting two goals: enjoyment and protection of parks. It is relatively easy to characterize parks as running into constant problems while attempting to meet the two often contradictory objectives - providing opportunities for understanding, appreciation and enjoyment and recreation, as well as protection/conservation. This has led to sometimes divisive debate, and Parks Canada is very sensitive to this view, which does not acknowledge historic realities. The Canadian Parks Service has existed since 1885, and there has been an evolution of reasons why parks were created. For example, in Banff National Park, tourism was the driver, whereas the new Arctic parks are much more biological preserves, while some PAs such as Gwaii Haanas have strong natural *and cultural* landscape protection functions. Thus, as national parks have evolved, we have seen the building of a diverse "product line" (*e.g.*, tourism, conservation, recreation) representing different states of the ideological balance over the years. Additionally, once infrastructure is created in a park, it is essentially "cast in stone". This presents an even greater and complex challenge for management agencies.

It is all too easy to target certain vulnerable PAs for criticism, for example, by saying that a park is being "loved to death" by its visitors. This perspective, however, is beginning to be viewed by the agency in terms of supply and demand management (Figure 6.4), rather than in terms of conflicting objectives (*e.g.*, parks may have a limited supply of access/accommodation in some highly attractive areas, which may have excess demand. The latter is usually due to a combination of pressures of visitation, and lack of application of the full range of direct and indirect management tools to deal with this).

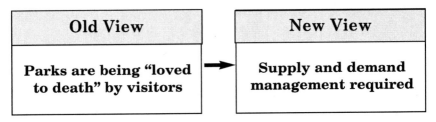

Old View	New View
Parks are being "loved to death" by visitors	Supply and demand management required

Figure 6.4: Views About Parks: Old and New.

Supply and demand management can move beyond "command and control" approaches (the hard end of management approaches), to incorporate any of the huge range of tactics illustrated in Table 6.3. This echoes the need to manage visitors, *and* impact, *and* resource. Although there is a new move to examine and incorporate a range of hard and soft management approaches, it is fair to say that it is still common to find a "limits" based perspective high in the list of management tools that are being adopted in PAs - a command and control approach. Other management tools need more emphasis. It is not the purpose of this chapter to systematically discuss all management tools available for PAs. However, it is useful to note that the range of tools employed could focus very much more on those that manage the demand, and the visitor, specifically.

Visitor Management

Visitor management is an important aspect of any form of tourism in sensitive areas, whether in a PA or an adjacent region or community. Examples of specific visitor management tools that could usefully be employed include those illustrated on Table 6.4 (Pam Wight & Associates, 1998b). It should be noted that although most of these tools address visitors *during* activities in the PA, some target the visitor *before* their arrival at the PA, and effective tools will also affect visitors *after* they leave.

Table 6.4 Examples of Visitor Impact Management Tools

VIM Tools	Examples
Target appropriate markets	Influence mix; attract specific types
Promotional tools	Agree where and when to promote a site; have alternatives
Educate and inform	Use Tourism Information Centres and materials to educate before arrival on site, and expectations, behaviour, etc.
Interpret and motivate	Inform and interpret to give greater understanding about sensitivities
Direct visitors	Use signage to influence behaviour
Influence behaviour	Develop code, guidelines, directed at visitors, community, operators, etc.
Guides/Stewards	Use on-site personnel to supervise, protect, inform, interpret positively
Involve community	Involve schools, groups, especially regarding maintenance and improvements
Involve community agencies	Involve agencies and individuals in developing code or guidelines for site and community

Voluntary Approaches: Codes and Guidelines

Canada developed an excellent Code of Ethics and Guidelines for Sustainable Tourism a decade ago (TIAC, 1992). Unfortunately they had poor industry distribution and application. There have been strong moves over the last decade, to introduce more sustainable forms of tourism, and to demonstrate to visitors this sense of responsibility. This has been found among countries, destination regions, cities, hospitality chains, groups of separate businesses, and individual businesses. One particular form of voluntary activity which has proliferated, is guidelines or codes for visitors or operators.

An example in Britain is the Welsh Ceredigon Marine "Heritage Coast", which was the first to have its boundary extended out to sea. It developed a Code of Conduct to encourage responsible use of the area (Table 6.5). This is displayed on leaflets and interpretation boards, and is included in the local Tide Tables.

The range of topic areas that are covered by the Welsh Code contrasts with a number of Canadian destinations, which have tended to develop a single focus code, such as for whale watching. An exception is on the west coast of Vancouver Island, where Pacific Rim National Park Reserve staff collaborated with marine operators to develop an expanded range of voluntary Guidelines related to:
- shoreline wildlife viewing;
- seabirds viewing;
- pinnipeds viewing
- killer whales / orca viewing;
- gray and humpback whale viewing; and
- Grice Bay wildlife viewing (a specific sensitive location).

The Pacific Rim Guidelines not only covered wildlife viewing, but also: getting into position; viewing; leaving the area; and even distance viewing and waiting.

Table 6.5 Welsh Code of Conduct Covering Diversity of Topics

Ceredigon Marine Heritage Coast: Code of Conduct	
Boats	• Operate with care and attention to safety of occupants and other sea users
Dolphins	• Maintain a steady speed and course, or slow down gradually • Don't chase, maneuver erratically, turn toward, or attempt to touch or feed
Seals	• Don't interfere with seals or pups on beach • Control dogs and keep away from seals
Birds	• When sailing, keep 100 m out from cliffs in breeding season (specified) • Don't sail directly towards rafts of birds resting or feeding on the sea • Avoid unnecessary noise close to cliffs
Fishing	• Don't discard tackle, take home for proper disposal
Jet Skis	• Don't launch or operate in the area (heritage coast)
Divers	• Observe BSAC Code of Conduct
Beaches	• Take home all your litter • Keep to dog by-laws • Replace shore rocks you move, to keep alive the animals who live underneath

Interpretation: An Underutilized Management Tool

Visitor management tools not only are often neglected, but each one has a range of dimensions that should be explored. As only *one* example, interpretation is a sadly underutilized tool. Interpretation can and should achieve much more than simple transmission of information. To be used as a visitor management tool, interpretation has to affect visitors' behaviour. Motivating them, through appeal to their emotions, is a very effective way to do this. Interpretation may have multiple objectives (Figure 6.5).

Learning	• What they learn/remember
	• This is commonest application of interpretation
Behavioural	• What they do
	• Helps focus on what you want visitors to do, and how to use information given
Emotional	• Must occur first, to alter behaviour or attitudes
	• Helps visitors remember topic because of strong feelings created; helps feel surprise, anger, guilt, pride and other desired emotions

Figure 6.5: Interpretation Objectives.

It is the information/learning aspects of interpretation that have commonly had the greatest emphasis. However, in the context of resource management, behavioural objectives are most important, because they can help shape visitors' behaviour and thus lessen resource impact. Emotional objectives also are critical, because they motivate visitors to change their behaviour, and also help visitors to "take away" important messages and values. In the context of the *independent* visitor to PAs who may not have access to commercial interpretive tours, it is important that adequate emphasis is given to non-verbal interpretive messages. These may be *during* the visit (*e.g.*, in interpretive displays or literature), or even *before* the visit (*e.g.*, in tourism literature, or on Internet web sites).

New Technologies to Manage the Resource and Human Use
It is interesting to note that innovative management tools are emerging from new technologies. These may assist in managing both the visitors and the resource, with the combined effect of managing impact.

An area that is often *not* well addressed relates to visitor transportation, movement and management. It is in this area that many of sustainable tourism's greatest challenges and criticisms occur. This may be because the challenges are larger than the individual business or destination scale. Recently, some exiting new developments in the field of software tools for management have emerged. Two such are Archaeolink and Caledonian Trails, both developed in the UK (Wight, 1998b).

Archaeolink Interpretive Park

Archaeolink is a 20 hectare park in Scotland including actual archaeological sites, and an indoor/outdoor interpretive centre. Indoor elements include an interpretive video, interactive computer educational tools, interpretive galleries, displays, the usual range of themed gift areas and food and beverage service. Outdoor elements include a Pictish farmstead, being worked by historical interpreters (volunteers and staff), a Roman Marching Camp and hill fort, and an interpretive playground. Of interest here, is the computer software "**ArchaeoQuest**", which was developed by Delphic Productions Ltd. in the UK. There are two elements of the software - **Browse**, and **Quest**.

ARCHAEOBROWSE: ArchaeoBrowse allows the visitor to look at all the regional archaeological sites identified on the program. A map of NE Scotland with all the sites is displayed, with icons representing sites, and each category of site can be highlighted (Table 6.6). Individual sites may belong to multiple categories, as follows:

Table 6.6: ArchaeoBrowse Categories

4000 BC - 1000 BC	1500 BC - 500 AD	300 AD - 700 AD
The Early Farmers	Tribal Power	The Picts
Stone Circles	Hill Forts	Symbol Stones

By selecting a site, one can browse it in a variety of ways.

- *Images* - seeing a range of picture views of the full area/structure, or individual details of interest about the site, and four to eight images, with a very small description of each.
- *Information* - this provides a series of panels describing the history and other details to a very interested user, and four to eight panels of details.
- *Video* - this provides an aerial experience of the site, which is particularly useful for sites which may better be interpreted from the air.
- *Main Map* - this enables the browser to return to the main map to change selections.

The visitor then can decide which sites are of most interest for them to visit in person.

ARCHAEOQUEST: ArchaeoQuest is intended to assist the tourist to visit the sites of interest to them, however, it also has important site management features. It allows visitors to enter details about their interests and how they travel, and is designed to respond not only to visitor interests and ability, but also to characteristics (such as party size) and to site conditions. The categories of question are fairly straightforward (Table 6.7).

After the questions have been answered, the on-screen map can print an individualized route, with sites selected according to stated interest and capability areas. Part of the data which is contained within the software relates to site constraints. For example, if there is *not* adequate parking for certain sizes of parties at certain sites, they are eliminated from the route selection.

Table 6.7 ArchaeoQuest Question Categories

Visitor Questions	Answer Options
Party size?	• 1, 2, 3-4, 5-12, 13-20, over 20
Level of fitness?	• Low, average, high
Mode of transportation?	• Foot, bike, car, coach, public transportation
Time available?	• 1 hour, <3 hours, <6 hours, 1 day, more than a day
Level of archaeological knowledge?	• Low, average, high
Eventual destination today?	• A series of regional towns are presented for selection on the map
Topics of interest?	• A menu of choices is presented. These choices are the same as those in the Browse menu.

This author contacted the software developers, and determined that the following aspects could easily be built into the software:

- expanded or contracted geographic area;
- inclusion of many types of destinations (natural, heritage, parks, trails, coastal routes, urban, facilities or attractions, recreation activity sites, etc.);
- other categories of questions about the visitor/party; and
- live links with the sites/destinations listed (this would enable those which had a large party that day, or where the car parks were full, or where there was some site degradation, to exclude themselves from the site selection process. Similarly, natural attractions that had a seasonal sensitivity, could exclude themselves from the process).

The point is, that whatever the destination, it would be possible to select which sites or attractions would feature on a software program, for commercial and/or environmental management or other purposes. This could have tremendous applications for the more popular parks and PAs; and computer terminals could be in multiple locations both inside and *outside* the PA, so as to assist in rerouting visitors and protecting the resource. It also could have application in historic sites and urban locations.

CONCLUSIONS: INTEGRATING A RANGE OF DIMENSIONS AND APPROACHES IN TOURISM PLANNING AND MANAGEMENT

A number of interrelated components are involved in sustainable development - economic, social, political, cultural and ecological. All these dimensions need to be considered to contribute effectively to sustainable tourism. In the past, tourism plans often were rooted in a single or limited perspective, thus having limited utility. A new generation of tourism plans is evolving to help destinations realize more of tourism's benefits while avoiding its range of potential pitfalls.

There have been many distinct and often different points of view in PAs, but those with voice tend to be the resource manager. Other perspectives are often missing - those of local communities/cultures, tourism operators and visitors. Tourism in destination areas must be able to meet the needs of the tourism sector, the local community, the tourism resource and the visitor.

PA managers generally have to manage for protection, as well as for other values such as visitor enjoyment. To obtain the greatest benefits of sustainable tourism in PAs, tourism planning and development must have the active maintenance of the natural and cultural resources as a prime consideration. To achieve this, the products developed must respect the cultural values and environment of the place, and incorporate other perspectives. PA managers are coming to the realization that good PA planning incorporates the perspectives of all stakeholders.

This paper discussed early stages of integrated planning to help optimize the tourism outcomes in and adjacent to two co-operatively managed protected areas (Gwaii Haanas and Aulavik National Park). Each adapted the approach to their own situation, but both were able to develop a clearer understanding of the tourism system and its outcomes. In both cases, the first objective was to develop an understanding of the local tourism system (inputs and outcomes) and to define the optimal outcomes for those systems, in consultation with the local communities, stakeholder groups, visitors and the travel industry.

Most tourism destinations are conscious of the need not only to *develop*, but also to *manage* for sustainable tourism. This presents a special challenge in PAs, particularly those where the ecological integrity of the destination may be of prime consideration.

A common response to visitor or resource problems in PAs has tended to be "command-and-control" oriented (a classic example being the call for "determining the carrying capacity", which is an impractical approach). Reasons for this "hard" approach may possibly be because it is simpler, particularly in times when agencies themselves are struggling with a lack of resources, ranging from staff, to time, to funding.

PAs have given less consideration to "softer" management approaches, yet there are many underutilized management strategies and tactics. For example, visitor impact management tools have tremendous potential, including voluntary and collaborative approaches, as demonstrated in Pacific Rim National Park Reserve, or Wales' Marine Heritage Coast. These require good cooperation and communication between resource managers and commercial operations, and mutual understanding of perspectives.

Other useful management approaches focus on integrating the management of visitors, their impacts and the resource. In particular, educational approaches have excellent potential for visitor influence, that is important since visitors themselves may be an active partner in accomplishing sustainable tourism. Much will depend on how well they are reached and "touched", whether by natural area managers, or by tour operators. Interpretation is a management tool that has tended to focus on transmitting information. But interpretative approaches also can include behaviour modification and motivation. Ensuring that emotional and behavioural interpretation objectives are reached, is essential to altering visitor behaviour and attitudes. The benefits of a comprehensive visitor management approach include the ability to influence visitors *before*, *during* and *after* their visit.

Besides the large range of strategies and tactics available for PA management, a number of specific tools are emerging to assist in tourism management. For example, some software programs include great benefits to fulfil a number of PA management objectives: resource protection; visitor behaviour management; and visitor enjoyment and satisfaction, as illustrated at Archaeolink in Scotland.

The integrated approach to tourism *planning* aims to develop effective, sustainable tourism plans that reflect the shared perspectives of the stakeholders in the tourism system, the full range of potential tourism impacts and the realities of the market place. It has proven useful in bringing these views together in ways that can help tourism to make its full contribution to the quality of life, the economy and the environment of the host area. The integrated approach to tourism *management* uses the range of strategies and tactics available, integrating "command and control", incentive, educational and voluntary approaches. It aims to bring all parties "on side", and by engaging or collaborating with visitors and commercial operators, can actively contribute to resource protection.

A main message of this chapter is that there are many tools in the PA manager's toolbag. The challenge is to move from the status quo, to integrate other stakeholder perspectives, and apply those tactics and tools collaboratively, in a manner appropriate to the place, the community and the visitor.

REFERENCES

Bianchi, R. (1994) "Tourism development and resort dynamics: an alternative approach," in C. Cooper and A. Lockwood (eds.), *Progress in Tourism and Hospitality Management*, Vol. 5, Chichester, England: Wiley: 181-193.

Buckley, R. and Pannell, J. (1990) "Environmental impacts of tourism and recreation in national parks and conservation reserves," *Journal of Tourism Studies*, 1(1): 24-32.

Cole, D.N., Petersen, M.E. and Lucas, R.C. (1987) *Managing Wilderness Recreation Use: Common Problems and Potential Solutions*, Ogden, UT: USDA Forest Service, Gen. Tech. Rep. INT-230.

Consulting and Audit Canada (1995) *What Tourism Managers Need to Know*, Spain: World Tourism Organization, June.

Dowling, R.K. (1993) "Tourism planning, people and the environment in Western Australia", *Journal of Travel Research*, 31(4): 52-58.

Getz (1987) "Tourism planning and research: traditions, models, and futures," in *Proceedings of the Australian Travel Research Workshop*, hosted by the Western Australia Tourism Commission, November 5-6, Bunbury, Western Australia, Australia.

Hall, C.M. and McArthur, S. (1998) *Integrated Heritage Management: Principles and Practice*, London: The Stationery Office.

Hinch, T. and Butler, R. (eds.) (1996) *Tourism and Indigenous People*s, London: International Thomson Business Press.

International Working Group on Indicators of Sustainable Tourism (1993) *Indicators for the Sustainable Management of Tourism*, for the Environment Committee of the World Tourism Organization, Winnipeg: Industry, Science and Technology Canada, and International Institute for Sustainable Development.

Manidis Roberts (1997) *Developing a Tourism Optimization Management Model (TOMM)*, Final Report, Adelaide: South Australian Tourism Commission.

Mathieson, A., and Wall, G. (1982) *Tourism: Economic, Physical, and Social Impacts*, UK: Longman Group Limited.

McCool, S.F. (1991) *Limits of Acceptable Change: A Strategy for Managing the Effects of Nature-Dependent Tourism Development*, Paper presented at Tourism and the Land: Building a Common Future Conference, Whistler, BC: December 1-3.

McIntosh, R., Goeldner, C. and Ritchie, J.R.B. (1995) *Tourism: Principles, Practices, Philosophies*, Toronto: John Wiley & Sons, Inc.

McNeely, J.A. and Thorsell, J.W. (1989) "Jungles, mountains, and islands: how tourism can help conserve the natural heritage," *World Leisure and Recreation*, 31(4): 29-39.

McVetty, D. (1997) *Segmenting Heritage Tourism Party-Visits on Dunedin's Otago Peninsula: A Strategic Approach*, Masters's Thesis, University of Otago, Dunedin, New Zealand.

Pam Wight & Associates (1998a) *Visitor Market Analysis for Aulavik National Park*, Canadian Heritage, Winnipeg, MB: Parks Canada Western Canada Service Centre.

_____ (1998b) *Saskatchewan Bird Trail, Part 2: Community Planning Guide*, Regina: Saskatchewan Wetland Conservation Corporation.

_____ (1999) *Market Analysis for Gwaii Haanas National Park Reserve/Haida Heritage Site*, Prepared for the Archipelago Management Board, Queen Charlotte City, BC: Heritage Canada.

Wight, P.A. (1994) "Limits of acceptable change: a recreational tourism tool for cumulative effects assessment," in Kennedy, A.J. (ed.), *Cumulative Effects in Canada: From Concept to Practice*, Calgary, AB: Fifteenth Symposium held by the Alberta Society of Professional Biologists, Calgary, 159-178.

_____ (1996) *Planning for Success in Sustainable Tourism*, Presentation to "Plan for Success" Canadian Institute of Planners National Conference, Saskatoon, Saskatchewan, June 2-5.

_____ (1998a) "Tools for sustainability analysis in planning and managing tourism and recreation in the destination," in C.M. Hall and A.A. Lew (eds.), *Sustainable Tourism: A Geographical Perspective*, Harlow, UK: Wesley Longman Ltd., 75-91.

_____ (1998b) *Innovative Visitor Management and Movement Tools: Economic, Environmental and Marketing Benefits*, Presented to Moving the Economy, an International Sustainable Transportation Conference organized by Transportation Options, The Green Tourism Association, & City of Toronto, July 9-12.

World Commission on Environment and Development (1987) *Our Common Future*, WCED, New York: Oxford University Press.

Chapter 7

The Heritage Shopping Village:
Profit, Preservation and Production

Clare J.A. Mitchell
University of Waterloo

The post-war period in North America has been one of great change for rural communities. While some continue to experience loss of population and economic activity associated with the shift from an industrial to post-industrial economy, others have taken on new roles within the settlement system (Barnes and Hayter, 1992; Gill and Reed, 1997). The production and sale of handcrafted products and experiences is one example of the expanded role taken on by a growing number of Canadian towns and villages. The emergence of these "heritage shopping villages" has attracted the interest of several North American researchers (Dahms, 1991; Getz, 1993; Mitchell, 1998; Mitchell *et al.*, 2001). Recently, a normative model was presented that provides an explanation for the origin and evolution of these unique places (Mitchell, 1998). To date, this model has been applied to three Canadian communities. In this chapter I present a comparative analysis of two of these sites, Elora and St. Jacobs, Ontario. The ultimate goal is to illustrate the model's ability to predict the future of communities whose development is based on the commodification of tradition and heritage.

ORIGINS

The appearance of heritage shopping villages can be attributed to the twin forces of demand and supply; to the desire to purchase "signposts" of the past and to their provision by enterprising entrepreneurs. The drive to collect historic mementoes is part of a broader societal trend to accumulate what Bourdieu (1984) calls "symbolic capital". Since the 1970s, Bourdieu argues, the middle class consumer has been engaged in the purchase of products that illustrate their individual tastes and distinctions. While for some this is reflected in the purchase of upmarket apparel or electronics, for others, the attainment of heritage, as either tangible product or aesthetic experience (Jameson, 1984), fulfills this post-modern quest for the unique.

The emergence of this new consumption behaviour has been explored by many (Featherstone, 1990; Zeppel and Hall, 1991; Cloke and Goodwin, 1992; Park and Coppack, 1994). It is widely agreed that the tendency to look to the past is a reflection of society's desire to root itself in the present. Konrad (1982: 412), for example, purports that this trend is driven by "a psychological need for continuity, the desire to transcend contemporary experience" and "the urge to know one's roots". Harvey (1990: 427) furthers the argument by linking these new desires to economic forces, such as globalization and time-space compression. In his own words:

> the more global interrelations become... the more spatial barriers disintegrate, so more rather than less of the world's people clings to place and neighbourhood or to nation, region, ethnic groupings or religious beliefs as specific marks of identity. Such a quest for visible and tangible marks of identity is readily identifiable in the midst of fierce time-space compression... There is still an insistent urge to look for roots in a world where image streams accelerate and become more and more placeless.

As the demand for heritage products has emerged, so too have the landscapes that satisfy these desires. We may attribute their development to the actions of at least three stakeholder groups, each driven by what Barnes and Duncan (1992) call "discourses", or the frameworks that embrace particular combinations of narratives, concepts, ideologies and social practices, each relevant to a particular realm of social action (Mitchell and Coghill, 2000). It is the materialization of these discourses (Schien, 1997) that has resulted in the creation of heritage shopping villages; landscapes that prove an irresistible lure to consumers in search of nostalgia.

Entrepreneurs are the first group who play a dominant role in the development of these post-modern communities. These are individuals with considerable vision, who see changing economies or technologies, as opportunity, rather than threat. Their investment of time, money and expertise sees the creation of new products whose consumption creates capital for reinvestment. The desire to generate profit has driven these individuals to invest in the purchase and restoration of historically significant buildings and in the construction of venues where heritage products are sold. Through successful marketing (or what Sternberg, 1996, calls iconography), these communities are sold as packaged experiences; an activity that generates custom and, hence, capital, for reinvestment.

Next, are the preservationists. Here are included two groups, differentiated by motive. First, are those whose actions reflect a desire to enhance the heritage landscape. Committees of Council, local residents or interest groups each invest time, money or expertise to restore architecturally significant structures to their former state. Second, are those driven to prevent destruction. Activist groups that emerge to combat development initiatives, which might comprise the community's historical integrity, are prevalent actors in this category. While driven by different motives, these organizations, or individuals, also foster the creation of the heritage landscape.

Finally, are the producers, or creators of artistic heritage. Visual, performing or literary artists contribute to the stock of both tangible and intangible heritage within a community. These individuals are driven by several discourses (Mitchell and Coghill, 2000). For those artists who do not sell their craft, the need to produce (*i.e.*, create) or to preserve a time-honoured artistic tradition, may be the primary motivations driving their actions. Their very presence and volunteer activity (*e.g.*, displays of craftsmanship) contributes to the ambience, and thus to the experience of visitors within a community. For others, the need to profit also may be a motivator and one that arises out of a need to fund the creative process. The sale of authentic crafts (pottery, stained glass etc.) provides the tangible products so desired by consumers driven to accumulate visible and tangible marks of identity.

It is the combined actions of the profit, preservation and production-driven stakeholders that promote evolution of a heritage shopping village. Not only are their actions responsible for the creation of this new landscape, but also for destruction of the old. It is to the model of creative destruction that we now turn.

THE PROCESS OF CREATIVE DESTRUCTION

The creation of new landscapes inevitably results in destruction of the old. This was recognized originally by Shumpeter (1942), and later by Harvey in the context of his cycle of accumulation (1985; 1987; 1988). In an earlier paper, I extended the argument by suggesting that the magnitude of this destruction will depend on the domination of a profit-motivated discourse (Mitchell and Coghill, 2000). In the absence or unsuccessful intervention of individuals embodying other discourses (production and preservation), the destruction of the original landscape may be total. This is evident in urban localities where investment in "spectacles" (Jameson, 1984; Harvey, 1987; Britton, 1991; Hollinshead, 1997), has resulted in the replacement of ageing industrial districts that developed under a fordist regime. Similarly, in a rural setting, industrial buildings or venues that provide goods for a local market, are transformed by entrepreneurs who wish to reap the benefits associated with tourism consumption.

As Mitchell and Coghill (2000) observe, the transformation of rural landscape takes more than a tangible form. The influx of visitors, which inevitably accompanies the creation of these spaces, will be seen by many as a threat to a way of life (Lowenthal, 1985; Brown and Giles, 1994; Herbert, 1995; Hall and McArthur, 1996). Ultimately, what is destroyed is the "rural idyll", an image of rural life that is happy, healthy, problem-free "safely nestling with both a close social community and a contiguous natural environment" (Cloke and Milbourne, 1992: 359). This is a process that can be operationalized in the model of creative destruction.

The model is based on the relationship among three variables that have been dealt with in some detail in the literature: entrepreneurial investment (Bryant, 1989; Harvey, 1989a and b; McGuirk *et al.*, 1996; Hall and Hubbard, 1996; Wood, 1998); consumption of commodified heritage (Urry, 1990; Bunce, 1994; Kilian and Dodson, 1996); and destruction of the rural idyll (Mingay, 1989; Short, 1991; Cloke and Milbourne, 1992; Halfacree, 1995; Gill and Reed, 1997). The premise underlying the model is that the desire to accumulate capital drives investment in the production and sale of tradition and heritage. These investments entice an increasing number of consumers, whose expenditures provide entrepreneurs with profit for reinvestment. As the landscape unfolds, it results in destruction of the old; in the replacement of the pre-commodified landscape with one that is crowded and congested, far-removed from the rural idyll.

The process of creative destruction occurs in five stages. In the first stage, the commodification of tradition or heritage is initiated. Investments that are made during this period generate financial benefits and cosmetic improvements. The attitudes of local residents are very favourable, and the rural idyll remains intact. The next period, that of advanced commodification, is marked by acceleration in investment levels. New businesses are opened, while others are converted to meet the demands of the visiting population.

The community is marketed extensively resulting in escalation in visitor numbers. Those involved in the tourism industry extol its virtues, while others point to the disadvantages associated with growing popularity. It is at this stage that the community begins to witness a partial destruction of the rural idyll (Mitchell, 1998).

The period of early destruction is one where surplus value is reinvested into businesses that provide for the needs of the expanding visitor population. While many of these investments are in keeping with commodification, other stray from this theme. As the landscape continues to evolve, numbers of tourists escalate, generating significant problems, including crowding and congestion. A growing number of residents perceive the erosion of their community and, ultimately, a further destruction of their idyllic rural landscape. The period of advanced destruction is also one of continual investment. During this stage consumption levels continue to rise and an out-migration of local residents may occur as individuals witness "the disintegration of the sense of community and cohesion" that formerly characterized village life (Mitchell, 1998: 277). The end of this phase is reached when residents perceive a complete destruction of the rural idyll, thus moving the community into a state of post-destruction. While several scenarios are possible (Mitchell, 1998), I suggest here that what emerges is the fully-fledged recreational, or tourist, shopping village; one that appeals not to the heritage-seeking consumer, but to the mass tourist market. Residents who remain learn to adjust to life in this new landscape, a landscape that no longer contains any vestiges of the rural idyll. The following discussion seeks to determine if this process has occurred in two villages of southern Ontario.

THE VILLAGES OF ST. JACOBS AND ELORA

St. Jacobs and Elora are excellent sites to test the model of creative destruction. According to the model, heritage landscapes emerge when three criteria are present (Mitchell, 1998). First, a community must be accessible to a large and relatively affluent population.

Second, some elements of a heritage environment must be in existence before commodification begins. Third, entrepreneurial spirit must be present. Each one of these criterion was found in the two study sites, thus ensuring the creation of these post-modern landscapes.

The villages of St. Jacobs and Elora are located on the banks of the Conestoga and Grand Rivers, respectively, in the midst of a densely populated region of southern Ontario (Figure 7.1). They lie within the urban fields of Kitchener-Waterloo (population approaching 300,000) and the Greater Toronto Area (population of about three million), both of which are accessible via a limited access highway. Such accessible locations provided the threshold population necessary to support the offering of a diverse array of heritage products.

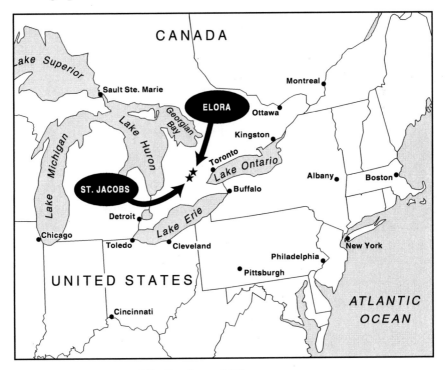

Figure 7.1: Location of St. Jacobs and Elora.

A favourable location does not guarantee success. For a heritage shopping village to develop, some aspect of heritage must be present before commodification begins. According to Herbert *et al.* (1989) heritage takes three forms; natural, built or cultural. Natural heritage refers to the physical environment encompassing a diverse array of flora, fauna or geographical features. Architecturally significant structures (buildings, bridges etc.) comprise the built heritage while local customs and traditions are representative of cultural heritage. Each is viewed as having value and worthy of preservation, and alone, or in combination, lay the foundation upon which a commodified landscape may unfold.

Each of these characteristics can be found in the villages. In the case of Elora, however, natural heritage has been at the root of its success. As described by Mitchell and Coghill (2000), the community is located on a spectacular site, one that influenced both the development of the original streetscape and the establishment of an artistic heritage. This site was described by Westhues and Sinclair (1974: 16) who observed that "the juncture of the two rivers is surrounded by picturesque hills and, below the juncture, nature has carved a deep gorge which offers rare natural beauty amid the mainly flat terrain of southern Ontario".

The power provided by the falls, located above the gorge, was the sole reason for the establishment of the village streetscape (Connon, 1974). Numerous manufacturing plants (including a gristmill, woollen mill, foundry, distillery, knitting mills and furniture, brush, carpet and organ factories) emerged after 1842, housed in structures built from locally quarried stone (Allan, 1982). This contributed to the creation of a unique streetscape, one that would later provide a venue for the sale of commodified products.

The natural setting also played a vital role in the development of a rich artistic heritage. It was suggested by a local reporter that "as one of the most scenic and historic areas in Ontario, Elora has

long been famous as a community of arts and crafts people"
(Anon., 1991: 3). As early as the 1920s, visual artists were drawn
to Elora for inspiration (Connon, 1974). A.J. Casson, a member of
Canada's famous "Group of Seven" for example, spent much time
in the village during the 1920s and 1930s. The work of Casson and
others created a rich heritage of artistic talent, which led to the
emergence of Elora as a focal point for cultural activity (Bunting
and Mitchell, 2001). When combined with its scenic attributes and
pleasing streetscape, Elora proved to be an irresistible lure in the
eyes of entrepreneurs (Mitchell and Coghill, 2000).

Cultural heritage has played a major role in St. Jacob's success.
Located in the heart of Ontario's "Mennonite Country", the village
of St. Jacobs traditionally functioned as a rural service centre "providing a limited range of goods and services to a nearby population
of Old Order Mennonites" (Mitchell, 1998: 278). These are a cul-
turally unique people, who maintain a lifestyle that is historically
and religiously linked to traditions of the sixteenth century (Buck,
1978). Their traditional style of dress, horse and buggy transportation and agrarian lifestyle stands in stark contrast to the behaviour
of urban residents located in nearby Kitchener-Waterloo. It is this
presence, coupled with recognition of the community's advantageous location, which prompted a local entrepreneur to invest in
redevelopment of the village.

Entrepreneurial activity has been at the root of both community's success. In St. Jacobs, the transformation has been led almost
single-handedly by one individual, and his development company,
who sought to create "a warm and small-town atmosphere . . .
pleasing to both tourists and residents of the area" (Anon., 1977:
24). The situation in Elora is considerably different since investments have originated with many entrepreneurs, both local and
non-local. As Mitchell and Coghill (2000) conclude, "to date, no
one individual can claim responsibility for its present structure. It is
the time and investment of many, which is responsible for placing

Elora on the path of creative destruction".

METHODOLOGY

The purpose of this chapter is to determine where each community sits in the evolutionary model and to offer an explanation for their current states. To meet these objectives, information is presented on the three variables that drive each stage of the model. First, Dun and Bradstreet Reference Directories and a variety of other secondary sources (newspaper articles, planning reports etc.) are used to provide indirect data on investment (evolving business composition). Second, estimated consumption levels (*i.e.*, visitor numbers), derived from various local and provincial organizations, are described. Finally, resident attitudes towards tourism are revealed from survey information that was collected in 1994 (St. Jacobs) and 1998 (Elora) (Table 7.1). In combination, these sources provided sufficient information to determine where each community is situated in the evolutionary model.

Table 7.1: Business Structure 1965-1999

	Elora	St. Jacobs
Businesses 1965 1999	49 158	35 151
Restaurants 1965 1999	1 12	0 8
Retail outlets 1965 1999	26 54	15 104

Source: Dun and Bradstreet, Reference Directories (1965, 1999).

THE CREATIVE DESTRUCTION OF ELORA AND ST. JACOBS

The evolution of St. Jacobs and Elora has been described in some detail in two publications (Mitchell, 1998; Mitchell and Coghill, 2000). The purpose of this chapter is not to retrace the evolution of these communities in detail, but, rather, to describe and explain their current state. This is accomplished in two steps. First, I present information on the three variables described above (investment, consumption and resident attitudes), and from this suggest where they are currently found in the evolutionary model. Second, I offer an explanation for these findings. Readers are encouraged to consult the original papers for a more detailed discussion of the evolutionary path taken by these two centres.

Data on entrepreneurial investment are difficult to obtain. A surrogate measure, however, is readily found in Dun and Bradstreet Reference Directories. Here, data are presented on the functional structure of all North American communities. Since the directories have been available since the mid-1800s, they provide an excellent source of information on a community's evolving business structure.

Table 7.1 reveals that the villages of Elora and St. Jacobs have changed much during the past three decades. In 1965 both communities contained fewer than 50 businesses. By 1999, the number of firms in both centres had more than tripled. While growth rates have been very similar, data provided by Dun and Bradstreet suggest that the village of St. Jacobs has developed a much larger commercial sector. Not only does the community offer more than 100 retail outlets, but also 12 restaurants can be found lining the streets of the downtown commercial district. In contrast, Elora boasts only 50 shopping venues, with fewer than 10 dining facilities. Nonetheless, while differences do exist, it is clear that both communities have experienced considerable growth since the mid-1960s; a trend indicative of their emergence as viable shopping destinations.

While Dun and Bradstreet is a useful source of information, it is limited in that one can not glean from the Directories which businesses present in a community cater to a tourist clientele. For this we must turn to secondary sources, such as newspaper articles and marketing material. Table 7.2 identifies some of the most significant investments that have been made since 1970, as described in these diverse sources.

Table 7.2: Examples of Major Investments

	Elora	**St. Jacobs**
1970-1980	The Elora Country Mill The Courtyard Shops The Elora Festival	St. Jacobs Country Mill The Stone Crock Restaurant Forge and Anvil
1980-1990	The Village Common	Jakobstettal Guest House Olde Factory Shops Benjamins Snyder's Merchant Riverworks Retail Centre
1990 - present	The Antique Warehouse	The Antique Warehouse The Schoolhouse Theatre The Factory Outlet Mall The Country Inn

Source: Mercedes Development Corporation (interview); fieldwork.

Several similarities in business composition can be observed from this table. For example, the catalyst for development in each community was the purchase and conversion of an historic mill. In St. Jacobs, the mill was purchased in the early 1970s and converted initially into a venue for the production and sale of reproduction pine furniture. Later renovations saw the mill transformed into a multi-tenant retailing centre, providing visitors with a variety of products created on-site by artisans, or what Dorst (1989) calls, "meta-craftsmen". In the same decade, the Elora gristmill was converted into a unique up-market inn and restaurant. As described by a local reporter (Anon., 1982: B16):

> the twenty-two guestrooms at The Mill are tastefully
> decorated in Early Canadian with pine furnishings,
> some antiques and quality replicas. There are pine or
> brass beds and pine accessories. Each room has hand-
> made quilts . . . and no two rooms are alike. Stepping
> into a room at the Elora Mill Country Inn and
> Restaurant is like taking a step back into a different
> century without giving up any of the modern conven-
> ience.

A second similarity revealed in Table 7.2 is the provision of the performing arts. A plethora of these events has emerged in Elora since 1970. The Elora Festival, for example, is an annual event that was established in 1979 and today attracts an international clientele. Its venues (including a barn and quarry), provide unique settings to celebrate local (and in some cases, national) artistic talent. While St. Jacobs has not promoted the arts to the same degree, the recent opening of the School House Theatre suggests that this is a direction the community hopes to take in the future.

Table 7.2 also points to a third similarity in functional structure. Since 1990, both communities have seen the establishment of an antique warehouse. Providing more than 65 vendors, each of these facilities offers a wide array of antiques and country collectibles. In both cases, the venues have been constructed outside the main commercial area, reflecting the continual expansion of tourism beyond the central business districts.

While sharing these similarities, it is evident from Table 7.2 that more money has been invested in St. Jacobs than Elora. In addition to the initiatives already described, St. Jacobs also boasts a number of large-scale developments including Riverworks (with more than 30 shops), a Factory Outlet Mall, and a Best Western

Hotel. While the former retailing centre is located in the downtown, the latter two structures are found some distance from the St. Jacob's core. However, each of these developments is marketed as part of a larger tourism package. The spatial separation of venues is overcome with the provision of a horse-drawn trolley. This vehicle not only transports visitors between attractions but also provides a nostalgic experience for those who choose to climb aboard.

As the infrastructure in St. Jacobs and Elora has evolved, so too have visitor numbers. While no accurate figures are available, several estimates have been made that reveal the increased popularity of both communities. The difference in levels of visitation, however, is striking. In the village of Elora, visitor numbers have increased since 1984. However, as revealed in Table 7.3, growth in visitation has not been consistent. In fact, between the mid-1980s and mid-1990s, visitor numbers plummeted (for a detailed explanation, consult Mitchell and Coghill, 2000). It is only since 1998 that numbers have begun their upward climb. Present levels, however, are far below those found in St. Jacobs. By 1989 it was estimated that more than 1 million people had visited this community. Ten years later, a value more than twice that was reported; one that is 10 times higher than recorded in Elora. This difference is not surprising, given the variations in investment that were described previously.

Table 7.3: Visitor Numbers

Dates	Elora	St. Jacobs
1984	225,000	-
1989	-	1 million
1992	100,000	-
1998	287,997	2.3 million

Source: Corporation of the Village of Elora (1987); Sinasac (1989); Elora Chamber of Commerce (1999).

One would expect that a community attracting large numbers of visitors would encounter a significant amount of resident dissatisfaction. A resident survey conducted in St. Jacobs reveals this to be the case. Table 7.4 shows that in 1994 a large percentage of St. Jacobs' residents were aware of a variety of adverse effects of tourism. Congestion and lack of parking spaces were seen by many as being a negative consequence of development. Additional complaints noted included a loss of local businesses and increased crime, leading to safety concerns. While these and other comments also appeared in the Elora surveys, they were mentioned somewhat less frequently by respondents.

Table 7.4: Disadvantages of Tourism (percent noting disadvantage)

	Elora N = 150	St. Jacobs N = 64
Congestion	22.0	78.0
Lack of parking	12.0	61.9
Reduced access and availability of services	4.0	16.1
Safety concerns	0.0	11.1
Crime	0.0	6.3
Rising costs	4.0	3.2
Destruction of natural environment	4.0	1.6
Ignorance of local concerns	0.0	1.6

Source: Resident surveys: 1998 (Elora) and 1994 (St. Jacobs).

While residents in both communities acknowledged the disadvantages of tourism, a larger percentage did not hesitate to comment on the positive externalities associated with the sale of heritage products (Table 7.5). In particular, many spoke of the increased income and employment opportunities that have resulted. Others commented on less tangible benefits including beautification of the landscape and the creation of a feeling of pride amongst local residents. Thus, despite the costs associated with tourism, in both communities many felt that development has many positive implications. Whether these benefits were seen to outweigh the costs was revealed in the answer to several additional questions.

Table 7.5: Advantages of Tourism (percent noting benefit)

	Elora N = 150	St. Jacobs N = 64
Generates income and employment	54.0	69.9
Restoration	0.0	14.3
Beautification	14.0	14.3
Recognition	8.0	0.0
Enhanced cultural environment	6.0	0.0
Price	4.0	0.0
Meet new people	0.0	1.6
Enhanced sense of community	0.0	3.2

Residents were asked to consider what impact tourism developments have on their quality of life. In Elora, the vast majority (over 95 percent) noted either an improvement, or no change, with only four percent stating their quality of life had deteriorated. In contrast, more than a third of residents surveyed in St. Jacobs felt that development has had a detrimental impact. These findings are not surprising and, in part, reflect variations in the magnitude of the tourism sector in each community.

Residents also were asked to comment on their desires for future development. In Elora, nearly one-quarter (22 percent) believed that there is room for expansion, with nearly one-half stating that tourism initiatives should be limited. This again contrasts markedly with the situation in St. Jacobs. Here, more than 80 percent of respondents felt that council should halt the development process, with only three percent in favour of additional growth. Thus, it appears that residents in St. Jacobs have less favourable attitudes towards development than do those in Elora; a situation that leads one to conclude that the villages occupy different stages in the model of creative destruction.

Results presented here, and described in greater detail in previous works (Mitchell, 1998; Mitchell and Coghill, 2000), suggest that St. Jacobs is farther along the path of creative destruction than is Elora. In an earlier paper, we concluded that Elora exists in a prolonged state of advanced commodification; one characterized by relatively modest investment levels, visitor numbers and negative attitudes towards tourism. In contrast, I placed St. Jacobs (at least in 1994), on the brink of advanced destruction; one identified by very high investments, visitor numbers and levels of resident dissatisfaction towards tourism. Since this conclusion was drawn prior to the opening of the hotel, it is highly likely that the village has now moved into the next period of advanced destruction. Additional research in the community will determine if, indeed, this is the case.

DISCUSSION

The conclusion that Elora and St. Jacobs occupy different positions in the model is an interesting finding and warrants further explanation. I attribute this difference to three factors: relative location; the presence of multiple stakeholder groups and the spatial structure of the commercial district. Each of these factors is considered briefly below.

Earlier in this chapter it was suggested that location is a key factor influencing the success of a heritage shopping village. It was determined that both communities are situated in highly favourable locations, accessible to Canada's most densely populated urban region. While both share a similar location within southern Ontario, the village of St. Jacobs is, in fact, found in a more advantageous setting. Located immediately north of Waterloo, the village has emerged as a year-round shopping destination for nearby urban residents. The same advantage does not accrue to Elora, which is found approximately one half hour away from the nearest census metropolitan area. While some stores operate year-round to serve local residents, others are seasonal and rely to a great extent on the summer tourist trade.

This study has revealed that investors have played a major role in the transformation of both landscapes. However, it appears that two other stakeholder groups, driven by different discourses, have been active in the village of Elora since development was first initiated. First, are the preservationists, whose actions have been motivated by both the desires to enhance the heritage landscape and to prevent its destruction. The former is reflected in the ongoing efforts of various public and private sector organizations (*e.g.*, the Local Architectural Advisory Committee) to preserve Elora's unique heritage (Mitchell and Coghill, 2000). The latter is illustrated by the actions of local residents who have fought periodically to prevent the implementation of development proposals (*e.g.*, boat tours with amplified commentary and mobile food operators) that might compromise Elora's heritage image (Bryan, 1992; van Ray, 1998; Anon., 1999). While preservationists also have been at work in St. Jacobs, their involvement has come at a much later phase in the community's evolution. Their actions, however, have prevented the physical expansion of the downtown commercial district (Mitchell, 1998); a move that merely prompted developers to seek out new sites in which to drive the cycle of destruction.

The creators of handcrafted products are the second group whose presence has shaped both the landscapes of St. Jacobs and Elora. In the former community, artists are housed in structures owned by the primary developer. These facilities are designed both for the production and sale of handcrafted objects. While some Elora venues serve both a production and consumption function, most appear to focus primarily on the latter. This suggests, therefore, that production occurs in a separate venue, either within Elora or at another, more distant location. This spatial separation of functions may be responsible, at least in part, for the unwillingness of some Elora artists/proprietors to provide consistent store hours; a predicament that is not found in St. Jacobs where all stores owned by the primary investor hold common hours of operation.

As Mitchell and Coghill (2000) conclude, the actions of multiple stakeholders may be responsible partially for Elora's current position in the evolutionary model. While profit-driven entrepreneurs have been active, they do not dominate in Elora, but, rather, co-exists alongside other stakeholders, the preservationists and the producers. This situation differs somewhat from that in St. Jacobs. Here, entrepreneurial drive to accumulate profit appears to have been the dominant motivation behind the process of landscape transformation and one that ultimately has led to its more advanced position in the model of creative destruction.

Finally, the unique physical layout of the central business district also may have played a role in prolonging Elora's stay in the stage of advanced commodification. Unlike St. Jacobs, where all downtown retail activity is conducted along the main street, Elora contains two spatially separate commercial districts. First is Mill Street West, which caters to the tourist market. Second is Upper Metcalfe Street, an area that provides for the basic needs of local residents (Corporation of the Village of Elora, 1987). As observed by Coppack (1985: 123) "Elora visitors usually confine themselves to the "tourist mainstreet" a small section of the downtown bordering the river. They do not in any significant numbers encroach on the residential community". This spatial separation has facilitated relatively amicable relations between Elora residents and visitors. This situation does not exist in St. Jacobs and may, in part, be responsible for the higher levels of resident dissatisfaction noted earlier.

CONCLUSIONS

The villages of St. Jacobs and Elora are unique communities. Their natural, architectural and cultural heritage has facilitated their transformation into very successful heritage shopping villages. In both cases, entrepreneurial investment in the restoration of historic structures and the sale of heritage products and experiences has given rise to a vibrant tourist economy; one that is promoted both locally and nationally. These efforts have been successful in luring visitors who are in pursuit of an experience that encompasses the purchase of specialized products in an historic setting. In the village of Elora, residents appear to be generally happy with the level of tourism development that has occurred, suggesting that the community is in a state of advanced commodification. In contrast, the prevalence of resident animosity in St. Jacobs leads one to conclude that the community (in 1994) was on the brink of advanced destruction. I attribute this difference to three factors; location; the degree of entrepreneurial domination in the development process; and the spatial structure of the central business district. These findings suggest that the process of creative destruction appears to be at work in these southern Ontario communities. They also suggest, however, that extraneous influences, that are not explicitly accounted for in the model, also impact the evolutionary process. While these processes do not weaken the premise of the model, they must be taken into account in future studies documenting the establishment and development of these post-modern communities.

REFERENCES

Allan, R. (1982) *History of Elora*, Elora, ON: Elora Women's Institute.

Anonymous (1977) "St. Jacobs gets new shops", *Elmira Signet*, 2 February, 24.

_____ (1982) "Elora Mill has personality plus", *Fergus-Elora News Express*, 4 Aug., B14-17.

_____ (1991) "Meet the Elora marketing committee", *Fergus-Elora News Express*, 30 Dec., 3.

_____ (1999) "Residents speak out against vendors," *Fergus-Elora*

News Express, 2 Feb., 2.

Barnes, T. and Duncan, J. (eds.) (1992) *Writing Worlds: Discourse, Text and Metaphor in the Representation of Landscape*, London: Routledge.

Barnes, T.J. and Hayter, R. (1992) "The little town that did: flexible accumulation and community response in Chemainus, British Columbia", *Regional Studies*, 26: 647-663

Bourdieu, P. (1984) *Distinction: A Social Critique of the Judgement of Taste*, Cambridge: Harvard University Press.

Britton, S. (1991) "Tourism, capital and place: towards a critical geography of tourism," *Environment and Planning D: Society and Space*, 9: 451-478.

Brown, G. and Giles, R. (1994) "Coping with tourism: an examination of resident responses to the social impact of tourism," in A. Seaton (ed.), *Tourism, the State of the Art*, Chichester: John Wiley and Sons, 755-764.

Bryan, A. (1992) "Merchants oppose street vendors", *Fergus-Elora News Express*, 24 May, 7.

Bryant, C. (1989) "Entrepreneurs in the rural environment", *Journal of Rural Studies*, 5(4): 337-348.

Buck, R. (1978) "Boundary maintenance revisited: tourist enterprise concentration and Old Order Amish survival: exploration in productive co-existence", *Journal of Travel Research*, 18(1): 15-20.

Bunce, M. (1994) *The Countryside Ideal: Anglo-American Images of Landscape*, London: Routledge.

Bunting, T.E. and Mitchell, C.J.A. (2001) "Artists in rural locales: market access, landscape appeal and economic exigency", *The Canadian Geographer*, 45(2): 208-285.

Cloke, P. and Milbourne, P. (1992) "Deprivation and lifestyle in rural Wales, 11, Rurality and cultural dimension", *Journal of Rural Studies*, 8(4): 359-71.

Cloke, P. and Goodwin, M. (1992) "Conceptualizing countryside change: from post-Fordism to rural structural coherence", *Transactions of the Institute of British Geographers*, 17: 359-371.

Connon, J.R. (1974) *The Early History of Elora Ontario and Vicinity*, Waterloo, ON: Wilfrid Laurier University.

Coppack, P. (1985) *An Exploration of Amenity and Its Role in the Development of the Urban Field*, PhD Thesis, Waterloo, ON: Department of Geography, University of Waterloo.

Corporation of the Village of Elora (1987) *Economic Analysis: Official Plan Background Studies*, Elora: Corporation of the Village of Elora.

Dahms, F. (1991) "Economic revitalization in St. Jacobs, Ontario: ingredients for transforming a dying village into a thriving tourist destination", *Small Town*, May-June: 12-18.

Dorst, J. D. (1989) *The Written Suburb*, Pennsylvania: University of Pennsylvania Press.

Dun and Bradstreet (1965) *Reference Books*, July issues, Toronto, ON: Dun and Bradstreet Ltd.

Dun and Bradstreet (1999) *Reference Books*, July issues, Toronto,

ON: Dun and Bradstreet Ltd.

Elora Chamber of Commerce (1999) *Unpublished Tourist Information*, Elora: Elora Chamber of Commerce.

Featherstone, M. (1990) "Perspectives on consumer culture", *Sociology*, 24(1): 5-22.

Getz, D. (1993) "Tourist shopping villages: development and planning strategies", *Tourism Management*, 14(1): 15-26.

Gill, A. and Reed, M. (1997) "The reimaging of a Canadian resource town: postproductivism in a North American context", *Applied Geographic Studies*, 1(2): 129-147.

Halfacree, K. (1995) "Talking about rurality: social representations of the rural as expressed by residents of six English parishes", *Journal of Rural Studies*, 11: 1-20.

Hall, T. and Hubbard, P. (1996) "The entrepreneurial city: new urban politics, new urban geographies?" *Progress in Human Geography*, 29(2): 153-174.

Hall, C. and McArthur, S. (1996) "The human dimension of heritage management", in C. Hall and L. McArthur (eds.), *Heritage Management in Australia and New Zealand*, Melbourne: Oxford University Press, 2-21.

Harvey, D. (1990) "Between space and time: reflections on the geographical imagination", *Annals of the Association of American Geographers*, 80: 418-434.

_____ (1989a) "From managerialism to entrepreneurialism: the transformation in urban governance in late capitalism", *Geografiska Annaler*, 71B(1): 3-17.

_____ (1989b) *The Condition of Postmodernity*, Oxford: Oxford University Press.

_____ (1988) "The geographical and geopolitical consequences of the transition from fordist to flexible accumulation", in B. Sternlieb and J. Hughes (eds.), *America's New Market Geographies: Nation, Region and Metropolis*, Rutgers, NJ: Centre for Urban Policy Research, 101-136.

_____ (1987) "Flexible accumulation through urbanization: reflections on 'postmodernism' in the American city", *Antipode*, 19(3): 260-286.

_____ (1985) *The Urbanization of Capital: Studies in the History and Theory of Capitalist Urbanization*, Baltimore, MA: John Hopkins Press.

Herbert, D. (1995) *Heritage Tourism and Society*, London: Mansell Publishing.

Herbert, D. Prentice, R. and Thomas, C. (1989) *Heritage Sites: Strategies for Marketing and Development*, Aldershot: Avebury.

Hollinshead, K. (1997) "Heritage tourism under post-modernity: truth and the past", in C. Ryan (ed.), *Tourist Experience: A New Introduction*, London: Cassell, 170-227.

Jameson, F. (1984) "Post-modernism or the cultural logic of late capitalism", *New Left Review*, 146: 53-92.

Kilian, D. and Dodson, B.J. (1996) "Forging a postmodern waterfront: urban form and spectacle at the Victoria and Alfred Docklands", *South African Geographical Journal*, 78(1): 29-40.

Konrad, V.A. (1982) "Historical artifacts as recreational resources", in G. Wall and J. Marsh (eds.), *Recreational Land Use: Perspectives on its Evolution in Canada*, Ottawa: Carleton University Press, 393-416.

Lowenthal, D. (1985) *The Past is a Foreign Country*, Cambridge: Cambridge University Press.

McGuirk, P., Winchester, H. and Dun, K. (1996) "Entrepreneurial approaches to urban decline: the Honeysuckle redevelopment in inner Newcastle, New South Wales", *Environment and Planning A*, 28(10): 1815-1841.

Mingay, G. (1989) T*he Rural Idyll*, London: Routledge.

Mitchell, C.J.A., Atkinson, R.G. and Clark, A. (2001) "The creative destruction of Niagara-on-the-Lake", *The Canadian Geographer*, 45(2): 285-300.

Mitchell, C.J.A. and Coghill, C. (2000) "The creation of a heritage townscape: Elora, Ontario", *The Great Lakes Geographer*, 7(2): 88-105.

Mitchell, C.J.A. (1998) "Entrepreneurialism, commodification and creative destruction: a model of post-modern community development", *Journal of Rural Studies*, 14(3): 273-86.

Park, C. and Coppack, P. (1994) "The role of rural sentiment and vernacular landscapes in contriving sense of place in the city's countryside", *Geografiska Annaler*, 76B(3): 161-72.

Schein, R.H. (1997) "A place of landscape: a conceptual framework for interpreting the American scene", *Annals of the Association of American Geographers*, 87(4): 660-680.

Short, B. (1991) *Imagined Country*, London: Routledge.

Shumpeter, J.A. (1942) *Capitalism, Socialism and Democracy*, New York: Harper and Row.

Sinasac, T. (1989) "A visitor's village", *Highlights*, October-November: 26-29.

Sternberg, E. (1996) "A case of iconographic competition: the building industry and the postmodern landscape", *Journal of Urban Design*, 1(2): 145-162.

Urry J. (1990) *The Tourist Gaze: Leisure and Travel in Contemporary Societies*, London: Sage.

van Ray, C. (1998) "Karaoke machine-amplified commentary sinks Grand River boat tour proposal in Elora", *Fergus-Elora News Express*, 27 May, 13.

Westhues, K. and Sinclair, P. (1974) *Village in Crisis*, Toronto: Holt Rinehart and Winston of Canada Limited.

Wood, A. (1998) "Making sense of urban entrepreneurialism", *Scottish Geographical Magazine*, 114(2): 120-123.

Zeppel, H. and Hall, C. (1991) "Selling art and history: cultural heritage and tourism", *The Journal of Tourism Studies*, 2(1): 29-44.

Chapter 8

First Nation Casino Gambling and Tourism

Barbara A. Carmichael
Wilfrid Laurier University

ambling is a universal cultural phenomenon: one of a relatively small number of activities that occur in nearly all societies in every period (Abt *et al.*, 1985). However, it is a controversial activity sometimes legally accepted and sometimes outlawed. It has been called the "pariah" or "leper" industry (Stansfield, 1996) and received criticism from the church and other religious groups (Cabot, 1996). It was referred to by a seventeenth century writer as "an enchanted witchery, gotten betwixt idleness and avarice", (cited in Abt *et al.*, 1985: 4). Despite such negative views with regard to gaming morality, the demand for opportunities to gamble is deeply rooted within society. Recent growth and economic prosperity in casino gaming in both the United States and Canada reflect the high demand for gambling as a leisure pursuit. It forms an exciting stimulus, an escape from the mundane and a form of adult play. Gambling is an opportunity to experience risk in a controlled setting. However, gaming is rarely advocated for its own sake, that is as a harmless and worthwhile recreational activity (Campbell and Smith, 1998). More often, it has been linked to serving the greater good, such as generating income for governments so taxes may be reduced, funding charities, creating employment and attracting tourists.

Casino gambling and its rapid diffusion across North America during the 1990s represents an exciting example of tourism dynamism. Casinos may be important tools for sustainable economic development, especially if they attract visitors from outside their local regions. In this situation, basic or new money is drawn into local economies from tourist spending. Tourists spend both at the casinos and at surrounding amenities and attractions.

Casinos have developed at different scales, types of location and under different ownership. Some were in existing tourist areas and contributed to the attraction mix, for example, Casino Rama, Ontario, Canada. Others developed into mega-resorts in themselves, for example, Foxwoods Resort Casino, Connecticut, USA. Eadington (1995) categorized casinos according to their physical structure and characteristics into four types: a) casinos in historic or refurbished structures; b) casinos on riverboats; c) casinos in purpose-built facilities with limited non-gaming amenities; d) casinos in purpose-built facilities with extensive non-gaming amenities and attractions. Casinos also can be classified in terms of where they are located: a) distant from urban population concentrations in areas with natural tourist attractions; b) outside of urban population concentrations in settings that may or may not have natural touristic attractions but which are conveniently located relative to urban concentrations; c) in urban centres but established in such a manner that access by the local population is discouraged, constrained or prohibited; and, d) in major centres that are openly accessible to resident populations (Eadington, 1995). Ownership is a third way to classify casinos; they may be publically or privately owned, or they may be operated on or off Indian land. In short, the patterns of casino development and their links with tourism are widely variable and there is no one model for US or Canadian casinos.

Large casino developments were identified by McIntosh *et al.* (1994) as a major force in the tourism industry. Casinos, like theme parks, resorts, golf courses and any other tourism attraction bring with them benefits and costs. In considering tourism growth, communities are faced with a situation in which they want to stimulate the economy but are nervous about the appropriateness of such development. Furthermore, different groups within communities hold different perceptions of, and attitudes toward, casino tourism impacts. This is particularly true for a controversial attraction like a casino, where attitudes are likely to be more polarized and in the situation of gaming on First Nation land, where the community is further divided on an ethnic basis. Perceptions of benefits and costs will affect attitudes toward casino development and toward the developers.

The purpose of this chapter is to examine the issues raised when a casino develops and brings change. Changes occur in society, economy and environment at both local and regional scales. Such changes are perceived in different ways and may or may not bring sustainable economic development. The focus of the chapter is on a specific type of casino development: Indian gaming. Two case studies are used to discuss the issues raised by Indian gaming. One example is taken from the USA: Foxwoods Resort Casino in Connecticut, the largest casino in the western hemisphere. The second example is taken from Canada: Casino Rama in Ontario, the largest First Nation casino in Canada. First, an overview is provided of the development of Indian gaming in the US and Canada. Second, a review is presented of some of the author's recent research on the two sample casino developments on Indian Reservation land.

INDIAN GAMING IN THE UNITED STATES
Growth and Scale of Development
The Indian casino market is a rapidly growing portion of the US casino industry. According to International Gaming and Wagering Business, revenues from Indian reservation casinos in the US increased from $700 million in 1991 to 2.9 billion in 1994 (1997 Casino and Gaming Market Research Handbook). More recent figures show that Indian gaming revenue in 1999 was $8.9 billion or 10 percent of the total gaming industry (http://www.indiangaming. org/library/index.html). Gross gambling revenues represent dollars wagered minus payouts. However, revenues are unevenly spread with 22 tribal operations accounting for 56 percent of the revenue.

In the US, in 1999, the total number of federally recognized tribes is 558 of which 198 tribal governments engaged in gambling. Twenty-four States had tribal compacts and there were 326 tribal gaming operations. According to the National Indian Gaming Association, 200,000 jobs have been created for employees working directly at the casinos (75 percent of employees are non-Indian and 25 percent are Indian).

Sovereignty Issues

The key to understanding the rise of Indian gaming is the desire for sovereignty (Ferber and Chon, 1994). Indian Nations on federally recognized reservations are recognized as "dependent sovereigns" (Stansfield, 1996). Sovereignty, according to the American Political Dictionary, means " the supreme power of the state, exercised within its boundaries, free from external interference". However, without a sound economic base such independence is hard to achieve. Thompson and Dever (1994: 5) state that "money allows people to survive. If the people of a nation cannot survive, they cannot be sovereign, for sovereignty demands a continuity for the people". Gaming provides a tool for restored sovereignty for First Nations. The Indian Gaming Regulatory Act (IGRA) passed by the United States Congress in 1988 declared its purpose as being "to provide a statutory basis for the operation of gaming by Indian tribes as a means of promoting tribal economic development, self sufficiency and strong tribal governments" (cited in Thompson and Dever, 1994: 5). Congress also recognized the need to shield tribal interests from organized crime and to ensure that the tribal members received the gaming revenues. At the time the Act was passed, Native Americans living on reservations suffered from high unemployment and lack of capital for investment. Many were dependent on Federal Aid that only allowed for substandard living. Land was held in trust by the US Government and thus could not be used as collateral for loans (Ferber and Chon, 1994). Gaming represented a route to economic development and is perhaps one of the few possibilities because of the poor quality of the land base on much of the reservation lands. Economic independence, as many tribal leaders argue, is the only way to ensure the continuation of separate Native American Nations (Ferber and Chon, 1994).

The Indian Gaming Regulatory Act

The Indian Gaming Regulatory Act delineated three classes of gaming (Table 8.1). Class I and II are easier to introduce than Class III. For Class III gaming to be permitted, the tribe must enter into a compact with the State. The tribe-state compact is a legal agreement that establishes the kind of games offered, the size of the facility, betting limits, regulation and security. If a state refuses to enter into negotiations in "good faith" for Class III games, a tribe may seek federal court mandate for negotiations. If the State continues to refuse, the court can appoint a mediator who is empowered to select a proposed compact and the Secretary of the Interior can certify the compact.

Table 8.1: IGRA Categories of Gambling

Class	Description
Class I	Social games, prizes of minimal value and traditional forms of Indian gaming engaged in as part of tribal ceremonies and celebrations.
Class II	Bingo and similar games, pull tabs, tip jars, punch boards, lotto, instant bingo and some card games excluding house banking cards, such as blackjack and baccarat and excluding certain non-banking card games.
Class III	All other forms of gaming including banking card games, slot machines, craps, pari-mutual horse racing, dog racing and lotteries.

Since the IGRA was passed in 1988, many tribes have negoti-
ated with their surrounding States and opened casinos with Class
III capability. The belief is now that gaming is like the "white buffalo", a spiritual symbol that represents the replenishment of the
American Indian people (Connor, 1993). However, the buffalo
analogy has been interpreted also in a negative sense. Long (1995)
suggests that the reference by some of gambling as the "new buffalo" indicates a concern that gambling could leave tribes once again
without an economic alternative should gaming revenues decline.
The IGRA created a framework for regulation and oversight of tribal gaming with four independent levels: tribal, state, federal
(including the Department of Justice, the Internal Revenue Service,
the Federal Bureau of Investigation and the Bureau of Indian
Affairs) and finally the National Indian Gaming Commission
(Anders, 1998).

INDIAN GAMING IN CANADA

Canadian First Nation groups are keenly aware of how Indian tribes
in the US have improved their lot through gambling but they are
unable to follow a similar path as a result of a different legal situation. Campbell and Smith (1998: 23), in reviewing the evolution of
Canadian gaming laws, identify two trends: "a clear transition from
criminal prohibition to legalization, and a consistent pattern of lesser federal responsibility and greater provincial authority over gambling matters". Indian gaming is not addressed separately by the
federal government as it is in the US. Indeed, for some years now,
Canada's Indian policy has been in a state of flux and although
assimilation is still approved, bands are allowed more self government and less governmental interference (Tobias, 1991). In 1985,
the provinces were given exclusive control of gambling and computer, video or slot devices were legalized. This transfer of authority for gambling to the provinces circumvented the right of First
Nations to create and operate gambling ventures. As a result, some
First Nations have opened casinos illegally for short periods or
have opted to work cooperatively with the provinces (Campbell

and Smith, 1998). Agreements between provinces and First Nations have been reached in Saskatchewan, Manitoba, Ontario, Quebec and Nova Scotia. First Nation leaders have long argued that neither the provinces nor the federal government have jurisdiction over the reserves and, therefore, no right to control casinos there.

However, in order to get a share of the casino profits First Nations have compromised their sovereignty issues but often after a long dispute. For example in Saskatchewan in 1994, the Province agreed to develop two First Nations casinos, one in Regina and one in Saskatoon. These casinos were developed in partnership with the Federation of Saskatchewan Indians in a profit sharing contract for 74 provincial bands. However, this agreement followed a bitter year long fight over aboriginal casinos in the Province in which one group challenged the Province over their sovereignty rights by opening a casino illegally (Marshall and Rudd, 1996).

In Ontario, Casino Rama was developed and chosen to represent First Nation interest. Bids from a shortlist of 14 bands were assessed in 1994 for this pilot project native casino. The Chippewas of Mnjikaning First Nation (Rama) was chosen mainly as a result of its profit sharing proposal, the support of the local region and its location in a tourist area close to Toronto. The profit sharing criterion for the bids was criticized by the First Nations as they felt they were being forced to fight among themselves. This criterion became a major issue after the casino opened in July 1996. It took until June 2000 for the moneys from profit sharing to be disbursed as the claim from the unrecognized Metis tribe, had to be first resolved. The Casino Rama Revenue Agreement transferred more than $400 million in net revenues from Casino Rama to a First Nation Fund. The Fund is shared among 134 First Nations in the Province to promote economic development and self sufficiency. "It is important that all parties be treated fairly" said Chief Lorraine McCrae of Mnjikaning First Nation. "This meant we had to consider factors such as isolation and population in addition to a base amount in determining the final distribution formula. While ensuring complete fiscal transparency, we also had to decide how best the revenues should be spent. It was agreed that economic development, health, education, culture and community development would be the five areas of investment" (News Release, Ontario Lottery and Gaming Corporation, 2000). Again, there were disagreements among First Nations as to the ways in which the profits should be divided.

DIFFERENCES BETWEEN CASINO DEVELOPMENT IN US AND CANADA

In Canada, there is a lack of a unified, cohesive national policy or legislation on First Nation gambling similar to the Indian Gaming Regulatory Act. This means that provinces are negotiating in an ad hoc manner with First Nations, while maintaining control over gaming legalization. Nevertheless, as in the US, the trend is towards increased development of gaming. Profit sharing schemes allow First Nations in some parts of Canada to share in gaming revenues without themselves developing casinos on their land. This may not be the ideal solution for some bands especially if they have seen successful casino developments across the border in the US. For example, Foxwoods Resort Casino "has become the holy grail of aboriginal gaming". Chief Len Tomah of Woodstock First Nation in New Brunswick stated, after he visited Foxwoods, "What impressed me most was the economic development and the self esteem put back into the people. Now they are bringing the tribe back together" (McDonald, 1994).

Indian gaming is more widespread in the US as a result of the IGRA. Indeed, gaming in general is more widespread. More research has been conducted on the impacts of gaming in the US. The US Federal Government commissioned a national study of the social and economic impacts of gambling in 1999 whereas no such undertaking has been launched in Canada. There is a National Indian Gaming Association and Information Center in the US (http://www.dgsys.com/~niga/). No such organization exists in Canada.

There are a number of other distinctive features of Canadian gaming. These are summarized in Table 8.2.

Table 8.2: Comparison of Gaming in US and Canada

Gaming in US	Gaming in Canada
privatization of casino ownership	provincial government ownership and in some cases management
widespread riverboat casinos	only one riverboat casino (Northern Belle, Windsor, Ontario)
gaming winnings taxed	gaming winnings not taxed
sports betting restricted	sports betting not restricted
Indian Gaming Regulatory Act	lack of unified, cohesive policy on Indian Gaming

Based on findings of Campbell and Smith (1998).

EXAMPLES OF INDIAN GAMING
US Case Study: Foxwoods Resort Casino, Connecticut
Development:
A quiet rural area in southeastern Connecticut has experienced a period of rapid change and tourist development as a result of the opening of Foxwoods Resort Casino by the Mashentucket Pequot tribe in February 1992. From the perspective of the tribe, the casino development has provided the passport to economic success. The tribe was officially recognized as a sovereign nation in 1983 but its early business ventures met with little success (see Carmichael and Peppard (1998) for a more detailed discussion of historical development). However, the success of bingo, which they introduced in 1986, provided an avenue for future growth. The

Indian Gaming Regulatory Act in 1988 gave federally recognized tribes the right to negotiate with the states for control of any games of chance already operating within that state. This enabled Mashentucket Pequots to negotiate for the operation of games like blackjack, craps, poker and roulette, which were allowed in Connecticut at charitable "Las Vegas" nights. After much opposition from the State, the tribe gained permission from the Secretary of the Interior for a high stakes casino expansion to the existing bingo hall and for Class III gaming. This rapid casino development brought both benefits and costs. There were positive impacts on tourism patterns, employment opportunities and economic development as well as social costs such as traffic congestion and perceived environmental threats (Carmichael, 1994; 1998). The casino has an excellent market location midway between New York and Boston and boasts to be the largest casino in the western hemisphere.

Perceived Impacts and Changing Resident Attitudes:
In each of three years (1992, 1993 and 1995), a 5 percent systematic random sample of telephone numbers was selected for the towns that surround the Mashentucket Peqout reservation. In 1992, 284 people were reached of whom 193 responded (68 percent response rate). In 1993 more people (310) were reached and more responded (247) for a 79.7 percent response rate, and in 1995, 203 of 285 households responded, a 71.2 percent response rate. Questions focussed on perceived positive and negative impacts of casino development, attitudes towards the tribe and attitudes towards casino gambling as an economic development tool and reasons for these attitudes. Personal variables also were included. Residents were asked if they had participated in a number of supporting (positive) or opposing (negative) behaviours with regard to the casino, for example, writing letters to newspapers, speaking at town meetings, displaying signs, speaking with or writing to government officials. This data set was used to investigate local residents perceptions of the effects of casino related development on

themselves, their town and the region. Survey data for three years provided a longitudinal look at how perceptions of the casino's impacts have changed. In addition, the surveys provided data that permitted modeling of the relationships between specific perceptions (Carmichael *et al.*, 1996). Data from the 1995 survey were used to investigate US local resident perceptions of casino impacts, attitude towards casino development, attitude toward their Native American neighbours and toward casino gaming as an economic development tool. A further purpose was to apply a matrix model, which explores the linkages between resident attitudes and behaviours. This model had been well referenced in the tourism literature but as yet had not been tested empirically (Carmichael, 2000).

There were both strongly positive and strongly negative perceived impacts by the residents of the host towns as the result of this new attraction. Among the positive results of the casino were the creation of new jobs and improvement in the prospects of local businesses. The economic effects were largely perceived as positive but generally the host communities perceived that the casino development would cause more negative effects. A majority of respondents believed that traffic had worsened, that the historic value of their towns had eroded, and that their towns had become less desirable places in which to live since the casino was developed (Carmichael *et al.*, 1996). These results are consistent with previous studies on the impact of casinos (Stokowski, 1996; Pizam and Pokela, 1985). Next, the linkage between perceptions and attitude toward the casino was investigated. Stepwise regression analysis revealed that attitudes toward the casino were significantly related to some of the personal variables, perceived casino impacts, attitudes towards the tribe and attitudes towards casino gaming ($R^2 =$ 62 percent). The dependent variable for this model was defined as agreement with the statement "it would be better if the casino had never been built" using a five point Likert Scale where 1=strongly agree and 5=strongly disagree.

Survey results revealed that 30.7 percent of respondents reported that the attitudes toward the tribe have worsened since the casino opened. Respondents were asked to report whether their attitudes toward the tribe had improved, stayed the same or worsened since the casino was built. The link between perceptions and attitude toward the tribe was modelled using a multi-nomial logit model. Negative opinions toward the tribe were affected by the distance from the casino (the closer the respondent, the more likely an opinion would worsen), perception of negative environmental effects and a lack of positive business and tax base effects. In addition, opinions got worse if the town became a less desirable place to live and if the respondent, or friends or family did not work at the casino, which reinforces the findings of Pizam (1978). More details on the multinominal logit model used to explore these relationships are reported in Carmichael *et al.* (1996).

One model developed in the geographical literature to describe cultural contact (Abler *et al.*, 1975) was suggested by Murphy (1985) to have application in understanding resident attitudes toward tourism. This model takes into account variation in resident attitudes and behaviours within the same area. A four cell matrix is used to classify persons by their attitudes and behaviours. On any given issue one's attitude may be negative or positive and one's behaviour active or passive. Therefore, four combinations are possible:

1. active-positive: aggressively promoting a position in favour of something.
2. active-negative: aggressively opposing something.
3. passive-positive: passively agreeing with and accepting something.
4. passive-negative: resigned acceptance of something one disagrees with.

Figure 8.1 shows this model and the arrows across the boundaries indicate that attitudes can change. However, the model does not indicate the relative importance of the four categories or the anticipated direction of change over time. Neither does it allow for neutral categories on either dimension.

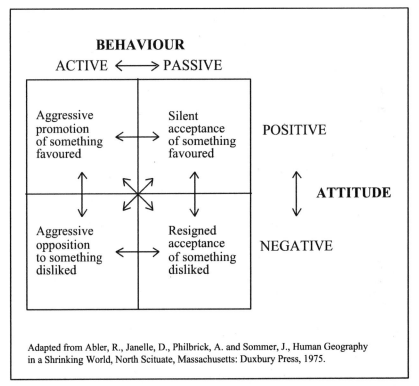

Figure 8.1: Matrix Model Classifying Residents by their Attitudes and Behaviours.

A composite variable was developed to measure attitudes toward the casino. The composite variable was obtained by combining and averaging attitude scores from a number of variables measuring perceptions of recreational opportunities, tax base, additional income, employment, real estate values, crime, historic value of the town, traffic, natural environment and quality of life. These

variables were measured on a five point Likert Scale as recom-
mended by Maddox (1985) and Lankford and Howard (1994) in
their tourism impact research studies. The composite variable scale
for attitudes toward the casino was tested for reliability and con-
struct validity (Carmichael, 2000).

Behaviours reported by survey participants were grouped
according to whether the behaviour was positive or negative or the
respondent took no action at all and a new categorical variable was
created. Like the attitudinal dimension, the behavioural dimension
also was modified to include three categories: negative actions, no
actions, positive actions. This was justified to test out the congru-
ence between positive and negative attitudes and positive and negative behaviours. The neutral and do nothing categories also make
sense intuitively.

Table 8.3 shows the frequencies of residents who fall into the
categories designated by the modified matrix model. While the
majority of residents performed none of the specific actions investigated, the table clearly shows the linkage between positive attitudes and positive actions and negative attitudes and negative
actions. The findings reveal that negative attitudes and behaviours
were more frequent than positive ones. Chi square analysis showed
statistically significant relationships between attitude toward the
casino and action (chi square 19.4801, significance .0006). Further
details and examples of the application of the matrix model are provided in a publication by the author in *Tourism Management*
(Carmichael, 2000).

Research on casino impacts and resident reactions is timely
since casino gaming is the most rapidly growing force in tourism
development in the 1990s. Tribes continue to negotiate with their
states and states increasingly turn to gaming in the hopes of generating revenue without tax increases. The growing importance of
Indian gaming raises the question of the responses by non Indian

communities to the owners of these enterprises. While developers may prefer to 'capture' their guests within resort complexes so that they have little contact with the surrounding host communities, large numbers of casino visitors inevitably bring changes that impact on local quality of life.

Table 8.3: Attitude Toward Casino and Action

	Behaviour			
		Negative action	No action	Positive action	Total
	Positive	3	20	10	33
	Neutral	9	26	3	38
	Negative	23	66	4	93
Attitudes toward casino*	Total	35	112	17	164

chi square 19.4801 significance .0006
*Composite variable taking values between 1 = most negative and 5 = most positive.
Positive 3.2-5.0, neutral 2.9-3.1, negative 1-2.8 (Broadening the neutral category to 2.5-3.5 yields a similar high chi square value).
Source: Carmichael, 2000.

Canadian Case Study: Casino Rama, Orillia, Ontario

Development:

As discussed previously, Casino Rama is developed to provide a First Nation casino in Ontario. Casino Rama is an Ontario Casino Corporation (OCC) project on the Chippewas of Mnjikaning (Rama) First Nation land near Orillia. The casino opened in July 1996 and it is the region's largest tourist attraction and the largest

First Nation casino in Canada. It is operated by Carnival Hotels under contract with the OCC and the Rama First Nation. The objectives of Casino Rama are:

a) to ensure that the casino provides increasingly progressive economic opportunities to aboriginal peoples both within and external to the operation;
b) to act as a catalyst for economic development for the host First Nations and surrounding communities;
c) to provide revenues for all First Nations in Ontario;
d) to promote the tourism and hospitality industries;
e) to create jobs
    (Ontario Casino Corporation, Annual Report, 1996-1997).

Casino Rama is one of three large casinos developed by the Province of Ontario. The others are located at Windsor and Niagara Falls.

Casino Rama and Sustainable Economic Development:
Casinos have become major tourism economic development strategies, particularly for First Nations. The revenue sharing scheme now in place through Casino Rama requires disbursement of revenues to First Nations across Ontario. There is no doubt that casinos have the ability to generate high revenues. However, while they provide opportunities for employment, they also frequently lead to more hidden costs such as crime, demands on public infrastructure and problem gambling. Understanding and balancing the costs and benefits of casinos as a sustainable development tool requires more comprehensive assessments than focusing just on employment and tax revenue gains. In this section a conceptual framework is presented for assessing a casino's role in sustainable economic development. This framework suggests that there are five functions for this assessment: environmental; socio-economic; productionist/ experiential; budgetary and political. To illustrate their relevance to sustainability, this framework is applied to Casino Rama.

According to the Bruntland Report, sustainable development is "economic activity which meets the needs of the present without compromising the ability of future generations to meet their needs" (WCED, 1987). Since the introduction of the concept of sustainable development, most economic activities, including tourism, have been considered and discussed in the context of the idea (Nelson *et al.*, 1993). Butler (1993: 29) gives a working definition of sustainable development in the context of tourism as "tourism which is developed and maintained in an area (community, environment) in such a manner and at such a scale that it remains viable over an indefinite period and does not degrade or alter the environment (human and physical) in which it exists to such a degree that it prohibits the successful development and well being of other activities and processes". Sustainable development in this context may be likened to the symbiotic relationship between tourism and conservation as discussed by Budowski (1976) in which both tourism and conservation are organized in such a way that they both benefit from the relationship in that a better quality of life is achieved.

Sustainable development is not the same as sustainable tourism (or sustainable profits), which is tourism that is economically viable in an area insofar as it is maintained because it is marketable and profitable. Sustainable development within the context of tourism in communities should not damage the environmental or social integrity so the impacts of tourism need to be carefully assessed. In addition, in promoting tourism in the context of symbiotic development, the full range of needs as perceived by current tourists or people at leisure must be considered (Butler, 1991). Much of the current research on sustainability focuses on the physical rather than the human environment. According to Garrod and Fyall (1998: 202): "The wider literature of sustainability tends to concentrate more on the use of natural resources, but it can be argued that human-made and socio-cultural resources are just as important in the context of tourism, if not more so." Within the context of casinos, the physical environmental impact is only one part of the sustainability issue.

Casino developments, like any other form of economic activity, need to fulfil a number of functions if they are to bring lasting improvements to local economies. While casinos draw on the local market, they also have the ability to attract considerable numbers of tourists from outside the region. Their role as tourist attractions depends on market access and competition, their social acceptability and the political climate in which they are allowed to operate, as well as the nature of the experience that they offer. Local resident endorsement of casino operations and their perceptions of casino impacts on their community, quality of life and environment are important considerations in understanding sustainability. Furthermore, backward linkages and job creation in local tourism and non-tourism enterprises are key factors in economic development that may or may not result from the casino's entry into the local economies.

A conceptual framework is suggested for assessing casino sustainability according to five functions: environmental; socio-economic; productionist/experiential; budgetary and political (Carmichael, 2001). The five functions are summarized in Figure 8.2 and have applicability at either the attraction level, within the host community or within the context of a wider region.

Environmental Function
Objective: To maintain or enhance the environmental base for tourism.
Casinos are located in a variety of different environments. They may function as part of a tourism attraction mix within attractive physical and cultural environments. As part of the built environment, tourism planners need to be concerned about appropriate building design, scale of development and environmental impact assessment. Developments in rural areas may be more sensitive than those in urban areas that already have lost green space.

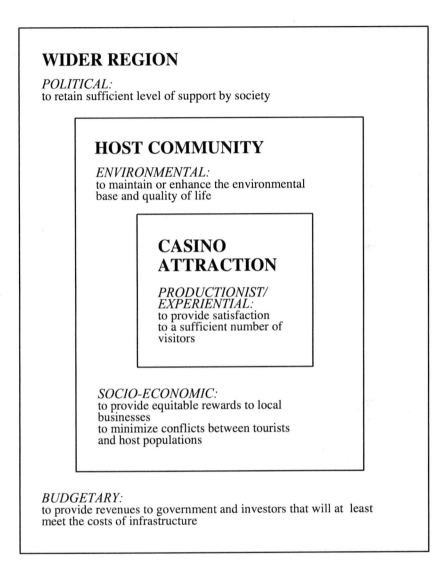

Figure 8.2: A Conceptual Framework for Assessing a Casino's Role in Sustainable Economic Development.

When Casino Rama developed, residents were concerned about increased traffic, especially at the Atherley Bridge which crossed a narrow strait between Lake Simcoe and Lake Couchiching. Marina operators were concerned over the loss of business at this location because of construction and bridge widening. Other residents were concerned about their increased commuting time into Orillia as a result of casino traffic on Route 11 (personal interviews conducted by the author, 1997). Ramera residents and cottagers along the lake shore near Rama Reserve were concerned about the possibility of commercial strip development in Ramera (personal interviews conducted by the author, 1997). As yet, such development has not occurred although the Mnjikaning band have opened a small shopping mall and gas station and plan to house their concert series and entertainment in a more permanent structure. Before the temporary casino was built, an environmental impact assessment was undertaken for a permanent casino on the lakefront. However, the decision was made by the band to forgo this development and concentrate their expansion at the initial location away from the lake. This decision was made mainly from cost reasons rather than from environmental concern. Concern over lake pollution levels has led to a McMaster University environmental monitoring study of plant organisms in Lake Couchiching in an attempt to monitor the effects of lakeshore developments and waste disposal (personal interview, conducted by the author, 1997).

Socio-Economic Function
There are two objectives to be discussed within this context:

a) to provide equitable rewards to individual entrepreneurs and resort communities, and
b) to minimize conflicts between tourists and local people.

Objective: a) To provide equitable economic rewards to individual entrepreneurs and resort communities.

Most casinos have proved to be highly profitable business enterprises. Economic impact studies reveal their direct, indirect and induced effects. The establishments are labour intensive and multiplier effects are created as workers spend their wages within the employee catchment region. As such, we may argue that casinos are growth poles or catalysts for economic development especially if they draw in basic money. However, we may take a different perspective and argue that casinos may be sink holes not growth poles.

The extent to which casinos cannibalize the product of local businesses is a key research question in assessing the socio-economic function of sustainability. The substitution effect is defined as the power of one good to replace another good with no change in the utility or satisfaction of a customer. The extent to which other forms of gaming activity (horse racing, dog tracks, lotteries) suffer from the introduction of casino gaming suggests that the substitution effect exists despite the growth in real personal incomes and growth in spending on leisure and recreation.

In the case of Casino Rama, the economic impacts are considerable. In 1999, business operations at Casino Rama generated $489 million dollars of economic activity for the Orillia region and 3,674 full year equivalent jobs. Casino Rama employees spend $51.8 million annually; $30.1 million of which is in the Orillia area. This spending generated $49 million of economic activity and 312 full year equivalent jobs (Pannell, Kerr Forster and Canadian Tourism Research Institute, 2000). The casino employs 2,700 full time employees, 600 of whom are Native Canadians. The unemployment rate in Rama reserve dropped from 80 percent to 10 percent once the casino opened. The Orillia Human Resource Centre of Canada reports that local employment patterns are changing as seasonal jobs are giving way to more permanent jobs. Between 1996 and 1998 the number of jobs in the Orillia area rose by 38 percent (Ontario Casino Corporation and Ontario Lottery Corporation

(OLC) Annual Report 1998-1999).

Objective: b) To minimize conflicts between tourists and local people.

For tourism development to be sustainable local endorsement of the nature of the development is important. In the case of casinos where the core tourism product is the gambling experience, perhaps there are limited opportunities for tourist and host interaction. Therefore, this function may be less important for casino development than for other types of tourist development. An important research question in this context is to what extent are casino patrons visitors to other attractions in the area? And to what extent are casino visitors locals? A Casino visitor survey conducted in 1997 revealed that 66 percent of visitors were in the region for the sole purpose of visiting Casino Rama. Of the one-third of the visitors who planned to participate in other activities in the region 55 percent were visiting a restaurant, 51 percent were golfing, 50 percent were hiking or nature walking, 49 percent were sightseeing and touring and 37 percent were shopping (Resource Management Consulting Group, 1997). Most of the visitors (52 percent) were from southern Ontario. Visitors stated that they wanted to know more about surrounding tourist attractions. In some instances, they felt that residents resented the visitors who come to the area and questioned whether they would want increased tourism in conjunction with the casino.

Productionist/Experiential Function

Objective: To provide satisfaction to a sufficient number of tourists.
As well as safeguarding the natural and built environment and meeting the needs of the host community, the development should satisfy the needs of the tourists and visitors. In 1999, the casino attracted 4.6 million visitors, an average of 12,700 per day. During the first fiscal year of its operation, (eight months) attendance levels reached 2.5 million guests with $223 million in gross gaming revenues. By the second fiscal year (April 1998) attendance levels

had grown to 4.1 million with gross gaming revenues doubling to $407 million. Attendance levels continued to rise in the third year of operation (April 1999) with over 4.6 million patrons and $492 million in gross gaming revenues (Pannell Kerr Forster and Canadian Tourism Research Institute, 2000). Visitors in the 1997 customer survey rated their experience at Casino Rama very highly. On a scale of one to 10 , over 70 percent of the respondents scored their experience as eight or higher. In this case of casino gambling, there is no doubt about the activity's popularity. For some, however, it is popularity to the point of addiction. While most players do not develop a compulsive gambling problem, approximately 4-6 percent of the population is likely to suffer from this addiction (Ferris and Stirpe, 1995). The Ontario government has set aside a minimum of $10 million for the treatment, research and prevention of compulsive gambling (OCC and OLC Report, 1998-1999).

Budgetary Function
Objective: To provide revenues to provincial and local governments that will at least meet costs of infrastructure.
Part of the reason for the rapid growth in the number of casinos is that they are regarded by states and provinces as lucrative sources of income as an alternative to raising taxes. In hard economic times, cities, states/provinces and countries need money, but raising taxes in a recession is faulty economics and bad politics. The operation of Casino Rama generated a total of $192 million in taxes for all levels of government and an estimated $165 million of these taxes were generated by economic activity that originated in the local area (Pannell Kerr and Forster and Canadian Tourism Research Institute, 2000).

Political Function

Objective: To retain sufficient level of support by society.
By the 1990s, in North America, there has emerged a substantial increase in the legal and social acceptance of gaming. It has changed from being perceived as a vice available in very restricted locations to being more of a mainstream participatory activity (Eadington, 1995). Despite this, legalizing casino gaming usually proves difficult to implement. A Veto model suggests that a campaign to legalize casinos will be successful only if all major campaign factors are favorable (Dombrink and Thompson, 1990). These major campaign factors include: support by the political elite; support by the economic elite; dominance of economic issues in the campaign (the need for jobs and tax revenues); non-emergence of crime issues; lack of opposition from a rival gambling enterprise (particularly horse tracks) and financial advantages for proponents. Power relations are integral to this process and to the outcome.

However, as more jurisdictions accept casino gaming, the public are increasingly realizing the negative effects of casinos *i.e.*, compulsive gambling. Casinos are contentious attractions that create strong reactions among some groups in society. There will always be people who contend that gambling is immoral and gambling is inappropriate as an economic development tool. In the past, it was a highly restricted activity and today it is still highly controlled in location. As Eadington states "historically, legal commercial gaming has seldom existed in a stable environment.... If the image of commercial gaming moved strongly towards the negative pole, there is a real possibility that legislation prohibiting such gambling could again emerge" (Eadington, 1990: 157-8).

At present in Ontario, it is unlikely that more casinos will be opened. There is now a hierarchy in casino developments. The last round of introduction of smaller, charity casinos was implemented in 1999 and 2000 on a reduced scale from that originally planned.

Four charity casinos opened as opposed to the 44 charity casinos suggested in a Coopers and Lybrand (1996) report. These four casinos located in Sault Ste. Marie, Brantford, Point Edward and Thunder Bay fill a popular niche and all opened in areas which had resident approval. A fifth casino, the Great Blue Heron, Scugog Island is an example of a First Nation charity casino provided at this scale of development. The Ontario Government scaled down its plan for more charity casinos mainly as a result of resident opinion.

CONCLUSION

Issues related to casino development are not clear cut. Resident opinion varies widely about the morality of gaming and its appropriateness as an economic development tool. There are perceived benefits and costs in both economic, environmental and social factors. In the case of Indian gaming, gambling has been embraced mainly because of the positive economic spin offs and the potential for the integrity of sovereignty, which the revenues bring. Improved morale and pride in cultural heritage has followed economic success. In the case of Foxwoods, sponsorship of annual Schemutzens or Indian Dance festivals celebrate Indian cultures. A museum of Indian artifacts is also developed on site. Tribal members who can prove their Mushentucket Pequot heritage have been attracted back to the Reservation. A question over the legitimacy of the tribes' claim to recognition in 1983 was aired in a well researched book (Benedict, 2000). The impact of news coverage of this book will surely have influenced resident attitudes in the region. However, the casino is such a successful employer and generator of revenues that it is highly unlikely that it will be closed down even if such mistakes were made in the granting of tribal recognition. In the case of Casino Rama, the Indian presence is visible but only superficially. Several respondents from focus group research responded positively about the native art on the outside and inside of the casino but found there was little interpretation of the art (Resource Management Consulting Group, 1997). The

Rama casino differs from Indian casinos in the US in that the revenue sharing program shares the profits of the casino with other First Nations in Ontario. Casinos are indeed proving profitable and beneficial to First Nations in both US and Canada, whether as stand-alone private enterprises or in the form of public sector/private partnerships. Casinos like Foxwoods and Casino Rama are located close to major metropolitan areas and have enjoyed immediate success economically. However, in assessing their sustainability a wider viewpoint should be taken with communities and environments also being considered. Resident opinion and reaction in surrounding communities provides one of the indicators for such assessment.

REFERENCES

Abt, V., Smith, J.F. and Christiansen, M. (1985) *The Business of Risk: Commercial Gambling in Mainstream America*, Lawrence, KS: University Press of Kansas.

Abler, R., Janelle, D., Philbrick, A. and Sommer, J. (1975) *Human Geography in a Shrinking World*, North Scituate, MA: Duxbury Press.

Anders, G.C. (1998) "Indian gaming financial and regulatory issues", *Annals AAPSS*, 556: 98-108.

Anon (2000) "Agreement promotes economic development in First Nations", *News Release Communique*, Toronto, ON: Ontario Lottery and Gaming Corporation.

Benedict, J. (2000) *Without Reservation: The Making of America's Most Powerful Indian Tribe and Foxwoods, The World's Largest Casino*, New York: Harper Collins.

Butler, R.W. (1991) "Tourism, environment and sustainable development", *Environmental Conservation*, 18(3): 201-209.

Butler, R.W. (1993) "Tourism — an evolutionary perspective", in J.G. Nelson, G. Wall and R. Butler (eds.), *Tourism and Sustainable Development: Monitoring, Planning, Managing*, Waterloo, ON: University of Waterloo, Department of Geography Publications Series Number 37, 27-44.

Budowski, G. (1976) "Tourism and environmental conservation", *Environmental Conservation*, 3(1): 27-31.

Cabot, A.N. (1996) *Casino Gaming, Policy, Economics and Regulation*, Las Vegas, NV: UNLV International Gaming Institute.

Campbell, C.S. and Smith, G.J. (1998) "Canadian gambling: trends and public policy issues", *Annals AAPSS*, 556: 22-35.

Carmichael, B.A. (1994) "Casino gambling and tourism in rural and urban communities", *Proceedings of the Conference in Quality Management in Urban Tourism*, November, 10-12, Victoria, British Columbia.

_____ (1998) "Foxwoods Resort Casino, Who wants it? Who Benefits?", in K. Meyer Arendt and R. Hartmann (eds.), *Casino Gambling in North America*, Elmsford, NY: Cognizant Communications.

_____ (2000) "A matrix model for resident attitudes and behaviours in a rapidly changing tourist area," *Tourism Management*, 21(6): 601-611.

_____ (2001) "Casinos, communities and sustainable economic development", in S. McCool and N. Moisey (eds.), *Tourism, Recreation and Sustainability: Linking Culture and the Environment*, London: CABI Publications.

Carmichael, B.A. and Peppard, D. Jr. (1998) "The impact of
    Foxwoods Resort Casino on its dual host community:
    Southeastern Connecticut and the Mashentucket Pequot
    Tribe", in A. Lew and G.A. Van Otten (eds.), *Tourism on
    American Indian Lands*, Elmsford, NY: Cognizant
    Communications.

Carmichael, B.A., Peppard, D. Jr. and Boudreau, F. (1996) "Mega
    resort on my doorstep: local resident attitudes towards
    Foxwoods Casino and casino gambling on nearby Indian reser-
    vation land", *Journal of Travel Research*, 34(3): 9-16.

Connor, M. (1993) "Indian gaming: prosperity, controversy",
    International Gaming and Wagering Business, March 15-April
    14, 1, 8-12, 45.

Coopers and Lybrand (1996) *Ontario Charity Gaming Club
    Project*, Toronto, ON: Gaming Control Commission, Province
    of Ontario.

Dombrink, J. and Thompson, W.N. (1990) *The Last Resort:
    Success and Failure in Campaigns for Casinos*, Reno, NV:
    University of Nevada Press.

Eadington, W.R. (ed.) (1990) *Indian Gaming and the Law*, Reno,
    NV: University of Nevada.

_____ (1995) "The emergence of casino gaming as major factor in
    tourism", in R. Butler and D. Pearce (eds.), *Change in Tourism,
    People, Places and Processes*, New York, NY: Routledge, 159-
    186.

Ferber, S.R. and Chon, K.S. (1994) "Indian gaming: issues and
    prospects", *Gaming Research and Review Journal*, 1(2): 55-
    65.

Ferris, J. and Stirpe, T. (1995) *Gambling in Ontario: A Report from a General Population Survey on Gambling Related Problems and Opinions*, Addiction Research Foundation, Problem and Compulsive Gambling Project, Toronto, ON: York University, Institute for Social Research.

Garrod, B. and Fyall, A. (1998) "Beyond the rhetoric of sustainable tourism", *Tourism Management*, 19(3): 199-212.

Lankford, S. and Howard, D.R. (1994) "Developing a tourism impact attitude scale", *Annals of Tourism Research*, 21: 121-139.

Long, P. (1995) "Casino gambling in the United States: 1994 status and implications", *Tourism Management*, 16(3): 189-197.

Maddox, R.N. (1985) "Measuring satisfaction with tourism", *Journal of Travel Research*, 23(3): 2-5.

Marshall, L.H. and Rudd, D.P. (1996) *Introduction to Casino and Gaming Operations*, Englewood Cliffs: Prentice Hall.

McDonald, M. (1994) "Tribal gamblers", *Macleans*, 107(22): 32.

Mcintosh, R., Goeldner, C.R. and Ritchie, J.R.B. (1994) *Tourism, Principles, Practices and Philosophies*, 7th Edition, New York: John Wiley and Sons.

Murphy, P.E. (1985) *Tourism: A Community Approach*, New York, NY: Methuen.

Nelson, J.G., Butler, R. and Wall, G. (1993) *Tourism and Sustainable Development: Monitoring, Planning, Managing*, Waterloo, ON: University of Waterloo, Department of Geography Publications Series Number 37.

Pannell Kerr Forster and Canadian Tourism Research Institute (2000) *The Economic Impact of Casino Rama on its Neighbours*, Toronto, ON: Pannell Kerr Forster.

Pizam, A. (1978) "Tourism impacts: the social costs to the destination community as perceived by its residents", *Journal of Travel Research*, 16: 8-12.

Pizam, A. and Pokela, J. (1985) "The perceived impacts of casino gambling on a community", *Annals of Tourism Research*, 12: 147-65.

Resource Management Consulting Group (1997) *Community Casino Task Force 1997 Research: Visitor Survey and Focus Groups*, Ottawa, ON: Human Resources Development Canada.

Stansfield, C. (1996) "Reservations and gambling: native Americans and the diffusion of legalized gaming", in R. Butler and T. Hinch (eds.), *Tourism and Indigenous Peoples*, London: International Thompson Business Press, 129-147.

Stokowski, P. (1996) *Riches and Regrets: Betting on Gambling in Two Colorado Mountain Towns*, Ninot, CO: University of Colorado Press.

Thompson ,W.N. and Dever, D.R. (1994) "A Sovereignty Check on Indian Gaming", *Indian Gaming Magazine*, 5(5): 5-7.

Tobias, J.L. (1991) "Protection, civilization, assimilation: an outline history of Canada's Indian Policy", in J.R. Miller (ed.), *Sweet Promises A Reader in Indian-White Relations in Canada*, Toronto: University of Toronto Press.

World Commission on Environmental Development (WCED) (1987) *Our Common Future*, New York, NY: Oxford University Press.

Chapter 9

Tourism in the Coastal Zone: Perspectives from Hainan, P.R. China

Geoffrey Wall
University of Waterloo

Tourism is too important to be left to tourism specialists. There are a number of reasons for this. First, while one can debate whether or not tourism is an industry, there is widespread recognition that tourism is fragmented among many varied operations of differing sizes and with different products. These include transportation, attractions, accommodations, food and beverage suppliers, and souvenir producers and their outlets to name a few. Furthermore, much tourism training has a relatively narrow focus upon hospitality, *i.e.*, hotel and catering management, to the relative neglect of other aspects of tourism. To complicate matters further, tourism is a phenomenon that has links to many other sectors of the economy and many tourism issues are not solely tourism problems but involve relationships with agriculture, forestry, mining, environmental protection and a host of other activities that compete for scarce resources of land, labour, capital, energy, waste assimilation capacity and the like. Thus, it is important to consider tourism in relation to these other phenomena: a narrow focus is unlikely to be able to do justice to the wide variety of interrelated concerns. It also follows that policies designed to sustain tourism may not necessarily contribute to sustainable development more broadly conceived, for the perpetuation of tourism may not always be in the broader, long-term, interest (Wall, 1997).

The coast is a place where oceanic, atmospheric, terrestrial and human processes, including tourism, are juxtaposed and linked. Integrated Coastal Zone Management (ICZM) is an integrated, interdisciplinary, intersectoral and adaptive approach for addressing complex issues for the conservation and sustainable development of coastal resources. It is an holistic perspective that recognizes the interconnections between coastal systems and uses and encompasses the dynamic tasks of measurement, assessment, community participation, evaluation, planning, management and monitoring. It is directed at the maintenance of balance between the protection of valuable ecosystems and the development of related economies.

Operationally, ICZM focuses on three objectives: strengthening sectoral and inter-sectoral management, for instance through human resources development and institutional strengthening; preserving and protecting the productivity and biological diversity of coastal ecosystems, mainly through prevention of habitat destruction, pollution and over-exploitation; and promoting rational development and sustainable utilization of coastal resources.

The coast is an environmental setting that is often attractive to tourists and tourism developers. However, just as coasts themselves take many forms (*e.g.*, sand and rocky beaches, cliffs, estuaries, coral reefs, wetlands....) so the forms of tourism that occur in their vicinity are highly varied. The world's coasts are also the location of its major cities and are under growing pressure from population growth, industrial activity, port development, fisheries, conversion to aquaculture, offshore petroleum and gas production and so on. It is self-evident that tourism developed in ignorance of these trends may be inappropriate, inefficient and, in many cases, doomed to failure. Thus, the coast provides an excellent, perhaps extreme, example of the normal situation in which tourism is one among a number of activities with claims on access to resources and which may or may not be compatible in their use of those resources.

It is a truism to state that everything is related to everything else. Ideally, therefore, wise decisions should be informed by a complete knowledge of the system at hand, including factors external to the system that impinge upon it. Such an approach requires that one adopt a *comprehensive* approach and examine everything that may affect the issues of concern. Unfortunately, limitations of knowledge, time and resources mean that it is impossible to study everything. Therefore, to embark on a comprehensive study is to be destined to failure and to raise expectations which cannot be fulfilled.

An *integrated* perspective leads to a more modest and pragmatic approach through which a subset of important phenomena is examined, including their interrelationships, so that the whole is greater than the sum of the parts. However, as might be ideal for a comprehensive approach, no claim is made that all phenomena have been taken into account and that a comprehensive investigation has been undertaken. Thus, an integrated approach is more pragmatic than a comprehensive approach. However, an attempt is still made to consider the integration of phenomena but primary attention is devoted to phenomena that are perceived to be important on the basis of past experiences, scoping, political concerns or some other criteria (Mitchell, 1997: 56-7).

The adoption of both comprehensive and integrated perspectives requires that information of many types must be brought together, leading to the espousal of interdisciplinary and multidisciplinary approaches. A literature has emerged that attempts to distinguish between theses two approaches but this will not be pursued here. Suffice to say that disciplines have their own emphases and cultures, and the number of disciplines involved in an investigation has implications for the ease with which insights can be pooled and can be used to inform each other. Frameworks can be developed in advance in an attempt to facilitate integration of data and results or the task can be left to the latter part of a project when more information is available to guide what needs to be done. Both have their strengths and weaknesses and they are not mutually exclusive.

This paper presents the framework prepared to guide a project on integrated monitoring and management of the coastal zone in Hainan, China. Tourism is an important part, but only one part, of this project. Tourism has links to many other sectors. It will be argued that while it is legitimate, even necessary, to focus attention on single sectors, such as tourism, to do so in the absence of attention to links between sectors would be to provide an inevitably incomplete but also inadequate appreciation of the current situation, issues and options. However, it is not an easy task to embrace intersectoral linkages.

Prior to presentation and discussion of the framework, a brief description of the overall project, including the characteristics of the Province of Hainan, will be provided as context.

PROJECT STRUCTURE AND GOALS
The full title of the project is "Environmental Training for Integrated Monitoring and Management in the Coastal Zone of Hainan Province, China". The project is funded by the Canadian International Development Agency (CIDA) through the Canada-China Higher Education Program (CCHEP) with contributions in kind from the Chinese (Nanjing University) and Canadian partner institutions (University of Waterloo, University of Guelph and Wilfrid Laurier University) in liaison with local government authorities, particularly the Provincial Department of Land, Environment and Resources in Hainan. The University of Waterloo is administering the program under a contribution agreement with CIDA. The project began officially in 1997 and is expected to continue until the middle of 2003.

As a sub-tropical island province, Hainan is in a unique and special situation in China. It is a formally-designated special economic zone that has experienced substantial port developments and rapid urbanization. Its magnificent beaches, particularly in the south, are undergoing tourism development. In addition, the island contains substantial ethnic minorities whose livelihoods may be impacted by such changes. The environmental conditions in and around the island are generally currently quite good. However, development is likely to induce considerable land use changes with the prospects of environmental degradation if steps are not taken to protect fragile natural resources both in the interior and on the coast. Hence, there is a need to strengthen monitoring systems, to identify specific impacts and to prepare local institutions and officials to respond to the growing need to manage pressures on coastal resources.

The project is designed to addresses pressing needs to enhance Chinese capabilities in Integrated Coastal Zone Management (ICZM) through human resource development (HRD), institutional strengthening and the improvement of information management in the context of Chinese national and provincial development strategies. The program has been developing locally-based materials for instructional purposes and, at the same time, provide training and resources to enhance sustainable management of Hainan's sensitive tropical environment through the application of ICZM by local managers.

The key project beneficiaries are expected to be those local government agencies in Hainan charged with managing the coastal zone (and, through improvement in their performance, the people of Hainan); Nanjing University through strengthening of their capabilities in ICZM; and the Universities of Waterloo and Guelph, and Wilfrid Laurier University, through increases in their expertise with respect to resources and environmental management in China.

The project consists of three main components:

1. an educational component in which a suite of courses has been taught to approximately 50 participants, mostly local government employees, in Haikou, the provincial capital

in the north of the island. These courses have been accepted by Chinese educational authorities and Nanjing University as meeting the course requirements (excluding thesis) of the Master's degree at Nanjing University.

2.   a monitoring component in which selected aspects of both natural and human systems have been examined in an integrated manner. These activities have been concentrated in and around Sanya in the south of the island.

3.   an outreach component in which the importance of coastal resources, resources management and sustainable development is conveyed to a broad public in both China and Canada.

A key task and challenge of the project revolves around the word "integration" for, in addition to the usual challenges of coastal management involving land and water, natural and human systems, different disciplines and academic and governmental perspectives, the project must also embrace differences in language and culture.

A framework for integrated coastal zone management was developed to guide project activities and this will be presented.

THE ICZM FRAMEWORK

The framework can be summarized in a single sentence: forces for change give rise to stresses, which are analyzed using integrative concepts and methods, resulting in outputs in the form of human resources development, improved information and the ability to use it, and modified institutional arrangements, leading to enhanced capability to undertake integrated coastal zone management (Figure 9.1). This statement will be amplified under the following headings: forces for change; stresses; integrative concepts and methods; and measurable outputs.

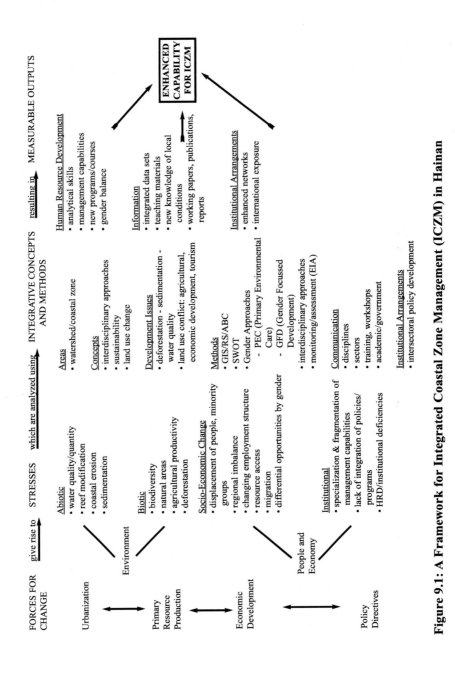

Figure 9.1: A Framework for Integrated Coastal Zone Management (ICZM) in Hainan

Forces for Change

The forces for change in Hainan include urbanization, primary resource production (*e.g.*, agriculture, fisheries, mining), economic development (*e.g.*, tourism, port construction), and policy directives associated with its status as a Special Economic Zone. These forces are giving rise to stresses on both the environment and human beings and their activities. Four key forces for change were identified. These were:

1. Population, particularly urbanization (Gu, 2002). The population of Hainan has grown substantially, both through natural increase as well as through migration. Hainan has large ethnic minority populations, particularly in the south-central part of the island (Xie, 2001). The population is not well-educated by Chinese standards and unemployment is high. Tourism offers the potential to provide economic opportunities for both minority and Han populations and is a substantial contributor to urban growth in both Haikou and Sanya, the main cities in the north and south of the island respectively.

2. Primary resource production includes agriculture (subsistence, commercial and plantations) and fisheries, including aquaculture. The island is an important producer of tropical fruit and vegetables as well as seed crops for the mainland. Large areas are in rubber and tea plantations. Some primary forests, particularly in the centre and southwest of the island, have ecotourism potential (Stone, 2002) and rugged areas of secondary forest are scenic but subject to swidden agriculture. Aquaculture is increasing rapidly in coastal locations. Iron ore deposits that were formerly exploited by the Japanese are no longer in production.

3. Aspects of economic development are included in the pre-

ceding two paragraphs. To these must be added offshore oil and gas and substantial port development. In spite of its key location in the South China Sea and its status as a Special Economic Zone, the economy is less vibrant than desired, particularly since the end of a speculative property boom in the mid 1990s. Tropical agriculture and tourism have been identified by the Government of Hainan as having great potential.

4. Policy directives of relevance include status as a Special Economic Zone, which facilitates international investment, as well as the arrival of international visitors, many of whom no longer require a visa (although the number of international visitors is still small). Also, Hainan has been declared the first Eco-province in China, although it is not clear at present exactly what this will mean.

Stresses

Stresses can be divided into two main categories: those associated with environment, and those associated with people and economy.

Environmental stresses can be divided into abiotic (such as water quality and quantity, reef modification, coastal erosion and sedimentation) and biotic (such as destruction of mangroves (Kennedy, 2001) and changes in biodiversity, natural areas, agricultural productivity and deforestation).

The people and economy division also can be divided into two groups: socio-economic change and institutional stresses. The former includes such phenomena as displacement of people, pressures on minority groups (Wang, 2003), regional imbalances, changing employment structure, changing access to resources, migration, and differential opportunities by ethnicity and gender. The institutional category includes overspecialization and fragmentation of management capabilities, lack of integration of policies and programs, and deficiencies in institutional capacities and in the capabilities of human resources (Liu, 2002).

Virtually all of the above have implications for or are modified by the development of tourism.

Integrative Concepts and Methods

Integration, or the amalgamation and combining of diverse forms of data and their interpretation, is a key concept in this paper. It is also something that is particularly difficult to do well. In the broadest sense, there are two main approaches that can be considered: participatory and technical. These approaches could be applied individually or in combination. Ideally, it would have been good to involve stakeholders in all aspects of the project to seek their interpretation of data and to assess their understanding and interpretation of linkages. However, this approach was difficult to adopt because of language complexities and the infrequent and limited stays of team members in the study area. Technical methods, as will be indicated below, can be used to analyze and integrate certain types of data although the interpretation of results and their local significance may require resolution in other ways.

More specifically, integration can be facilitated by careful research design and the adoption of concepts and methods that facilitate and even require the use of and/or interpretation of multiple types of information. Examples of such concepts and methods follow.

1. Choice of appropriate study areas. The coastal zone itself is an integrative concept, focusing upon both land and water and the interface between them. Of course, one can argue about the exact definition of the coastal zone and how it is to be determined, what attributes it should possess and how wide it may be. In fact, in a relatively small island, one could argue that even the interior is part of the

coastal zone because changes throughout the island have implications for the coast.

A watershed is another spatial unit with integrative elements. While the focus may be on the quantity and quality of water, this, in turn, reflects other changes in the system such as population growth, land-use change and industrial development. It also may draw attention to relationships between upstream and downstream locations.

2. Some concepts and approaches lend themselves more to integration than others. For example, interdisciplinary and multidisciplinary perspectives imply some degree of integration of different approaches and types of information. Assessments of sustainability require that attention be given to economy, environment and culture. Land use change and associated changes in water quality and quantity are key concepts. Land use itself may be an integrative concept in that it is the product of a combination of natural capabilities and human decisions and activities. Both land use and water reflect both physical and human processes and were used to identify areas of stress and documented in a demonstration area that incorporates a watershed and the adjacent coastal zone. Gender is a theme that cuts across many types of resource use and economic sectors. Somewhat similarly, tourism can be used as an integrative theme, because of its multiple dimensions. The fragmentation and complexity characteristic of tourism that have been highlighted above can be turned to advantage if tourism is used as a focal activity or lens through which observations can be interpreted.

3. Many development issues require an integration of information, both economic and environmental, if they are to be addressed adequately (Hu, 2003). For example, defor-

estation is likely to have economic underpinnings with implications for water quality and sedimentation. Land use conflicts, perhaps reflecting development possibilities associated with tourism that may, for example, be viewed as being in competition with traditional agriculture and lifestyles, require the weighing of multiple perspectives and types of information (Wang, 2003).

4. Numerous techniques lend themselves to manipulation of varied types of data and may in fact require a diversity of information sources. Their application and outputs may require complex inputs and interpretation, perhaps involving multiple skills and even interdisciplinary teams. Examples of such techniques are geographical information systems, remote sensing, the ABC (abiotic, biotic and cultural) method (Bastedo, 1986), SWOT (strengths weaknesses, opportunities, threats) analysis (Wall, 2002), rapid rural appraisal, gender focused development, and environmental and social impact assessment.

5. Communication is both a challenge and an opportunity. In a situation involving people with different languages and cultures, with varied disciplinary backgrounds, representing different economic and other interests, as well as both academic and government (and occasionally private sector) perspectives, communication is difficult. On the other hand, the rich diversity of experiences and approaches that can be brought to the table, assuming that appropriate fora for exchange of information and training can be devised, can stimulate mutual learning and novel interpretations.

6. Institutional analysis, leading to the stimulation of dialogue between authorities with overlapping jurisdictions, can lead eventually to intersectoral policy development.

Thus, although it is much easier to list possibilities than to put them into practice, a wide variety of techniques, either singularly or preferably in combination, can be used to stimulate more integrated perspectives on the collection, analysis and interpretation of information.

Outputs

The project that has led to the preparation of this paper, has had practical objectives as its major goal - enhancement of the capability of governments in Hainan to better manage the growing pressures on the coast. Accordingly, the project has been designed and managed under a "results-based management" framework (Appian Consulting Inc., 2001) with all the strengths, weaknesses and bureaucratic requirements that this implies. It is important to recognize that this presenter, as the Canadian project director, and his team have no mandate to manage the coast of Hainan - nor should they! Rather, it is assumed that through human resources development, improved information availability and enhanced institutional arrangements, local capacity for better management of the coast of Hainan, *i.e.*, ICZM, would be achieved. Human resources development was interpreted as the enhancement of analytical (and integrative) skills and management capabilities, the promotion of greater gender equity and appreciation of the differential consequences of development for women and men, through the provision of new education and training opportunities.

One of the greatest impediments to ICZM is the lack of accurate and replicable data sets on linked environmental and human systems that can be used as a basis for informed decision making. The information base on which decisions could be made was enhanced through the development of teaching materials, new data sets, new knowledge of local conditions, and the provision of and training in the use of new equipment, as well as the preparation of reports and publications. Changes in institutional arrangements have taken place in Hainan, including the renaming of the main governmental department with which we collaborate, the initiation of the Eco-province initiative, and the enhancement of networks both within Hainan, nationally and internationally. However, it is not absolutely clear that either of the first two should be attributed solely to the existence of this project.

SUMMARY AND CONCLUSIONS

Tourism is a major force for change in Hainan and, thus, should be an important consideration in managing the coast and, indeed, the interior of this tropical island. However, to focus solely upon tourism would be to overlook the many interrelationships between tourism and other sectors leading to partial understanding. Yet, it is impossible to examine everything. Pragmatism requires that one relinquish a desire for a comprehensive in favour of an integrated approach.

A framework has been presented to guide project activities related to coastal zone management in Hainan. A review of this framework reveals that tourism is seldom mentioned explicitly (perhaps it should be!). On the other hand, almost all statements in the framework have implications for tourism research or training. Conversely, a detailed examination of tourism, in the absence of an appreciation of broader linkages, would lead to an impoverished understanding of issues facing Hainan and the role of tourism within them.

A little knowledge is a dangerous thing! It is natural that tourism trainers, planners and authors should concentrate on tourism but, unfortunately, it is contended that this all too frequently occurs to the neglect of the bigger picture and tourism's place within it. Yet, if tourism specialists do not take up the challenge of placing their subject in a broader context, is it reasonable to expect others to do it for them?

REFERENCES

Appian Consulting Inc. (2001) *A Results Approach to Developing the Implementation Plan*, Ottawa, ON: Canadian International Development Agency.

Bastedo, J.D. (1986) *An ABC Resource Survey Method for Environmentally Significant Areas with Special Reference to Biotic Surveys in Canada's North*, Department of Geography Publication Series No. 24. Waterloo, ON: University of Waterloo.

Gu, K. (2002) *Urban Morphology of the Chinese City: Cases From Hainan*, Unpublished PhD thesis in Planning, Waterloo, ON: University of Waterloo.

Hu, W. (2003) *Developing Environmentally Responsible Tourism in Tourist Attractions: A Case Study from Hainan, China*, Unpublished MAES thesis in Local Economic Development (Tourism Policy and Planning), Waterloo, ON: University of Waterloo.

Kennedy, S. (2001) *Protected Area Designation, Conservation and Community Development: Dongzhai Nature Reserve, Hainan, China*, Unpublished MES thesis in Geography, Waterloo, ON: University of Waterloo.

Liu, A.Y. (2002) *Human Resources Development and Planning for Tourism: Case Studies from P.R. China and Malaysia*, Unpublished Ph.D thesis in Planning, Waterloo, ON: University of Waterloo.

Mitchell, B. (1997) *Resources and Environmental Management*, Harlow, UK: Longman.

Stone, M. (2002) *Ecotourism and Community Development: Case Studies from Hainan, China*, Unpublished MA thesis in Planning, Waterloo, ON: University of Waterloo.

Wall, G. (1997) "Sustainable tourism - unsustainable development", in J. Pigram and S. Wahab (eds.), *Tourism Development and Growth: The Challenge of Sustainability*, London, UK: Routledge, 33-49.

Wall, G. (2002) "A SWOT analysis of tourism in Baoting, Hainan, China", *International Journal of Tourism Sciences (Korea)*, 2(1): 37-48.

Wang, Y. (2003) *Social Impacts of Tourism-Caused Displacement: A Case Study in Hainan, China*, Unpublished MA thesis in Planning, Waterloo, ON: University of Waterloo.

Xie, P. (2001) *Authenticating Cultural Tourism: Folk Villages in Hainan, China*, Unpublished PhD thesis in Planning, Waterloo, ON: University of Waterloo.

Chapter 10

Future Directions for Tourism

Richard Butler
University of Surrey

The task of predicting the future is something that has fascinated mankind since time immemorial (Kennedy, 1993). To predict trends and patterns from even stable and well documented phenomena is still difficult and prone to error, and to attempt to forecast trends and changes in something as esoteric and dynamic as tourism is almost impossible. Such forecasting is complicated by the fact that firstly, there is no certainty of what are true causal agents and secondly, most projections assume stable and continued relationships between dependent and independent variables. However, it is clear that many of the variables that influence tourism and leisure are not truly independent and are certainly interrelated, and thus predicting on the basis of activity participation alone is rarely accurate beyond the very short term. Rather it is necessary to understand behaviour, and the related perceptions, attitudes, values and motivational forces, before there can be any hope of predicting the future with any degree of accuracy. One way of doing this would be to identify clear indicators of change but as Paine *et al.* pointed out "despite the collection of an immense amount of data over the last two decades, there is no clearly defined set of indicators in the outdoor recreation field" (Paine *et al.*, 1980: 7). This comment, although two decades old, still has considerable relevance today in the context of both recreation and tourism.

There are several ways of examining the future, and considerable work has been carried out on describing and evaluating various approaches (Veal, 1999). In general the results of predictions have been disappointing, which perhaps explains why people keep trying (see for example, Kelly, 1987; Bergstrom and Cordell,

1991), coupled with the fact that few researchers or readers go back to verify if the projections came true. Statistically oriented methods tend to give reliable short-term forecasts for stable recreation activities for which considerable longitudinal data exist, but are poor for forecasting patterns of new, rapidly growing activities or those characterized by instability (Song and Witt, 2000). Qualitative predictions may be more suited for longer term projections and for speculation on activities not yet participated in, but are at best inspired guesswork (Anderson and Schneider, 1993). Even the most experienced researchers do not have high levels of accuracy when it comes to predictions. Of 14 items related to tourism anticipated to be in place by 1990 or earlier, based on predictions made in 1980, only six were even partially happening by 1994 (Hawkins *et al.*, 1980), and some are still not a reality in 2002.

It seemed pointless, therefore, to attempt to forecast in detail, or to speculate at length on what tourism might look like in the future. Rather, it was decided to discuss potential changes at a more general level, commenting on factors that do affect tourism and recreation behaviour now, and that are likely to affect them in the future, although not necessarily in the same way or with the same force. A major consideration to bear in mind is that in the short-term or even medium-term future, massive change in tourism is relatively unlikely, barring a major catastrophe such as global war. People do not abandon lifetime preferences and behaviours lightly, especially when they may have considerable amounts of money and time invested in equipment, property and skills. As well, constraints on their participation in tourism and recreation do not change quickly (Jackson and Scott, 1999). Change therefore, is likely to be incremental and gradual at an aggregate level, and evolutionary rather than revolutionary for the most part. Bevins and Wilcox (1980) demonstrated clearly that over a 20 year period there were few changes in participation levels in individual recreation activities of more than five percent, and the most common activities remained relatively constant in popularity over almost two decades. Almost all surveys from the time of the Outdoor Recreation Resources Review Commission (ORRRC, 1962) have found that in North America at least, there is great inertia and stability in recreation, leisure and tourism participation for most of the population (Gartner and Lime, 2000). There is also decreasing distinction between work and leisure (Sylvester, 1999,) and as many authors from Clawson and Knetsch (1966) onwards have noted, participants are seeking and participating in an experience rather than a single activity (Mannell, 1999).

In this discussion, attention is paid first to societal trends and potential changes in some of the demand shifters (Spencer, 1989; Cordell and Bergstrom, 1991; Teigland, 2000). Secondly, there is discussion of the anticipated effects of technology and the rate of change of attitudes and behaviour. Finally, there is a brief examination of the impacts of the anticipated changes in tourism patterns upon the environment and upon communities. A short conclusion attempts to pull together major threads and implications.

SOCIETAL TRENDS
Population
Perhaps the most definite trend in Western society in terms of the certainty of it continuing is the overall ageing of the population. The number of people in North America over the age of 65 at the end of the century is likely to be double what it was in 1971, and the only age cohort anticipated to show an absolute decline is the youngest (Spencer, 1989). Murdock *et al.* (1991: 239) concluded that the average age of the US population would increase from 30 in 1980 to 36 in the year 2000, and 41 by 2025. Some implications of this trend are already apparent, which may give some indications of the way patterns may change in the future.

The new elderly population is not, and will not be like previous older generations. While it can be expected to retain some of the same traditional and conservative values, it is a generation that has more money, better health, is better educated and has travelled more extensively than elderly generations before it (Nickerson and Black, 2000). Its recreational preferences and behaviour have been modified by the Great Depression, the Second World War, the Korean War, the post war boom, the 1960s, jet aircraft and terrorism. The generation that was 65 at the beginning of the 21st century however, did not experience the Depression, probably barely remembers even the second of the two World Wars and spent their adolescence in the post war boom of the 1950s. Those turning 65 in the year 2010 are of the baby boom generation. It can be expected, therefore, that the increasingly large elderly population will be more like current 40 to 50 year olds than current 70 to 80 year olds. Like the latter group, but probably much more effectively, many of them will reject old age and continue to travel and to engage in many activities that they engage in now. They will be less considerate of society's preconceived and stereotyped roles for them and will have the numbers and financial power to act as an influential force in society. While some are seeking out retirement pastures in the southern and south western states of the US, in British Columbia, around the Mediterranean or the Gulf of Mexico, many will choose or have to remain where they are, perhaps in condominiums or apartments, possibly travelling for long breaks during the winter, and taking other vacations and recreation trips during the late spring and early fall.

One effect of this pattern may be to increase the shoulder season accommodation occupancy rates and the use levels at many locations, and possibly slightly reduce peaking. However, because this large elderly population can be expected to remain active for more years than previous generations (Kelly, 1993), many destination areas will be busier in the future than at present. The impact is likely to be particularly great in many highly scenic areas (Cordell and Super, 2000), in heritage areas such as national parks and historic sites, and in northern and wilderness areas. This group has both time and money to spend on longer trips to remote areas, and many have the health and ability to accept considerable physical challenge. This population has enough experience not to want or to accept the ordinary or the familiar on every occasion. They have the time, and many of them the money and the inclination to behave like the allocentrics or near-allocentrics of Plog's (1974) psychographic segmentation. Some of them are already involved in exploration trips to the Arctic and Antarctica, heritage excursions to places such as Peru, India and the Pacific, mountain hikes in the Rockies and Andes, and natural history excursions throughout the world.

This group, as it grows and continues to be active, could pose considerable problems in natural areas. While many of its members may be extremely environmentally conscious and interested in heritage and natural history, that very interest may draw them in increasing numbers to the wilderness and protected areas such as national parks. They, or those catering for them, may demand additional developments and facilities such as roads, trails and lifts to allow them access to many parts of such areas. They are less likely to want campgrounds in these areas than they are to want good hotels. As they gain more and more political influence, if only because of sheer numbers, policies may have to change to accommodate them (Butler, 1998). There is nothing inherently wrong in this but additional conflicts may arise as a result in many areas over the degree and nature of development (Hammitt and Schneider, 2000).

Supply

Research has shown the importance of supply in shaping participation (Cordell and Bergstrom, 1991). It is difficult to foresee major changes in the overall pattern of the provision of tourism and outdoor recreation opportunities by the public sector in the short to mid-term future. New initiatives can be expected to result in additional areas becoming National Parks, especially in less developed areas, for example, Vietnam (Cresswell and McLaren, 2000). However, factors including budget limitations, continued reluctance by non-national governments and authorities to allow the creation of new national parks when required to release all rights to resources, and reluctance by some local populations to have national parks established close to their permanent homes all suggest new parks will not be of great size or number. While protection is now identified as the first priority in most national parks systems, the emphasis appears to have widened to include a wider range of developments (see for example Butler and Boyd, 2000). This may be a reflection of changing demands (related to special user groups, for example the aged and handicapped as noted above) and of political factors, including pressure from and on governments to stimulate tourism.

In the future it is possible that parks will have to be shown to be commercially valuable to continue to receive public sector support if present trends continue. This could be translated into additional and more varied developments in accommodation, services and recreation activities than previously allowed, with possibly some expansion of the system as compensation. To the wilderness purist such developments would be anathema, but to politicians probably highly attractive. Alternatives to national and similar parks are not likely to appear, and could not be expected to provide the degree of protection to the environment afforded by these areas. Legal liability and problems of damage to and loss of property of landowners have proved to be the major obstacles, and changes in legislation have failed to resolve these problems. This tendency is more prevalent among exurbanites moving to the countryside to live, or owning recreational properties in rural areas than among long-time rural residents.

Private commercial developments, *e.g.* campgrounds, theme parks, ski areas, on the other hand, can be expected to continue to expand as market opportunities are perceived. Large scale theme parks on the scale of the Disney operations are not likely to appear in more than a few additional locations given market requirements and economic conditions, however smaller and more specific amusement and leisure facilities will be developed. In China for example, there has been a virtual explosion in smaller theme parks, so much so that the economic life cycle of many of them is extremely short (Bao, 2003). One innovation, which has been developed in some number in Northern Europe and Japan, has been climate-controlled aquatic leisure centres, featuring wave pools, artificial beaches and other water-based attractions under domes or in indoor settings. This is often part of a process of making the downtown parts of older urban areas more attractive to both residents and visitors for purposes of economic regeneration based on tourism and leisure uses. One feature of tourism in the last two decades in particular has been the growth of urban-centred short breaks, holidays of one to three overnights, often to capital cities or to historic or heritage urban centres, particularly in Europe. This trend has been accentuated by the rise of budget airlines serving smaller urban centres and less used airports at often extremely low prices (In Europe in the summer of 2002 it was possible to fly between some 40 urban centres for as little as $20, excluding tax). It is almost certain that, despite cultural and spatial variations, the patterns of participation will remain "sensitive to recreation opportunity (supply) growth rates" (Cordell and Bergstrom, 1991:1).

Cultural Mosaic

There is little doubt that the current patterns of tourism are different from those of the 19th century, although remnants of the older patterns still exist. One of the factors which has, and can be expected to continue to cause changes in these patterns is the cultural composition of countries. Immigration, especially in the last 100 years, has seen significant numbers of many different ethnic groups move around the world, mostly to developed countries (Hutchison, 2000). In recent years numbers have grown as civil wars, terrorism and other conflict have driven people from their homes, most recently from the Balkans and the Middle East. These immigrants often give clear and distinctive cultural identities to specific parts of a country or to different cities, for example Mennonites in Pennsylvania, Chinese in Vancouver, Italians in Melbourne, Caribbean emigrants in England, and Mexicans/Latin Americans in Southern California. Such groups bring with them very different and distinctive cultures and forms of recreation (Kraus, 1994). While immigrant groups bring additional variety in culture, in general minority groups participate less than majority groups in tourism and in many recreation activities, partly from economic disadvantage and partly because of different preferences.

It appears that, as in times past, the immigration mix will continue to change, with fewer emigrants from Western Europe and more moving from Asia, the Middle East, Africa and Eastern Europe. Murdock *et al.* (1991: 239) deduced that the minority population in the US would increase in proportion from 20 percent in 1980 to 33 percent by 2025, and that 78 percent of an expected 70 million new Americans will be from what are currently minority groups. It would be surprising if such groups did not succeed in introducing new patterns of behaviour in tourism and recreation, and thus indirectly result in a decrease or decline in growth of participation in more traditional patterns and activities. In the context of tourism, changes in the Visiting Friends and Relative (VFR) segment can be anticipated, as the VFR destinations will reflect the new patterns of emigration and immigration as new residents gain the economic security to return on a temporary basis to their former countries (where and when it is safe to do so).

Free Time

Many changes in employment related factors have not all materialized as anticipated some decades ago (Campbell, 1976; Nickerson and Black, 2000). The working-week in most developed countries has not declined to 25 hours or even 30 hours but remains around the 35 hour level, and there are even signs that significant numbers of employees, especially those in professional occupations, are working longer hours than before. The normal work week for most people is still five days long, and any minor gains in non-work time on a daily basis have been lost to increased travel time, especially for those living in metropolitan areas. This situation is not likely to improve at all for most people in the near future, and as people locate further away from their place of employment in major cities to escape urban problems including high accommodation prices, their travel times are likely to increase and their potential leisure time decrease. Only in the context of tourism has free time remained constant or increased for many people over the last two decades.

Although there has been widespread use of computer and information technology, which might have allowed considerable numbers of employees to work at home, by and large this has not occurred. Neither flexitime nor job-sharing has been accepted by employers or employees as eagerly and on as large a scale as once thought. While these innovations may see more participants in the years ahead, major changes in the working patterns and habits of most people are not anticipated in the next two decades at least. As noted below, however, the adoption of IT in the tourism industry has made major changes in behaviour possible and, with these, significant changes in patterns of tourism.

The inevitable problems of peaking and crowding resulting from seasonal variations in climate and in supply and demand for tourism are likely to remain for the foreseeable future (Baum and Lundtorp, 2001). Despite a range of attempts and procedures, most destination areas have been unable to overcome what is often seen as the 'problem' of seasonality, in part because of the difficulty of overcoming institutional arrangements and in part because of inertia to change established habits (Butler, 2001). Similar problems arise at weekends, especially those with holidays attached. While there has been a marked increase in short breaks, particularly in the off-season in many year-round tourism destinations, particularly major cultural and historic urban centres, the basic seasonal pattern of tourism and recreation for the main vacation of most people is unlikely to change significantly in the short to medium term future.

Family Structure

A major social change that has taken place throughout the developed world is the decline in the 'traditional' nuclear family, consisting of two adults of opposite sexes and two or more children, normally living relatively close to other family members. In a more mobile population the support and contact provided by the extended family members are becoming less common. Frequent job and location changes among many upwardly-mobile baby boomers have contributed to the disruption of traditionally stable family groups. The increasing incidence of single-parent families also has changed what was the normal lifestyle of families of the 1950s and 1960s and the full impacts of these trends on tourism and leisure are not known (Nickerson and Black, 2000). For many families, less parental time is available in most cases for participating in recreation outside conventional working hours, and the annual vacation, when there is one, becomes one of the few, if not the only, times of the year in which the family can participate in an extended period of leisure time together.

Other Factors

There are of course many other elements of change in society that affect tourism patterns (Lockwood and Medlik, 2001). The women's movement and feminism have certainly changed the level of participation in tourism and many forms of leisure and, perhaps more importantly, changed society's attitudes towards 'appropriate' gender-based recreation behaviour (Shaw, 1999). Old stereotypes and shibboleths can be expected to continue to decline in relevance and significance in the future, and fuller participation by women in all activities, will continue.

No specific comments have been made on increasing affluence or on the importance of employment, although both of these variables have long been accepted as major determinants of the nature and extent of participation in tourism and leisure. This is not because such relationships are expected to change in the future, rather the opposite, but employment in particular, and income to a lesser degree, are not as stable or permanent through the working section of the life cycle as for previous generations. 'Jobs for life' are now uncommon, and several career changes are experienced by an increasing number of people. Thus an increasing level of turbulence has entered the system, reflecting the uncertainty in many economic systems in the past two decades, and simple relationships between type of employment or specific levels of income are not as clear as they were (if they were ever really fully understood). It is not unreasonable to assume that levels of affluence may continue to rise at an aggregate level in the future but the overall process of the democratization of leisure may not continue for all groups or for the more expensive activities in the same manner that it has for the past half century or more. While the proportion of two income families has been increasing, there is a finite limit to the growth of such a phenomenon. Such growth is also dependent on job creation and may be driven as much by financial necessity as a desire for additional material goods.

Finally, for two decades at least, there has been a growing concern for the environment and indications that such feelings may have finally registered with political and corporate decision makers, as evidenced by the wide support for the concept of sustainable development and sustainable tourism (Wahab and Pigram, 1997; Hall and Lew, 1998; Butler, 1999a). Whether such indications will translate into major action to reduce environmental degradation and even to restore environmental quality remains to be seen. Efforts by the European Union to reduce the emphasis on 'factory' farming, particularly after such disasters as BSE and Foot and Mouth in the United Kingdom (and elsewhere in Europe) in the last decade may result in some rural areas being phased out of agriculture and into environmental protection, which may make them more attractive for rural tourism and recreation (Butler et al., 1998). Initially such action might not have major direct impact on tourism patterns, but if additional areas became unsuitable for tourism, for example, polluted water bodies, then spatial patterns may change significantly. A further result of increased environmental concern would be additions to the list of protected areas, although a political response may be that increased expenditures on environmental improvement may reduce the need for formally protected areas. Irrespective of these possibilities, increased participation in tourism in scenic resource-oriented areas is likely to continue in the future. Without significant changes and improvements in access, the patterns are not likely to change significantly, but use levels towards the fringe can be expected to increase. Additional pressure will continue to be felt on national parks and other natural or pristine areas (Butler and Boyd, 2000).

Technology and Rates of Change

One major factor, which has typified most societies, and particularly modern western society, is the rate of change of many once traditional attitudes and values and patterns of behaviour. The speed by which information is disseminated throughout the world has increased exponentially, and certainly with respect to communications and travel the last two centuries have seen the increasing development of time-space convergence. In tourism the developments in these two areas have been of crucial significance and will continue to be so in the future (Bengston and Xu, 1993; Buhalis, 2002). The ability to access information almost immediately has allowed the development of a wide range of services by tourism agencies, especially those in transportation and accommodation fields, and allows travel agents and others to almost instantly confirm travel and other requirements of would-be travellers (Buhalis, 2002). Reports on road conditions, space available in accommodation, weather conditions, facility opening hours and skiing conditions are just a few of the information services instantly available to potential tourists, whether by telephone, computer, or the increasingly sophisticated mobile telephone systems.

The availability of vast amounts of constantly updated information has increased astronomically in recent years, and will continue to increase the ease of substitution of various elements of the tourism experience in the future. The combination of personalized mobility, perhaps slightly increased leisure time, improved transportation facilities, increased affluence and a vastly increased supply of opportunities have given the tourist of the 21st century an incomparably wide range of options to select from. Whereas in earlier times decisions would have to be made days or even months in advance to book accommodation and make travel arrangements, and were difficult, if not impossible to change, now decisions can often be made on the day of departure or even during travel, on aspects such as trip duration, route, destination location and activities to be engaged in. The growth of the new communication technology in particular has both allowed and created change in conventional patterns.

The rise of budget airlines, in Europe in particular, has been dependent to a considerable degree on reducing costs in operations, and one of the significant cost reductions has been in commissions on bookings. Airlines such as Easyjet and Ryanair now receive over 80 percent of their bookings by internet by passengers directly and the percentage is still increasing. Airlines such as these seized the opportunities offered after September 11, 2001, when conventional airlines reduced seats and services, and expanded their operations in western Europe so successfully that passengers carried have increased by up to 40 percent on a monthly basis in the year since the terrorist attack in New York. Such growth cannot be expected to continue, but it has made air travel available to many people who did not fly before, mainly because of cost, and has probably changed their perceptions of potential holiday destinations and travel on a permanent basis. If one is able to travel from London (albeit an outlying airport) to Italy and back for about 100 dollars (excluding taxes), such destinations become feasible not only for vacations, but also for short breaks such as weekend visits. One indication of this is a marked increase in pre-wedding 'stag' (and 'doe') nights in locations such as Dublin or Amsterdam for parties from England, as the costs of accommodation and alcohol are so much cheaper than in England that the low costs of the air fare are more than compensated for. As well, the environment may perhaps be more appealing and is certainly more exotic and exciting than one's home town. Such minor individual changes in behaviour are a small but perhaps a significant indication of the way that IT and transportation technology are changing spatial and social patterns of tourism and leisure, at least in western Europe. The venture of Virgin airlines to introduce budget air travel into Australia, Air Canada's Tango and Jazz services in North America, and the long established (although sometimes short-lived) no-frills airlines in the USA are all indicative of the same process, a willingness to change the way of doing business and offering services. Not since the advent of charter airlines in the 1960s have such radical changes in established patterns been introduced, and the effects are likely to be as significant in the first decades of the 21st century as those pioneering efforts in the first decades of the second half of the 20th century.

Such initiatives have not appeared in other forms of transportation to the same degree. Passenger rail travel in North America does not attract large numbers of tourists. A few lines, such as the privatized route through the Rockies from Calgary to Vancouver, attract tourists, but otherwise the car and the plane remain predominant. In Europe, the development of high speed and efficient train service is used mostly for commuting and business travel, but does also cater for tourist journeys, especially the Eurostar services from London to Paris, Brussels and beyond via the Channel Tunnel. In Britain, the undercapitalized and less reliable and efficient system still carries a considerable leisure and tourism market, but this is in part a reflection of both inertia and shorter distances than strong preference. In boat traffic there has, of course, been a major expansion in the cruise ship industry, with boats being constructed and put into service of quite amazing size, some now over 100,000 tons, and the market is continuing to grow. Not surprisingly, this market has now begun to divide into recognized segments, based in part on price, and in part on location, on theme or focus, and on service attributes. The range of cruise ship destinations runs from Pole to Pole, and virtually all oceans and seas, although the two major locations still remain the Caribbean and the Mediterranean. Educational, sports, sexual inclination, cultural and natural history themes are only a few of the specific interests catered for on cruises. Increasingly also, the time dimension of cruising has changed from the conventional week or two week cruise to ones of two day duration to semi-permanance, with the launching of the "Residensea". This is a very large cruise boat that is intended to be a permanent, albeit mobile, home, for the affluent, visiting locations such as Rio de Janeiro, Monte Carlo, and New Orleans each year in time for specific events such as Carnival, Grand Prix and Mardi Gras. The cruise ship part of tourism has emerged as one of the most competitive and hence most dynamic elements in tourism in the last three decades.

This dynamism in tourism represents a revolutionary element to the evolutionary change that is most common in tourism. The process of change has undoubtedly speeded up over the last half century, and this is evident in the compressed life cycle of destinations and activities (Butler, 1999b). New activities have appeared in tourism and leisure that have certain elements in common. They all utilize "new" technology in terms of materials (fibreglass, resins, plastics); they all appeal to a young audience (primarily 10 years to

30 years); they are all individual activities; they all require physical activity, agility and practise; and they all allow the demonstration of talent and performance (Butler, 1998). Examples include snow-boarding, snowmobiling, surfing, yachting, scuba diving, jet skiing, downhill skiing, para sailing and sky diving, while recent interest in four-wheel drive and other off-road vehicles is also not unrelated. These activities offer challenge and excitement to what is increasingly being accepted to be a bored society (Ewert and Schreyer, 1990). As well, they are glamorous, possess a positive image (hence the role they play as the backdrop in many lifestyle commercials), and perhaps of some importance to many participants, are activities the preceding generation did not participate in to any great degree, if at all. In those activities in which there was participation, for example downhill skiing, new forms, freestyle, ballet and mogul skiing, have developed, and equipment and clothing have changed dramatically from the conservative forms of two decades ago. Participation in these activities often is not simply engaging in an activity but making a social, economic and personal statement about oneself and one's style or lack of it. Many destinations are now catering for these new activities, often facing some difficulties in accommodating these with the established activities, for example, downhill skiing and snowboarding, although as time goes by, conflict and competition gradually disappear as the new forms become more established and accepted.

One can speculate therefore that activities which may appear in the future will be those that offer the following features; challenge and excitement at a personal level; the opportunity to improve and to display that improvement; the opportunity to engage in the activity, both in conjunction with others and alone in an outdoor setting; the opportunity to make a personal statement through participation, for example, by personalizing equipment or technique; and the utilization of new technology in the form of equipment and means of access to use areas.

Several problems can be expected to continue in the future relating to technological innovation. These include conflict between participants in the new forms of tourism and in more traditional forms over use of resources and incompatibility; conflicts between participants in the new activities and non-users of the same areas, including indigenous people in some areas; philosophical conflicts over the acceptability of the new activities, both under any circumstances, and in specific areas; safety concerns, both for users and non-users; legal problems stemming primarily from liability and trespass issues; and licensing and operating regulations where appropriate. Bengston and Xu (1993: 252) note also that technological innovations and changes in human preference and attitudes can make previously ignored features significant as tourist resources, such as cliffs with up-drafts for hang-gliding, (perhaps in much the same way as the establishment of national parks on hitherto 'worthless' land represented a new evaluation of resources a century or more ago) (Hall, 2000). These pose additional allocation and management problems for those controlling such features.

These are not new problems and have been present in some form since fire and the wheel were invented, but as noted above, where the rate of introduction and acceptance of innovations is so rapid, the ability of users and non-users to adapt to the innovations is often overtaken by events. Hopefully some of the lessons learned from innovations such as the snowmobile can be applied to new situations to avoid a repetition of mistakes and omissions in the future. Over the years however, there seems to have been a hardening or polarization of attitudes between many groups over such issues as environmental protection, native peoples' and others' rights to areas and resources, and increasing use of the legal system to acquire or prohibit access to areas. There is, unfortunately, little reason to expect this trend to change significantly, at least in the near future, and thus we will almost certainly be faced with continued problems to resolve relating to compatibility and acceptability of new forms of tourism in the areas in which they will be used and with non-users and local residents (Butler and Hinch, 1996).

CONCLUSIONS

The picture that has been drawn of future tourism patterns is perhaps not an overwhelmingly positive one. Growth in almost all aspects of leisure, recreation and tourism is anticipated, but such growth is expected to be incremental and in similar directions to what is witnessed today. This is because many of the current participants will still be active for several decades into the future, and will be exposing their children to many of the same activities they themselves have been engaging in for many years. Expansion into new areas in a spatial sense is almost inevitable, both because of crowding, reduction in environmental quality and lack of opportunity for new development in old areas, and because technological innovations allow and encourage such expansion, but there are a decreasing number of appropriate new locations and an increasing number of existing areas facing problems from tourism penetration.

Some suggestions have been made above about the nature of these innovations particularly in the context of types of activities which may appear. Most of the innovations are likely to be variations on activities engaged in now, as are most of the innovations in equipment and transportation, such as the increasing portability of many items and increasingly computerized information dissemination and recording systems for users and managers of destinations.

There is at least one factor which may cause some change in the global patterns of tourism behaviour and make some of these predictions less valid, and that is climatic change brought about by what is known as the 'Greenhouse Effect'. Global change, with predicted effects including rising sea levels, declining inland lake levels, declining rainfall in some areas, changes in vegetational and hence wildlife distribution and regeneration, all resulting from a warming of the planet could have major effects in many areas (Agnew and Viner, 2001). The increases in temperature, while not major from a human perceptive point of view, could have major effects on both summer and winter recreation patterns, especially winter recreation in currently near-marginal areas. Wall (1993) has shown the serious results of climate change on tourism and recreation in North America, and Lamothe and Périard (1988) examined the implications for skiing tourism in Quebec. The predictions are much more negative for winter recreation than they are positive for summer recreation, and while they are only possible scenarios, the implications are extremely serious. In addition, while beaches may increase in area in some locations, some rivers and streams may have reduced flow, possibly to a level prohibiting many forms of water-based recreation such as sailing and fishing. Oceans are expected to rise if global warming occurs, and many beaches and communities will disappear beneath the waves, along with significant parts of the USA as well as complete island states in the Pacific and Indian Oceans. The social and particularly the economic upheaval and necessary readjustments could result in even greater change in recreational and tourist behaviour in the world at large. Global change may not be inevitable and may not be a long-term phenomenon but rather a short-term misinterpretation of the climatic record. However, the very possibility serves to remind humanity of the fragility and interdependence of the earth's physical and human systems. Much tourism is tied closely to the environment and requires a clean and healthy environment if participants are to derive enjoyment and satisfaction from their pleasure experiences now and in the future, whatever direction it may take.

The discussion in this chapter has been based on the assumption that there would be no catastrophic change in the global situation such as nuclear war, a major economic depression as in 1929, or massive medical or environmental tragedies. Such events would, in varying degrees clearly render much, if not all, of the previous discussion meaningless. It is impossible to conclude the chapter without some reference to the events of September 11, 2001 and their effects on tourism. The attacks on the United States had significant short-term effects on tourism globally. The American market is the largest tourism market in the world, as the American economy is also the largest, and any major change in these is felt throughout the world. As Americans (and some others, although for a much shorter period of time) stopped flying, especially abroad, world tourism went into a significant decline. The decision of many Americans not to fly abroad was not necessarily logical, given that the four flights that were highjacked were all internal American flights, but the overall reluctance to fly is understandable. The results are still being felt at the time of writing; airlines have gone bankrupt and continue to be threatened with this fate, despite a relatively small (less than 10 percent for the most) decline in traffic, and in the immediate months after the attack, severe declines were experienced in the travel, accommodation and services sectors of tourism in almost all parts of the world. It is likely, despite the instant pronouncements of the World Tourism Organization and the World Travel and Tourism Council to the contrary, that over the 12 months from September 11, 2001 world international tourism arrivals will show at most a very slight decline, and some areas will not experience any decline in numbers. That is not to say that the events of September 11 did not have major significance. The Gulf War of 1991 did not produce an overall decline in world tourism (although it did have severe regional effects), so it is unlikely that a single event, even as major as the attacks on the US, could do so, but the psychological effects of the attacks were significant and have produced major changes in security and travel arrangements with large costs in terms of finance and time for all involved, suppliers and tourists alike. Despite this, the Foot and Mouth outbreak in the United Kingdom and the collapse of Ansett Airline in Australia, both in 2001, are deemed to have had greater effects on tourism in the United Kingdom and Australia respectively, than the events of September 11 (a conclusion based on comments made at the World Tourism Convention in Hobart, November 2001). The fact that the event took place in the United States, headquarters of much of the world's leading media and tourism companies perhaps resulted in the over anticipation of the longer term effects of what was an international tragedy.

Irrespective of the exact influence of such an event, it does serve to dramatize the increasing turbulence and chaos that exists in tourism (Faulkner and Russell, 1997). While the inertia and stability noted earlier are still strong features of tourism, the increasing rate of change of technology and of knowledge dissemination, the reduction in controls on travel and information flows, and the overall impact of globalization ensure that while a butterfly flapping its wings in Amazonia may or may not cause a typhoon in Japan, an entrepreneur in one sector of tourism can certainly cause significant change throughout the industry (Russell and Faulkner, 1988). Thomas Cook proved this almost two centuries ago, but the speed with which a change can occur and the dimensions of that change are now vastly different. We can only conclude that tourism will continue to change, excite, frustrate and impact the world and people's lives in the future as it has done in the past, but exactly how it will do this remains to be seen.

REFERENCES

Agnew, M. and Viner, D. (2001) "Potential impacts of climate change on international tourism", *Tourism and Hospitality Research*, 3(1): 37-60.

Anderson, D.H. and Schneider, I. (1993) "Using the Delphi process to identify significant recreation research based innovations", *Journal of Park and Recreation Administration*, 11: 25-36.

Bao, J. (2003) "The tourism area life cycle and theme parks in China", in R.W. Butler (ed.), *The Tourism Area Life Cycle: Applications and Modifications*, Clevedon: Channel View Publications.

Baum, T. and Lundtorp, S. (2001) *Seasonality in Tourism*, London: Pergamon.

Bengston, D.N. and Xu, Z. (1993) "Impact of research and technical change in wildland recreation: evaluation issues and approaches", *Leisure Sciences*, 15(2): 251-272.

Bergstrom, J.C. and Cordell, H.K. (1991) "An analysis of demand for and value of outdoor recreation in the United States", *Journal of Leisure*, 23(1): 67-86.

Bevins, M.I. and Wilcox, D.P. (1980) *Outdoor Recreation Participation-Analysis of National Surveys, 1959-1978*, Vermont Agricultural Experimental Station Bulletin 686, Vermont: University of Vermont.

Buhalis, D. (2002) *Tourism: Information Technologies for Strategic Tourism Management*, New York, NY: Financial Times Prentice Hall.

Butler, R.W. (1998) "Rural recreation and tourism", in B. Ilberry, (ed.), *The Geography of Rural Change*, Harlow: Longman, 211-232.

_____ (1999a) "Sustainable tourism: a state-of-the-art review", *Tourism Geographies*, 1(1): 7-25.

_____ (1999b) "Tourism - an evolutionary perspective", in J.G. Nelson, R.W. Butler, and G. Wall (eds.), *Tourism and Sustainable Development: A Civic Approach*, Geography Publications Series No. 52, Waterloo, ON: University of Waterloo, 33-62.

_____ (2001) "Seasonality in tourism: issues and implications", in T. Baum and S. Lundtorp (eds.), *Seasonality in Tourism*,

London: Pergamon, 5-22.

Butler, R.W. and Boyd, S.W. (2000) *Tourism and National Parks: Issues and Implications*, Chichester: John Wiley and Sons .

Butler, R.W., Hall, C.M. and Jenkins, J. (1998) *Tourism and Recreation in Rural Areas*, Chichester: John Wiley and Sons.

Butler, R.W. and Hinch, T. (1996) *Tourism and Indigenous Peoples*, London: International Thompson Business Press.

Campbell, C.K. (1976) "Future symptoms in Canadian outdoor recreation", Research Committee (ed.), *Park and Recreation Futures in Canada: Issues and Options*, Toronto, ON: Ontario Research Council on Leisure, 83-147.

Clawson, M. and Knetsch, J. L. (1966) *Economics of Outdoor Recreation*, Baltimore: Johns Hopkins Press.

Cordell, H.K. and Bergstrom, J.C. (1991) "A methodology for assessing national outdoor recreation demand and supply trends", *Leisure Sciences*, 13(1): 1-20.

Cordell, H.K. and Super, G.R. (2000) "Trends in Americans' outdoor recreation", in W.C. Gartner, and D.W. Lime (eds.), *Trends in Outdoor Recreation, Leisure and Tourism*, Wallingford: CABI Publishing, 133-144.

Cresswell, C. and McLaren, F. (2000) "Tourism and national parks in emerging tourism countries", in R.W. Butler and S.W. Boyd (eds.), *Tourism and National Parks: Issues and Implications*, Chichester: John Wiley and Sons, 283-300.

Ewert, A. and Schreyer, R. (1990) "Risk recreation: trends and implications for the 1990s", in J.T. O'Leary, D. Fesenmaier, T.

Brown, D. Stynes and B. Driver (eds.), *Proceedings of the National Outdoor Recreation Trends Symposium III*, (Vol. 2) Indianapolis, MN: Leisure Research Institute, 480-489.

Gartner, W.C. and Lime, D.W. (2000) *Trends in Outdoor Recreation, Leisure and Tourism*, Wallingford: CABI Publishing.

Hall, C.M. (2000) "Tourism, national parks and aboriginal peoples," in R.W. Butler and S.W. Boyd (eds.), *Tourism and National Parks: Issues and Implications*, Chichester: John Wiley and Sons, 57-72.

Hall, C.M. and Lew, A.A. (1998) *Sustainable Tourism: A Geographical Perspective*, London: Addison Wesley Longman.

Hammitt, W.E. and Schneider, I.E. (2000) "Recreation conflict management", in W.C. Gartner and D.W. Lime (eds.), *Trends in Outdoor Recreation, Leisure and Tourism*, Wallingford: CABI Publishing, 347-346.

Hawkins, D.E., Shafer, E.L. and Rovelstad, J.M. (1980) *International Symposium on Tourism and the Next Decade: Summary and Recommendations*, Washington, DC: George Washington University.

Hutchison, R. (2000) "Race and ethnicity in leisure studies," in W.C. Gartner and D.W. Lime (eds.), *Trends in Outdoor Recreation, Leisure and Tourism*, Wallingford: CABI Publishing, 63-72.

Jackson, E.L. and Scott, D. (1999) "Constraints to leisure", in E.L. Jackson and T.L. Burton (eds.), *Leisure Studies - Prospects for the Twenty-First Century*, State College, PA: Venture

Publishing Inc., 299-322.

Kelly, J.R. (1987) *Recreation Trends Towards the Year 2000*, Champaign, IL: Management Learning Laboratories Ltd.
_____ (1993) *Activity and Aging: Staying Involved in Later Life*, Newbury Park, CA: Sage Publications.

Kennedy, P. (1993) *Preparing for the Twenty-First Century*, New York: Random House.

Kraus, R. (1994) *Leisure in a Changing America: A Multicultural Perspective*, Riverside, NJ: MacMillan Publishing.

Lamonthe, P. and Périard, D. (1988) "Implications of climate change for downhill skiing in Quebec", *Climate Change Digest*, 88-03, Ottawa: Environment Canada.

Lockwood, A. and Medlik, S. (2001) *Tourism and Hospitality in the 21st Century*, Oxford: Butterworth Heinemann.

Mannell, R.C. (1999) "Leisure experience and satisfaction", in E.L. Jackson and T.L. Burton (eds.), *Leisure Studies - Prospects for the Twenty-First Century*, State College, PA: Venture Publishing Inc., 235-252.

Murdock, S.H., Backman, K., Hogue, N. Md., and Ellis, D. (1991) "The implications of change in population size and composition on future participation in outdoor recreational activities", *Journal of Leisure Research*, 23(3): 238-259.

Nickerson, N.P. and Black, R.J. (2000) "Changes in family and work: impacts on outdoor recreation and tourism in North America," in W.C. Gartner and D.W. Lime (eds.), *Trends in Outdoor Recreation, Leisure and Tourism*, Wallingford: CABI Publishing, 29-36.

Outdoor Recreation Resources Review Commission (ORRRC) (1962) *Outdoor Recreation for America*, Washington, DC: Government Printing Office.

Paine, J.D., Marans, R.N. and Harris, R.C. (1980) "Social indicators and outdoor recreation: the forgotten sector", in W. LaPage (ed.), *Proceedings 1980 National Outdoor Recreation Trends Symposium*, USDA Technical Reference NE 57, Broomall, PA: USDA North East Forest Experimental Station.

Plog, S.C. (1974) "Why destination areas rise and fall in popularity", *Cornell Hotel and Restaurant Administration Quarterly*, (February): 55-58.

Russell, R. and Faulkner, B. (1998) "Movers and shakers: chaos makers in tourism development", *Tourism Management*, 20(4): 411-420.

Shaw, S.M. (1999) "Gender and leisure", in E.L. Jackson and T.L. Burton (eds.), *Leisure Studies - Prospects for the Twenty-First Century*, State College, PA: Venture Publishing Inc., 271-282.

Song, H. and Witt, S. (2000) *Tourism Demand Modelling and Forecasting: Modern Econometric Approaches*, Netherlands: Elsevier.

Spencer, G. (1989) *Projections of the Population of the United States by Age, Sex and Race: 1988 to 2080*, Current Population Reports, Series P-25, No. 1018, Washington, DC: Government Printing Office.

Sylvester, C. (1999) "The Western idea of work and leisure: traditions, transformations and the future satisfaction", in E.L. Jackson, and T.L. Burton (eds.), *Leisure Studies - Prospects for the Twenty-First Century*, State College, PA: Venture

Publishing Inc., 17-34.

Tiegland, J. (2000) "The effects on travel and tourism demand from three mega-trends: democratization, market ideology and post-materialism as cultural wave", in W.C. Gartner and D.W. Lime (eds.), *Trends in Outdoor Recreation, Leisure and Tourism*, Wallingford: CABI Publishing, 37-46.

Veal, A.J. (1999) "Forecasting leisure and recreation satisfaction", in E.L. Jackson and T.L. Burton (eds.), *Leisure Studies - Prospects for the Twenty-First Century*, State College, PA: Venture Publishing Inc., 385-398.

Wahab, S. and Pigram, J.J. (1997) *Tourism, Development and Growth - The Challenge of Sustainability*, London: Routledge.

Wall, G. (1993) *Impacts of Climate Change on Recreation and Tourism in North America*, Washington, DC: Office of Technology Assessment.

List of Contributors

Dr. Richard Butler
School of Management
University of Surrey
U.K.

Dr. Barbara Carmichael
Department of Geography and Environmental Studies
Wilfrid Laurier University
Waterloo, ON N2K 3C5

Dr. Clare J.A. Mitchell
Department of Geography
University of Waterloo
Waterloo, ON N2L 3G1

Dr. David J. Telfer
Department of Recreation and Leisure Studies
Brock University
St. Catharines, ON L2S 3A1

Dr. Dallen J. Timothy
Department of Recreation Management and Tourism
Arizona State University
Tempe, AZ 85287
U.S.A.

Dr. Geoffrey Wall
Department of Geography
University of Waterloo
Waterloo, ON N2L 3G1

Dr. David B. Weaver
George Mason University
formerly at:
School of Tourism and Hotel Management
Griffith University Gold Coast Campus
Queensland 9726
Australia

Pamela Wight
Pam Wight & Associates
Edmonton, AB

Dr. David Wilton
Department of Economics
University of Waterloo
Waterloo, ON N2L 3G1

University of Waterloo

Department of Geography Publication Series

Available from:
Geography Publications   Phone: 519-888-4567; Ext. 3278
University of Waterloo   Fax: 519-746-0658
Waterloo, Ontario, Canada   e-mail: bkevans@fes.uwaterloo.ca
N2L 3G1

http://www.fes.uwaterloo.ca/Research/GeogPubs/geogpub.html

Series

55 Andrey, J. and Knapper, C., editors (2003) *Weather and Transportation in Canada*, ISBN 0-921083-65-3, 305 pages.

54 Bunch, M.J. (2001) *An Adaptive Ecosystem Approach to Rehabilitation and Management of the Cooum River Environmental System in Chennai, India*, ISBN 0-921083-62-9, 484 pages.

53 Nicol, H. and Halseth, G., editors (2000) *(Re)Development at the Urban Edges*, ISBN 0-921083-61-0, 444 pages.

52 Nelson, J.G., Butler, R. and Wall, G., editors (1999) *Tourism and Sustainable Development: Monitoring, Planning, Managing, Decision Making*, ISBN 0-921083-60-2, 406 pages.

51 Olive, C. (1998) *Land Use Change and Sustainable Development in Segara Anakan, Java, Indonesia: Interactions Among Society, Environment and Development*, ISBN 0-921083-59-9, 350 pages.

50 Needham, R., editor (1998) *Coping with the World Around Us: Changing Approaches to Land Use, Resources and Environment*, ISBN 0-921083-58-0, 294 pages.

49 Sinclair, J., editor (1997) *Canadian Environmental Assessment in Transition*, ISBN 0-921083-57-2, 419 pages.

254

48 Mitchell, C. and Dahms, F., editors (1997) *Challenge and Opportunity: Managing Change in Canadian Towns and Villages*, ISBN 0-921083-56-4, 298 pages.

47 Filion, P., Bunting, T.E. and Curtis, K., editors (1996) *The Dynamics of the Dispersed City: Geographic and Planning Perspectives on Waterloo Region*, ISBN 0-921083-55-6, 427 pages.

46 Sanderson, M. (1996) *Weather and Climate in Kitchener-Waterloo, Ontario*, ISBN 0-921083-54-8, 122 pages.

45 Andrey, J., editor (1995) *Transport Planning and Policy Issues: Geographical Perspectives*, ISBN 0-921083-53-X, 261 pages.

44 Martopo, S. and Mitchell, B., editors (1995) *Bali: Balancing Environment, Economy and Culture*, ISBN 0-921083-52-1, 674 pages.

43 McLellan, A.G. (1995) *The Consultant Geographer: Private Practice and Geography*, ISBN 0-921083-51-3, 230 pages.

41 Andrey, J. and Nelson, J.G., editors (1994) *Public Issues: A Geographical Perspective*, ISBN 0-921083-49-1, 435 pages.

40 Sanderson, M., editor (1993) *The Impact of Climate Change on Water in the Grand River Basin, Ontario*, ISBN 0-921083-48-3, 248 pages.

39 Lerner, S., editor (1993) *Environmental Stewardship: Studies in Active Earthkeeping*, ISBN 0-921083-46-7, 472 pages.

38 LeDrew, E., Hegyi, F. and Strome, M., editors (1995) *The Canadian Remote Sensing Contribution to Understanding Global Change*, ISBN 0-921083-45-9, 462 pages.

37 Nelson, J.G., Butler, R. and Wall, G., editors (1993) *Tourism and Sustainable Development: Monitoring, Planning, Managing*, ISBN 0-921083-44-0, 306 pages.

36 Day, J.C. and Quinn, F. (1992) *Water Diversion and Export: Learning From Canadian Experience*, ISBN 0-921083-42-4,

236 pages.

35 Mitchell, B. and Shrubsole, D. (1992) *Ontario Conservation Authorities: Myth and Reality*, ISBN 0-921083-41-6, 388 pages.

34 Mitchell, B., editor (1991) *Ontario: Geographical Perspectives on Economy and Environment*, ISBN 0-921083-37-8, 311 pages.

32 Charette, R. and Krueger, R. (1992) *The Low-Temperature Hazard to the Quebec Orchard Industry*, ISBN 0-921083-30-0, 166 pages.

30 Coppack, P.M., Russwurm, L.H. and Bryant, C.R., editors (1988) *The Urban Field, Essays on Canadian Urban Process and Form III*, ISBN 0-921083-25-4, 249 pages.

29 Guelke, L. and Preston, R.E., editors (1987) *Abstract Thoughts: Concrete Solutions: Essays in Honour of Peter Nash*, ISBN 0-921083-26-2, 332 pages.

28 Dufournaud, C. and Dudycha, D., editors (1987) *Waterloo Lectures in Geography, Vol. 3, Quantitative Analysis in Geography*, ISBN 0-921083-24-6, 140 pages.

27 Nelson, J.G. and Knight, K.D., editors (1987) *Research, Resources and the Environment in Third World Development*, ISBN 0-921083-23-8, 220 pages.

26 Walker, D.F., editor (1987) *Manufacturing in Kitchener-Waterloo: A Long-Term Perspective*, ISBN 0-921083-22-X, 220 pages.

25 Guelke, L., editor (1986) *Waterloo Lectures in Geography, Vol. 2, Geography and Humanistic Knowledge*, ISBN 0-921083-21-1, 101 pages.

24 Bastedo, J.D. (1986) *An ABC Resource Survey Method for Environmentally Significant Areas with Special Reference to Biotic Surveys in Canada's North*, ISBN 0-921083-20-3, 135 pages.

256

23 Bryant, C.R., editor (1984) *Waterloo Lectures in Geography, Vol. 1, Regional Economic Development*, ISBN 0-921083-19-X, 115 pages.

22 Knapper, C., Gertler, L. and Wall, G. (1983) *Energy, Recreation and the Urban Field*, ISBN 0-921083-18-1, 89 pages.

20 Mitchell, B. and Gardner, J.S., editors (1983) *River Basin Management: Canadian Experiences*, ISBN 0-921083-16-5, 443 pages.

19 Gardner, J.S., Smith, D.J. and Desloges, J.R. (1983) *The Dynamic Geomorphology of the Mt. Rae Area: High Mountain Region in Southwestern Alberta*, ISBN 0-921083-15-7, 237 pages.

17 Wall, G. and Knapper, C. (1981) *Tutankhamun in Toronto*, ISBN 0-921083-13-0, 113 pages.

16 Walker, D.F., editor (1980) *The Human Dimension in Industrial Development*, ISBN 0-921083-12-2, 124 pages.

12 Nelson, J.G., Needham, R.D. and Mann, D. (1978) *International Experience with National Parks and Related Reserves*, ISBN 0-921083-09-2, 624 pages.

6   Bullock, R.A. (1975) *Ndeiya, Kikuyu Frontier: The Kenya Land Problem in Microcosm*, ISBN 0-921083-06-8, 144 pages.

Occasional Papers

18 Scott, D., Mills, B., Jones, B., Svenson, S., Lemieux, C., Wall, G. and McBoyle, G. (2002) The Vulnerability of Winter Recreation to Climate Change in Ontario's Lakelands Tourism Region, ISBN 0-92-1083- 64-5, 100 pages.

17 Wall, G., editor (2001) *Contemporary Perspectives on Tourism*, ISBN 0-921083-63-7, 304 pages.

16 Wall, G., editor (1993) *Impacts of Climate Change on Resource Management of the North*, ISBN 0-921083-47-5, 270 pages.

15 Wall, G., editor (1992) *Symposium on the Implications of Climate Change for Pacific Northwest Forest Management*, ISBN 0-921083-43-2, 244 pages.

13 Sanderson, M., editor (1991) *Water Pipelines and Diversions in the Great Lakes Basin*, ISBN 0-921083-39-4, 131 pages.

12 Wall, G., editor (1991) *Symposium on the Impacts of Climatic Change and Variability on the Great Plains*, ISBN 0-921083-38-6, 376 pages.

11 Wall, G. and Sanderson, M., editors (1990) *Climate Change: Implications for Water and Ecological Resources*, An International Symposium/Workshop, ISBN 0-921083-36-X, 342 pages.

10 Chalmers, L. (University of Waikato), and MacLennan, M. (State University at Buffalo, New York) (1990) *Expert Systems in Geography and Environmental Studies: An Annotated View of Recent Work in the Field*, ISBN 0-921083-35-1, 92 pages.

6 Bryant, C.R., LeDrew, E.F., Marois, C. and Cavayas, F., editors (1989) *Remote Sensing and Methodologies of Land Use Change Analysis*, ISBN 0-921083-29-7, 178 pages.

3 Bunting, T.E. (1984) *Kitchener-Waterloo - The Geography of Mainstreet*, ISBN 0-921083-02-5, 117 pages.

1 Diem, A., editor (1984) *The Mont Blanc-Pennine Region*, ISBN 0-921083-00-9, 186 pages.